Imperial Alchemy

The mid twentieth century marked one of the greatest watersheds of Asian history, when a range of imperial constructs were declared to be nation-states, either by revolution or by decolonisation. Nationalism was the great alchemist, turning the base metal of empire into the gold of nations. To achieve such a transformation from the immense diversity of these Asian empires required a different set of forces from those that Europeans had needed in their transitions from multi-ethnic empires to culturally homogeneous nations. In this book Anthony Reid, one of the premier scholars of Southeast Asia, explores the mysterious alchemy by which new political identities have been formed. Taking Southeast Asia as his example, Reid tests contemporary theory about the relation between modernity, nationalism and ethnic identity. Grappling with concepts emanating from a very different European experience of nationalism, Reid develops his own typology to better fit the formation of political identities such as the Indonesian, Malay, Chinese, Acehnese, Batak and Kadazan.

ANTHONY REID is a Southeast Asian Historian now again based at the Australian National University, Canberra, but previously at the National University of Singapore (2002–9), where he established the Asia Research Institute, and University of California, Los Angeles (1999–2002). His other recent books include *Southeast Asia in the Age of Commerce* (2 vols, 1988–93), *Charting the Shape of Early Modern Southeast Asia* (1999), *An Indonesian Frontier: Acehnese and Other Histories of Sumatra* (2004), and, as [co]editor, *Islamic Legitimacy in a Plural Asia* (2007), *Chinese Diaspora in the Pacific* (2008) and *Negotiating Asymmetry: China's Place in Asia* (2009).

T0364313

Imperial Alchemy

Nationalism and Political Identity in Southeast Asia

Anthony Reid

CAMBRIDGE
UNIVERSITY PRESS

CAMBRIDGE UNIVERSITY PRESS
Cambridge, New York, Melbourne, Madrid, Cape Town,
Singapore, São Paulo, Delhi, Mexico City

Cambridge University Press
The Edinburgh Building, Cambridge CB2 8RU, UK

Published in the United States of America by Cambridge University Press, New York

www.cambridge.org
Information on this title: www.cambridge.org/9780521694124

First published 2010

A catalogue record for this publication is available from the British Library

Library of Congress Cataloging-in-Publication Data
Reid, Anthony, 1939–
    Imperial alchemy : nationalism and political identity in Southeast Asia /
Anthony Reid.
        p. cm.
    ISBN 978-0-521-87237-9 (hardback) – ISBN 978-0-521-69412-4 (pbk.)
    1. Ethnicity–Southeast Asia. 2. Nationalism–Southeast Asia.
3. Southeast Asia–Ethnic relations. 4. Southeast Asia–History–1945–
I. Title.
    DS523.3.R44 2009
    320.540959–dc22
                                                            2009034656
ISBN 978-0-521-87237-9 Hardback
ISBN 978-0-521-69412-4 Paperback

Contents

List of maps	*page* vi	
List of figures	vii	
List of tables	viii	
Acknowledgements	ix	
Abbreviations	xi	

1	Nationalism and Asia	1
2	Understanding Southeast Asian nationalisms	25
3	Chinese as a Southeast Asian 'other'	49
4	Malay (*Melayu*) and its descendants: multiple meanings of a porous category	81
5	Aceh: memories of monarchy	115
6	Sumatran Bataks: from statelessness to Indonesian diaspora	145
7	Lateforming ethnie in Malaysia: Kadazan or Dusun	187
8	Imperial alchemy–revolutionary dreams	210

Glossary	219
References	221
Index	238

Maps

1 Southeast Asia, colonial and contemporary   *page* 24
2 Northern Sumatra   150
3 Sabah, showing Kadazan and Dusun concentrations   189

Figures

3.1 & 3.2　Aftermath of May riots in Kuala Lumpur,
1969 (3.1, top) and Jakarta, 1998
(3.2, bottom)　　　　　　　　　　　　　*page* 73

5.1　　　　Aceh government banner celebrates cessation
of hostilities between the Indonesian Republic
and GAM, 2002　　　　　　　　　　　　　140

5.2　　　　Debris of the tsunami surrounds the
miraculously intact main mosque of the
Aceh capital, December 2004　　　　　　　142

6.1　　　　Statue of Singamangaraja XII erected in Medan
to celebrate his national hero status, 1961　148

6.2　　　　Modern Toba Batak monument (*tugu*), erected
by the Manihuruk lineage, near Pangururang
(Samosir), to rebury the ancestors　　　　179

6.3　　　　Modern Church of GBKP with signature Karo
roof, Medan 2008　　　　　　　　　　　　182

6.4　　　　The North Sumatra provincial museum deals
with ethnic claims with a Toba–Batak designed
roof style, Malay entrance and horizontal
bands of decoration to represent seven different
ethnicities　　　　　　　　　　　　　　184

7.1　　　　Donald Stephens proclaims Sabah's entry
to Malaysia, 1963, with Tun Mustapha
seated centre　　　　　　　　　　　　　195

Tables

6.1   Batak migrants in Medan   *page* 169
6.2   Growth of Batak church membership in Jakarta   170
6.3   HKBP membership figures in major cities   170
6.4   Destination of children of Gunung, Tiga Binanga,
      Tanah Karo, 1995   172
7.1   Ethnic percentages in Sabah censuses   188
7.2   Sabah population by ethnicity and religion   206
7.3   Mean income of ethnic groups in Malaysian
      Ringgit, 2004   208

Acknowledgements

The foundation of this book was laid in four lectures I delivered at the University of Hawai'i in 1996 as John A. Burns Distinguished Visiting Professor in the History Department. The prior seed was planted in a period of field work in Sumatra and East Malaysia in 1995, made possible by my supportive then employer, the Research School of Pacific and Asian Studies at the Australian National University. The final writing became possible only through the generosity of the National University of Singapore (NUS) in allowing first a period of leave in Cambridge and later release from administrative responsibilities. The leave was spent as a Visiting Fellow at King's College, Cambridge. I am grateful to all of these institutions, and the individuals who animated them, for those wonderful opportunities.

During the times in the field in 1995 and subsequently, I acquired many debts, only the heaviest of which can be mentioned here. Two former colleagues and friends, both now sadly missed, introduced me to their beloved homelands in Karoland and Sabah respectively—the late Dr Masri Singarimbun and Dr James Ongkili. Sikap Sembayang, Nismah Tarigan and Manis Tarigan greatly facilitated research in Gunung, while in addition Juara Ginting, Yasin Karo-Karo and Mary Steedly constituted invaluable guides on the Karo; Fr Philippus Manala and his Capucin colleagues, Fr Tony Scerri, J. B. Simbolon, Professor A. Pasaribu and Ben Pasaribu with the Toba. Yasin also helped with questionnaires in Medan. In Sabah Jacqueline Kitingan, Benedict Topin, Penelope Husin, Herman Luping, Joanna Kissey and Rita Lasimbang were particularly helpful. In the preparation of this manuscript, and particularly the maps, Joyce Zaide and Henry Kwan Wai Hung were indispensable. In all things I am in debt to Helen Reid—muse, mentor and gentle critic.

During the long maturation since the 1995 fieldwork, each chapter passed through extensive and constant revision, and various forms of presentation. For chapters 1 and 2 these included a Kaplan Lecture, given at the University of Pennsylvania on 30 March 2000, several lectures in Singapore and Malaysia, and an article, 'National and Ethnic

Identities in a Democratic Age: Some Thoughts of a Southeast Asian Historian', in Oh Myung-Seok and Kim Hyung-jun (ed), *Religion, Ethnicity and Modernity in Southeast Asia*, Seoul, Seoul National University Press, 1998, 11–43. Chapter 3 has evolved as the situation of Chinese Southeast Asians changed, including an International Society for the Study of the Chinese Overseas (ISSCO) conference paper in 1998, a published lecture at the Academia Sinica in Taipei and presentations in Canberra and Singapore. The genesis of chapter 3 was a paper presented at the 15th Conference of the International Association of Historians of Asia, held in Jakarta in August 1998. A later version was published in *Journal of Southeast Asian Studies* **32**: 3 (2001). Chapter 5 also had diverse incarnations, including an article in *Asian Ethnicity* **15**, 3 (Oct 2004). An earlier version of chapter 7 was published in *Journal of Southeast Asian Studies* **28**, 1 (March 1997) 120–36. All these were milestones on the way to this book, and I acknowledge and thank all the editors and outlets involved. My final group of critics and long-suffering collaborators were my NUS graduate class in 2008, who taught as they learned.

Abbreviations

AKAR	Angkatan Keadilan Rakyat, People's Justice Movement
ASA	Association of Southeast Asia
ASAA	Asian Studies Association of Australia
ASEAN	Association of Southeast Asian Nations
BKI	*Bijdragen tot de Taal-, Land-, en Volkenkunde van Nederlandsche Indië*, published by the KITLV (see below)
BN	Barisan National, National Front (ruling party in Malaysia)
BP	*Borneo Post* (Kota Kinabalu)
BPS	Biro Pusat Statistik, Central Statistical Bureau
CIA	Central Intelligence Agency
DAP	Democratic Action Party (Malaysia)
DE	*Daily Express* (Kota Kinabalu)
EPU	The Economic Planning Unit, Prime Minister's Department, Malaysia
FEER	*Far Eastern Economic Review*
FMS	Federated Malay States
GAM	Gerakan Acheh Merdeka, Aceh Independence Movement
GBKP	Gereja Batak Karo Protestan, Karo Batak Protestant Church
GKPI	Gereja Kristen Protestan Indonesia, Indonesian Protestant Christian Church
HKB	Hatopan Kristen Batak, Batak Christian Association
HKBP	Huria Kristen Batak Protestan, Batak Protestant Christian Church
HKI	Huria Kristen Indonesia, Indonesian (formerly Batak) Christian Church
HUDA	Himpunan Ulama Daya Aceh, Association of Ulama of [traditional] Aceh Religious Schools
IAIN	Institute Agama Islam Negeri, State Islamic Institute
ISEAS	Institute for Southeast Asian Studies (Singapore)
JAS	*Journal of Asian Studies*

JMBRAS	*Journal of the Malaysian* [formerly *Malayan*] *Branch, Royal Asiatic Society*
JSEAS	*Journal of Southeast Asian Studies*
JSB	Jong Sumatranen Bond; Young Sumatrans' Union
KCA	Kadazan Cultural Association (later KDCA)
KD	Kadazan Dusun (two peoples) or Kadazandusun (one language)
KDCA	Kadazan Dusun Cultural Association (formerly KCA)
KITLV	Koninklijk Institute voor Taal-, Land-, en Volkenkunde (Leiden)
KLF	Kadazandusun Language Foundation
KMM	Kesatuan Melayu Muda; Young Malays' Union
KMT	Kuomintang (*pinyin*: Guomindang); Chinese Nationalist Party
MCP	Malayan Communist Party
MIB	Melayu, Islam, Beraja; Malay, Islam, Monarchy (Brunei)
NBAR	*North Borneo Annual Report*
NEP	New Economic Policy (Malaysia)
NII	Negara Islam Indonesia, Indonesian Islamic State
NST	Negara Sumatera Timur, State of East Indonesia
NZG	Nederlandsch Zendingsvereniging, Dutch Missionary Society
OUP	Oxford University Press
OSH	outrage at state humiliation (see chapter 1)
PAP	People's Action Party (Singapore)
PAS	Parti Agama Se-Malaysia; Pan Malaysian Islam Party (Malaysia)
PBS	Parti Besatu Sabah; Sabah Unity Party
PKI	Partai Komunis Indonesia, Indonesian Communist Party
PNI	Partai Nasionalis Indonesia, Indonesian Nationalist Party
PRRI	Pemerintah Revolusioner Republik Indonesia, Revolutionary Government of the Republic of Indonesia
PUSA	Persatuan Ulama Seluruh Aceh, All-Aceh Ulama Association
SANAP	Sabah National Party
SCA	Sabah Chinese Association
SIRA	Sentral Informasi Referendum Aceh, Aceh Referendum Information Centre
ST	*Sabah Times* (Kota Kinabalu)
TNI	Tentara Nasional Indonesia, Indonesian National Army
UMNO	United Malays National Organisation

UNKO   United National Kadazan Organisation (became UPKO
        in 1964)
UPKO   United Pasok-momogun Kadazan Organization (previously
        UNKO)
USDA   United Sabah Dusun Association
USNO   United Sabah National Organisation
VOC   Verenigde Oost-Indische Compagnie; (Dutch) United East
        India Company

1 Nationalism and Asia

The mid-twentieth century marked one of the greatest watersheds of Asian history. The relatively brief Japanese occupation of Southeast Asia and much of China, and its sudden ending with the atomic bombs of August 1945, telescoped what might have been a long-term transition into a dramatic and violent revolution. In essence, imperial constructs were declared to be nation-states, the sole legitimate model of twentieth century politics, sanctioned in the 'sovereign equality' principle of the United Nations charter (1945).

The world system of competitive, theoretically equal sovereign states, inadequately labelled the 'Westphalia system', had been carried into Asia over several centuries under the 'organised hypocrisy' of imperialism (Krasner 2001), which held that only 'civilised states' could be full members of the sovereign equality club. After 1945 that exclusivist hypocrisy was replaced by a more optimistic one, which held that every corner of the planet should be divided into theoretically equal sovereign states, in reality an extension to the planet of the system of sovereign equality which European states had painfully learned to practise among themselves. In Asia, which had very different experience of international relations of a largely unequal kind, what units would emerge to play this game of nominally equal sovereign states?

The growing literature on nationalism would suggest that the winners from the collapse of empires would have to be ethnically homogeneous nation-states. Yet each major Asian state looks like an anomaly, failing to undergo the kind of culturally homogeneous national assertiveness that broke up empires in Europe and the Americas under the new pressures of industrialisation and print capitalism. Imperial borders were sanctified by China, India, Indonesia, Burma and the Philippines, though each has experienced modernity under radically different conditions. The British and Spanish/American empires in Asia democratised without fragmenting into ethnically based states; India was of course rendered asunder, but on religious, not ethnic grounds. China stalled on democratisation partly out of fear that it would endanger the sanctified maximalist borders of the Manchu empire. Indonesia also reversed its experiment with democratisation in the late 1950s on the basis of similar fears, but returned to democracy in 1998 with only a modest challenge of ethnie nationalism around the edges.

The failure of Southeast Asian attempts to vary imperial boundaries in the name of historical, cultural or ideological claims illustrates the power of the alchemy. Thailand's wartime annexation of western Cambodia, some of eastern Burma, and northern Malaya (1941–5), Indonesia's annexation of (Portuguese) East Timor in 1975–99, the division of Vietnam in 1954–75 (even though coinciding with its pre-colonial history of division), the regional rebellions in Indonesia (1956–62), Cambodia's probing of its south-eastern border in 1978 and Vietnam's subsequent invasion of Cambodia, all failed in the long run to dethrone the power of imperial boundaries. The succession of Malaysia to Britain's untidy empire in the Malay World was fought by Indonesia in 1962–6 and opposed by the Philippines (which laid a claim to Sabah in 1962), yet in the long run it was only the departure of tiny Brunei (1962) and Singapore (1965) that diminished the imperial heritage. Burma has been the least successful in defending its extended imperial borders, yet no rebellion has been successful against even such a weak state. Since 1975, the only legally acknowledged change to borders has been the reassertion of an imperial one, as Indonesia's occupation of (Portuguese) East Timor was deemed a failure and reversed in 1999.

How do we explain this difference from the fate of empires in Europe? It was the task of nationalism to invent the new nation-states for the post-1945 world, but was this nationalism a different beast altogether from that of Europe? Could we imagine nationalism in Europe sanctifying the multi-ethnic borders created by the Hapsburgs, Romanovs and Ottomans, as we do in Asia for the empires of British, Dutch, Spanish, French and Manchus? If Asian nation-states were to perform this trans-formation from the immense variety and antiquity of their ethnic, political and civilisational forms, without fragmenting the leviathans of imperial construction, they would require a kind of magic—the imperial alchemy of my title. The base metal of empire would have to be transmuted into the gold of nationhood.

Two kinds of alchemy were at work here. The revolutionary alchemist was the most daring, insisting that the ideal model of the modern nation state should be implemented within the imperial borders without delay. His gold comprised the sovereignty of the people, the equality of all citizens under a unified and centralised state, and a complete break with past loyalties. Indonesia is my primary case, but the much more complex shadow of China looms always in the background.

Other imperial constructs decolonised and democratised in a series of federal compromises which left the outer shell of empire still able to act in the world as a nation-state with the same borders as the old. India is the classic case, but in Southeast Asia the example was followed in Malaysia's strikingly asymmetric form of federalism.

A burst of perceptive writing in the 1980s gave the phenomenon of nationalism a clear definition and a place in the history of the Western world. Benedict Anderson's brilliant *Imagined Communities* (1983), taken together with the work of Gellner (1983) and Giddens (1985), suggested that the West had sufficiently broken the spell of the nation-state and its assumptions to be able to analyse the phenomenon clearly.

The most striking feature of these three writers was their positioning of nationalism as the outcome of a certain historical conjuncture, which created homogeneities of readership, education, language, work-place and eventually, imagination. At a particular time the process of industrialisation called for a new ideology, which put the creation or maintenance of strong states corresponding with these homogeneities at the top of its priorities. 'A homogeneity imposed by objective, inescapable imperative [of industrialism] eventually appears on the surface in the form of nationalism' (Gellner 1983: 39).

These writers thereby stressed the essential modernity of nationalism and fatally punctured some common-sense ideas about its perennial naturalness. They did not proceed explicitly to predict the demise of nationalism as an outcome of the disappearance of these historic features, though the replacement of Anderson's 'print capitalism' by global electronic networks might have led in that direction. However, as Hobsbawm (1990) noted, the fact that nationalism aroused such scholarly interest in the 1980s was a sign that we could for the first time see beyond it.

There was a natural reaction on the part of those pointing to the durability of some ethnies, even without a supporting state, and to the ethno-linguistic foundation of most nation-states (Armstrong 1982; Smith 1986). But a larger scholarly industry developed around the quest to understand the unexpected outburst of ethnic violence in eastern and southern Europe as the Soviet and Yugoslav autocracies unravelled. Their question was 'why, at the close of the second millennium, there should be a resurgence of ethnic conflict and nationalism, at a time when the world is becoming more unified and interconnected?' (Smith 1995: 1). Journals, conferences and book series were initiated with titles like *Nationalism and Ethnic Politics*.[1] Having been profoundly neglected for so long, the complex issues of nation and identity were suddenly central to social science.

Much of this literature sought to disentangle the positive, inclusive elements of nationalism from its divisive ones, by utilising the distinction between territorial or civic nationalism and ethnic nationalism. Hans Kohn had long ago pointed out how differently nationalism developed east of the Rhine. 'French nationalism was born (as English and American had [been] before it) in a wave of generous enthusiasm for the cause of mankind; the opposing nationalisms ... were directed to laudable but narrower goals, self-centred but antagonistic' (Kohn 1944: 572–3). Anthony Smith (1986) elaborated this distinction. Whereas older experiments with nationalism represented a geographically bounded state (Britain, the US or France) eventually creating a culturally coherent nation, the ethnic model was the other way around: an ethnic group of unclear borders attempted to acquire appropriate borders and political status.

Liah Greenfeld's *Nationalism* (1992) was a careful historical analysis of the relationship of these two types in the context of European history. She saw the concept of nation developing in sixteenth century England in the sense of a sovereign people, entitled to representation in the body politic. It was thus a concept closely wedded to the emergence of democracy in early modern Europe. As it spread eastwards through Europe in the eighteenth century, however, the unique quality of the nation became more marked than its sovereign or democratic character. The sovereignty of this type of nation was held to lie in its distinctiveness, not its participatory civic character. While in the civic variant 'nationality is at least in principle open and voluntaristic', in the ethnic variant 'it is believed to be inherent—one can neither acquire it if one does not have it, nor change it if one does' (Greenfeld 1992: 11). In general, her analysis of 'five roads' shows Germany and Russia following this ethnic path; England and the US (in common with most anti-colonial New World nationalisms) the civic path; and France a more ambivalent path eventually veering towards the civic. By implication, her five exclusively European roads to the nation-state were exemplary types, as if Asian experience were irrelevant.

Walker Connor (1994) made a sterner distinction between nation and state, two very distinct categories often conflated in popular parlance. He wished to limit the use of nationalism and nation to what

---

[1] The journals *Nationalism and Ethnic Politics* and *Social Identities: Journal for the Study of Race, Nation and Culture* date from 1995 and 1997 respectively.

he specified as ethno-nationalism. An identification with a state should be distinguished as patriotism, so that the nation can be restricted to 'the largest human grouping predicated on a myth of common ancestry' (Connor 1994: 214). The nation is fictive kin; not a true descent group (since most **felt** nations, such as the English, Chinese or Thai, are immensely plural in terms of biological descent). Connor seeks to deal with the obvious fact that modern educated Europeans are fully aware of the ethnic diversity of their national backgrounds by claiming that despite this book knowledge, 'at a more intuitive or sensory level, they [English, French and Germans] "know" their nation is ethnically, hermetically pure' (*Ibid.*: 215).

This is unconvincing. Like many authors, Connor rightly associates the term nation with the dream of belonging, and seeks to separate it from states. But he creates further problems by seemingly accepting that state-created or state-dependent identities are nations despite his attempt to narrow the definition to fictive kinship.

In this book I propose to avoid the term 'nation' except as used by its advocates, as too profoundly emotive and ambiguous to be helpful in analysis. I will follow Smith in labelling a group which imagines itself kin as an **ethnie** and its political assertiveness as **ethnie nationalism**. By contrast the strong identities which modern states have been able to evoke through education, state ritual and the media I will call **state nationalism**. This is not intended to have the negative connotation which Anderson (1991: chapter 6) gave his 'official nationalism'. All modern states, democratic or authoritarian, ethnie-based, multi-ethnic or imperial, have powerful means at their disposal to evoke solidarity, for good or ill.

A typology for Asian nationalism

When we turn to Asia, it is immediately apparent that neither of these nationalisms covers the way the term nationalism was most frequently used in the twentieth century. Indian, Indonesian, Filipino, Sri Lankan and Burmese 'nationalisms' were all multi-ethnie solidarities directed against alien rulers, and in this sense without clear parallel in Western Europe or the Americas. This type we must qualify as anti-imperial nationalism. Once it had succeeded in replacing the imperial authorities in power it began to change into state nationalism, but retained for some time the emotional pull generated by successfully ending the painful racial humiliation of imperialism. It certainly has a great deal more potency in Asian states than is suggested by Smith's dismissive characterisation of what he calls 'colonial nationalism' as still-born, imitative and elitist (Smith 1991, cited in Tønnesson and Antlöv 1996: 11).

This tripartite typology of nationalism—ethnie, state and anti-imperial—has similarities with the three categories adopted by Tønnesson and Antlöv (ethno-, official and plural). Their tentative fourth category, class struggle, is much less convincing as a category of nationalism (Tønnesson and Antlöv 1996: 20–2). I also see the need for a fourth category, but rather to make better sense of nationalism in independent Asian states both before and after the high colonial period. I call this outrage at state humiliation (OSH), a category which is characteristically Asian as a reaction to the humiliations the state was seen to have undergone over two centuries at the hands of barbarians.

Each of these four categories is intended to be analytic rather than prescriptive. The distinction made by Kohn, Greenfeld and others is extremely important, between an exclusive ethno-nationalism which marginalises minorities and an inclusive civic nationalism which embraces all. But this is primarily a qualitative question of whether a particular nationalism is seen as malign or benign. Ethnie nationalisms may gain power in a vengeful mood which makes them ethno-nationalist, but they may also seek alliances and accommodations leading to a fruitful civic nationalism. I will retain the distinction between ethnie nationalism, as an analytic category, and ethno-nationalism, as a qualitative judgement.

This book is designed to make recent advances in understanding nationalism more helpful in understanding Asian phenomena by looking empirically at Southeast Asian cases. Southeast Asia has the great merit of diversity, with examples of almost every type of phenomenon to be found in the broader world outside Western Europe and its New World offshoots. These latter cases have generated the great majority of the careful analytic work, even that of Southeast Asianist Anderson. The immigrant societies of the Western Hemisphere are clearly atypical as purely territorial movements sharing language and culture with the imperial power. Even post-enlightenment Western Europe, though more helpful in its wide range of possibilities, represents one extreme, a system of compact and competing nation-states, within the broader Eurasian spectrum. While the categories generated from European examples are helpful, the work of adapting them to Asian experience largely remains to be done.

Ethnie nationalism

An ethnie will be defined as a group with a strong sense of being similar. As simplified by Smith (1986: 22–31), this belief in similarity is likely to consist of most or all of the following six elements:

a collective name,

a common myth of descent,

some shared history or set of traditions,

a distinctive shared culture, usually including language or religion,

an association with a territory, either present or past (though one of sacred sites and centres rather than boundaries),

a sense of solidarity.

For Asia in particular, **ethnie** has the advantage of escaping the positive emotive associations of 'nation', the currently negative (but once positive) ones of 'race', and the necessarily sub-national ones of ethnic group. Most Asian languages do not have these distinctions, or have them differently. When the Chinese term *minzu,* or its analogue in Korean (*min-jok*), or the Thai word *chat,* or the Malay/Indonesian word *bangsa* were developed into the object of modern national striving, they could be translated equally well as race or nation. These terms are still used in many Asian countries to exhort loyalty and devotion. It sounds shocking in English if they are translated as race; acceptably patriotic if they are translated as nation. To modern American, Australian, or West European ears the two concepts seem quite distinct, even if in the nineteenth century they did not. To Malays or Khmers they still do not.

State nationalism

The royal dynasties that dominated human history before the modern age had little need of nationalism. They ruled by divine right, not as representatives of a people; their armies, their officials and their subjects were diverse, often by design. For the most part therefore state nationalism is a feature of the post-Enlightenment regimes in the West and of twentieth century ones in Asia, which needed to rule in the name of a people and therefore to define and mould that people. In general only these modern regimes believed it their business to build homogeneity by providing a uniform education syllabus and monolingual media, and to persuade their people to fight and die for the national cause.

There are however some older Asian examples of identification with king, dynasty or territory which have features of state nationalism. Pre-modern Chinese described their collective identity by reference to a dynasty—'People of Han, or Tang, or Qing'. Nevertheless, the state's requirement that officials be recruited through examinations of certain classical texts created an unusual uniformity of high culture (see below).

Vietnamese and Korean rulers, although using similar examinations of the Chinese classics for their bureaucracy, placed great emphasis on the unique distinctiveness of their country from China. In Vietnam, later literati used the emperors who had successfully resisted China as the epitome of 'Vietnameseness'. The role of the rulers, in turn, 'was supposed to be that of a moral teacher whom the whole society revered and imitated' (Woodside 1976: 16).

In southern Asia monarchs often used religion to create homogeneities of culture. Southeast Asian kings exercised a power more charismatic and spiritual than bureaucratic and temporal, and they sought to build, patronise and control the most sacred sites and symbols of the land. A new religious order could be used to expand royal power by overriding local cults and spirits. Islam played this role for a time during the 'gunpowder empires' that accumulated unprecedented power in the sultanates of Aceh, Banten, Makassar and Mataram in the seventeenth century.

Theravada Buddhism proved more useful in the long term, however, in building a common consciousness among subjects of Thai, Lao, Khmer and Burmese kings. The monkhood (*sangha*) was a popular and widespread force in education, ritual and building a common mentality, and kings made it their business to patronise and reform it in the direction of state-directed homogeneity. The Mahavihara form of ordination practised in Sri Lanka proved an effective means for kings, from the fifteenth century to the eighteenth, to 'reform' the *sangha* along uniform foreign lines, and thereby bring the population into a similar mould under a royally appointed patriarch.

I argue therefore that state nationalism was a factor in some premodern Asian states. It came into its own, however, in the high modernist era of the 1950s to 1970s, when it sought with remarkable success to transform ancient Asian civilisations through mass education, state ritual and revolutionary rhetoric.

Anti-imperial nationalism

In twentieth century Asia and Africa, this facet of nationalism became so dominant that it was popularly thought to be the only valid variant. Most of the literature on South and Southeast Asia labels it 'nationalism' without further need for questioning. The uncolonised variants of nationalism, Chinese, Japanese and Thai, were wholly different in nature, combining state and ethnie nationalisms in different degrees. Yet because they were contemporary with the anti-imperial phenomena of southern Asia, they have been considered part of Asian nationalism when they have been analysed at all. Chinese nationalism, the most problematic case for the analyst, often presented itself as anti-imperial and occasionally sought common cause with anti-imperial nationalism elsewhere. The target of this anti-imperialism, however, quickly moved away from the Manchus who had very successfully colonised China for 250 years but were swiftly removed in 1911. More immediate antagonists then became the powers (European, American and Japanese) which had 'humiliated' China and dominated its Treaty Ports, and the Japanese who occupied militarily much of eastern and northeastern China from 1931 to 1945. This is more properly considered OSH (see below) than anti-imperial nationalism.

Further confusion is caused by the popular and political use of 'nationalist' as the label for anti-communist governments and parties in China, Korea and Vietnam. This obscures the way in which communist movements mobilised anti-imperial and ethnie nationalism against the state nationalism of the governments they opposed.

Yet anti-imperial nationalism was absolutely crucial as the key ingredient for the alchemy that sought to turn empires into nations in the middle of the twentieth century. It can be categorised by the following features:

- Reversal of the racial hierarchies of late imperialism, which had Europeans (or Japanese in Korea and Taiwan) at the top, outsider Asians (Chinese, Indians and Japanese in Southeast Asia) in the middle and 'natives' at the bottom.
- Adoption of the boundaries and unities created by the imperial power as the sacred space of the new national identity, within which all 'indigenous' people should bury their differences.
- A radically modernising agenda, condemning traditional monarchies and customs as 'feudal' and artificially sustained by colonialism.
- Glorification of one or more ancient polity deemed to represent the national essence before its humiliation or dismemberment.
- Support for economic self-sufficiency, a national language and national education, as keys to creating prosperity for the new national identity.

More than the other two forms, anti-imperial nationalism was the child of very specific conditions in the first half of the twentieth century. Imperialism changed its nature profoundly in the decades before and after 1900, as colonial governments extended their sovereignty to internationally agreed boundaries and assumed most of the unitary functions of nation-states elsewhere. The twentieth century imperial combination of creating a structure that looked like a modern nation state but lacked some of its key features (democracy, widespread education, equality before the law), and beginning to educate increasing sections of the population in modern Western ideologies, ensured the success of anti-imperial arguments. Marxism was attractive to many as a seemingly rational, non-racist and above all optimistic form of anti-imperial nationalism, using the arguments of Hobson (1902) and Lenin (1916) to show imperialism as a doomed form of capitalism.

Outrage at state humiliation (OSH)

This is an emotive variant very salient in the proud independent states of Asia. Although entangled with all three other types, it requires a separate categorisation because it cannot be subsumed into any of the other three. It is distinguished from mainstream ethnie nationalism in that its focus is the perceived humiliation of a state, rather than an ethnie, before outsiders deemed to be unreasonably powerful. It is not anti-imperial nationalism because it operates particularly in states that are formally independent, yet not as successful or powerful as their citizens demand. It is not state nationalism because it lives so uncomfortably with the compromises made by the state, and can be a major factor leading to its destabilisation or overthrow. As Jing Tsu (2005: 222) puts it, 'Beneath the surface of modernity and enlightenment lies an unabated restlessness expressed as passionate discontent with the self and nation.' We may understand the salience of this factor in Northeast Asia as a product of the success of state nationalism over many centuries in making the state unusually central in the self-identification of subjects. Although, or perhaps because, subjects had little influence on the remote and bureaucratic Confucian state, they accepted it as the principal feature of political identity in the competition with outsiders. State nationalism had done its job over many centuries in both China and Korea making the bureaucratic state more central to political identity there than in most European societies before the French Revolution. OSH nationalism therefore sought to recreate the state more powerfully, not to build a new polity more reflective of the ethnie.

The Boxer movement (1899–1900) and the May Fourth movement (1917–21) are the most spectacular formative manifestations of OSH in China, representing opposite rural/mystical and urban/reformist sides of Chinese outrage. The acceptance by the Yuan Shikai government on 9 May 1915 of Japan's twenty-one demands led quickly to protests around the country against 'national humiliation' and the demand above all that this humiliation must be remembered and the bitterness endlessly reiterated. Every year subsequently saw 9 May and several other days in May commemorated as 'national humiliation days'. When the Chinese Nationalist Party (KMT) achieved national power in 1927 the day was formalised as the party's major public ritual (Cohen 2003: 148–60; Callahan 2006). Maoism had little use for this kind of victimhood, but after the death of Mao OSH nationalism returned to China. 'National humiliation' commemorations returned with the 150th anniversary of the Opium War humiliation in 1990, the launching of an official textbook, *The Indignation of National Humiliation* and a rash of subsequent anniversaries of particular events (Callahan 2006). In 2001, inspired by the Army and perhaps aiming to channel the dangerous outbursts of popular outrage that occurred after the bombing of the Chinese embassy in Belgrade in 1999, the National People's Congress legislated a single 'National Humiliation Day'. Progress was slowed by debate over which of the many candidates to pick (the KMT had listed twenty-six such 'national humiliation days' in 1928), but eventually the first such day was celebrated in September (Callahan 2006; Tsu 2005: 222–4; *People's Daily* 29 April 2001). China's rise has done little to counter the effects of having shifted the national educational curriculum from an emphasis on Marxist philosophy to a state-as-victim framework for telling national history (Zheng 2009). OSH nationalism remains a destabilising popular sentiment, seen in the violent anti-Japanese demonstrations of 2005 and the Olympic torch fiasco of 2008.

The outrage felt in Northeast Asia at the weakness and humiliation of the civilisation and polity which had governed the largest concentration of people in human history was matched in Southeast Asia by frustration and rage at the weakness and humiliation of Islam, also heir to a proud tradition of perceived superiority to other political models. In the sixteenth to nineteenth centuries Indonesia's most powerful still-independent state, the sultanate of Aceh, remained independent largely because this type of nationalism was influential enough among ordinary Acehnese to arouse them against their monarchs who constantly sought political and commercial accommodation with the Europeans. As in China, this was a form of nationalism that repeatedly destabilised the state even though retaining that state as the centre of its political identity. It has operated in the form of popular resentment against more successfully modernising neighbours in the twentieth century—in China and Korea against Japan; in Laos against Thailand; in Cambodia against Thailand and Vietnam; in Malaysia against Singapore.

Overlapping time-scales

Much of the story of Southeast Asia in the first half of the twentieth century was one of anti-imperial nationalism prevailing over ethnie nationalism, though to a greater extent in some cases (Indonesia, Vietnam) than in others (Malaya, Cambodia). Anti-imperial nationalism had seemingly served its purpose by the 1950s with the independence of the major countries, but it was kept vigorous until 1975 by the Indo-China wars and the Cold War. It contributed much of the emotional capital for the state nationalism of the new independent governments, but was of rapidly decreasing effectiveness as a response to renewed ethnie nationalism. The issue then became how far state nationalism could use the early momentum of anti-imperial nationalism to create a new sense of identity coterminous with the state.

Could the alchemy of turning reviled imperial borders into sacred national ones be completed in time to stave off further challenges of ethnie nationalism and OSH, turning Acehnese and Bataks into Indonesians; Chinese, Malays and Kadazans into Malaysians? The argument will be that where this alchemy has succeeded with the most distinctive ethnies it has been by providing a larger stage on which to play out a reinvented modern ethnicity. Batak, Christian and Indonesian identities (or else-where, Balinese, Hindu and Indonesian identities) are able to coexist through a process of layering or nesting of identities. The alchemy has been much less successful in Malaysia where anti-imperial nationalism was weaker and a protective form of ethnie nationalism stronger.

The global context of course affects whether Asia might be expected eventually to follow a fragmenting path similar to Europe's towards nation-state-dom. If we accepted the European experience as normative we might have to assume rough times ahead as Asian nationalisms demanded cultural homogeneity in their nation-states. Following Chakrabarty (2000), however, it will be prudent to 'provincialise' Europe to the extent as seeing it as a particular case based on rather unusual European conditions. Comparing the situations of Europe, Northeast Asia and most of Southeast Asia will clarify the mix between global factors and regional ones; the translation of ideas; the apparent paradox that sovereign powers were being voluntarily surrendered in Western Europe while thousands died fighting for them in ex-Yugoslavia, the Caucasus, East Africa, Burma, Indonesia and China.

Post-nationalism: Europe and the global factors

There is much evidence that nationalism, as well as the nation-state that was its object, 'has already passed its peak', as Vaclav Havel put it before the Canadian Parliament (1999). The decline of anti-imperial nationalism in the post-colonial world appeared to coincide with the hugely increased mobility of capital and goods at the end of the century to suggest a new era of globalisation and interdependence. All parts of the world are affected by this greater integration, which provides some of the context for regional differences in nationalist expression.

The signs of a post-nationalist age may be summarised as follows:

- **The end of the Cold War**, and the collapse of the 'second world' of international communism, has also robbed the 'third world' and the 'non-aligned movement' of most of their meaning. Hindsight enables us to see how the balance of terror between two Superpowers encouraged the suspension of disbelief in the sovereign equality of extraordinarily dissimilar members of the United Nations, even the tiniest of which were wooed by the Superpowers.
- **The globalisation of capital markets and trade** has ridden the collapse of communism, so every government now woos foreign investment with as much zeal as nationalists once condemned it. The World Trade Organisation, created only in 1995, expanded rapidly to embrace 148 states (2004) and 97 per cent of the rapidly expanding world trade it regulated and encouraged. National elites know that their own national economies are drastically affected by changes elsewhere, and that the immediate cost of scaring off international capital is more unemployment at home. Even as late as the 1980s large countries such as China and the Soviet Union, and smaller ones including most of mainland Southeast Asia, were able to write their own economic stories, producing statistics that suited government needs. The end of the Cold War had as one consequence the genuine globalisation of data-gathering through the World Bank and the United Nations, forcing states to compete in the realm of gross national product (GNP) growth, welfare statistics and gini-coefficients rather than political rhetoric.
- **The media operates globally**, as increasing numbers obtain their news from electronic sources and multi-nationals take over many of the key services. It is difficult to read Benedict Anderson (1991: 37–46) arguing that the 'print capitalism' of newspapers with particular circulation areas was vital in creating nation-states, without pondering how the global media empires of today, the internationally syndicated columns and satellite TV hook-ups, may affect the growing irrelevance of those same nation-states. Three changes at least seem important here: (i) more widely available international alternatives to the national identity choices people make when they switch on;

(ii) specialist audiences for movements, ideologies, hobbies, interests, causes and identity politics more readily become global. Where this involves powerful changes of consciousness like feminism, ecology, fourth-world empowerment or democracy this brings world-wide pressures to bear on particular sovereign states, largely through the phenomenon we call non-governmental organisations (NGOs) (iii) the highly mobile elites of several multi-national regions or language groups, including the North Atlantic, eastern Asia, Africa south of the Sahara, the Arab World, the Chinese-reading world and Spanish America, are increasingly interested in supra-national journals and news sources which serve the planet or some sub-set of it, like CNN, Al-Jazeera, or *The Economist*. Far from representing Samuel Huntington's 'civilizations', these are imagined trans-national communities defined by language, ideology and temporary migration.

- **The international movement of labour** is not new, but has reached new heights after an anomalous period in the mid-twentieth century when nationalism tended to keep people at home. More than a million Chinese a year became labour migrants at the first peak in the 1920s, even though excluded from the migrant countries of the New World, to which streamed millions of Irish, Italians and Germans. A similar scale of movement was again reached in the 1990s, but now primarily moving from poorer tropical countries to wealthier temperate ones. Southeast Asia, one of the largest net importers of labour in the 1920s, became among the largest net exporters of people, particularly in the form of labour contracts to Japan, Taiwan, Hong Kong and the Middle East. Plummeting birth rates in most affluent countries, led by Japan, Korea, Hong Kong and Singapore, ensure that large-scale international migration will be needed to keep these economies functioning. The new migrants are more able than their predecessors to retain their old identities, for the reasons above.
- **Ideological changes** have weakened, if not ended, the assimilationist ideal of the melting pot, whereby receiving countries expected migrants to lose their old identity in favour of the state nationalism of their new country. Canada and Australia led the experiment with multi-culturalism in the 1980s, and the subsequent 'culture wars' in the United States reflected the same trend. Countries such as Mexico, China, India and Vietnam, which as late as the 1970s had denounced their millions who had deserted homeland for a better life elsewhere, realised the economic advantages to both sides of bi-cultural migrants, not only in the form of remittances home but in the international connections and skills the migrants possessed. The acceptability of dual nationality and multiple passports has gradually spread, with

the United States quietly accepting the widespread nature of the phenomenon at the end of the century. Wang Gungwu (1996) and Aihwa Ong (1999) have drawn attention to the new respectability of a sojourning mentality among Chinese, but the phenomenon of multiple identities has gone even further in Europe.

In all these areas the European community has been the pace-setter. Its members have seen the benefits since 1945 of subordinating national sovereignties in the interests of peace, a large market, economies of scale and regional specialisation. In structural terms Europe made multi-national regulation work. In popular terms it also established the limits of their peoples' tolerance of it, as demonstrated in the negative outcome of referenda in France and the Netherlands (2005) and Ireland (2008). At a global level European states have also been the champions of and exemplars for international regulation. An ever larger body of trans-national law in turn makes the sub-national autonomy of Flanders, Scotland, or Catalonia less threatening to practical arrangements (Keating 2001). Post-nationalism is to some extent a global phenomenon, but it claims its securest gains in previously fragmented Europe.

Enduring states: Northeast Asia

The Northeast Asian experience presents the major challenge to generalisations about the development of nationalism and the nation-state. The question here is not so much the perduring ethnie (mostly of Middle Eastern origin) that concerned Armstrong and Smith, but the perduring **states** of China, Korea, Japan and Vietnam. Each of these states has been in existence for a millennium or more, generating dynastic histories and literary works in a language that can be read by modern citizens. The boundaries between these four states changed scarcely at all in that period, even if China and Vietnam expanded greatly at the expense of 'barbarians' to west and south. As opposed to the modern states imagining an ageless community to match their contemporary identity, here are states with long memories of former dynasties and sages. Yet with a few exceptions like Prasenjit Duara (1995: 51–6), there has been little analysis of their experience in relation to the new literature.

To render the Chinese experience understandable in European terms, one must imagine a Roman Empire that did not fragment into dynasties and ethnies speaking different vernaculars, but repeatedly reconstituted itself after each dynastic crisis around the same core area and the same written language. The fragmentation did not occur because the written language was not phonetic, and therefore not organically connected to the spoken regional dialects. Literary uniformity was established from Han (analogous to Roman) times by the practice of rubbing paper sheets applied to stone tablets on which the official version of the classics had been inscribed. This primitive form of printing was gradually replaced by efficient wood-block printing onto paper, and by the eleventh century large numbers of books were circulating. Printing served to reinforce the imperial language, not the separate regional spoken vernaculars as happened in Europe.

Korea and Vietnam absorbed the Chinese system through direct rule in the first millennium of the Common era, but continued it in what may be considered the closest the world knew to nation-states before the sixteenth century. China itself was unashamedly an empire, indeed a world-empire believing itself the only legitimate power under heaven. But Korea and Vietnam negotiated their independence through warfare (primarily in the Vietnamese case) and consummate playing of the Chinese imperial game, under extremely testing circumstances of proximity to the world's strongest power. Both regularly sent tribute missions to the Chinese capital over many centuries, but at the same time refused any Chinese interference in their affairs. In their official pronouncements and histories they were at pains to assert their equality with China or, when the Middle Kingdom was under barbarian Mongol or Manchu rule, even their cultural superiority as more faithful upholders of the classics.

From the time the self-proclaimed 'First Emperor' or world-ruler (*Qin Shih Huangdi*) created the Chinese state and ended feudalism in the period 221–210 BC, it was governed bureaucratically and centrally, systematically divided into commanderies and prefectures. 'There can be no civilization on earth that has so long and full a record of state structures and official posts; there can be no other civilization to which the state itself has for so long been so central; ... an institution that is almost sacred in its unquestionableness' (Jenner 1992: 18). Measures, weights, coinage and the writing system were unified over the vast area embracing the lower Yellow and Yangtze rivers, and governors were expected to report regularly to the centre. The same centralised system was re-established by the Han (206 BC–220 CE), the Tang (618–907 CE) and later dynasties. The system of examining young scholars on their knowledge of the Chinese classics was introduced as early as the sixth century CE in China (or in embryo the second century BC), the eighth in Korea and the eleventh in Vietnam. In principle these literati chosen on merit administered the state in accordance with the Confucian norms they had studied. In practice there were of course warlords and powerful families in all three cases, but the norm continued through to the end of the nineteenth century.

Japan was a compact archipelago like the British Isles, the boundaries of which were determined by nature, not shifting as was the fate of most of the Eurasian land mass. English historians sometimes trace the national idea back as far as the fourteenth century, but it was not until the sixteenth century that Westminster ruled all the British Isles, and not until the late nineteenth century that English prevailed as the language of the whole archipelago. Britain's state nationalism never succeeded in convincing the Irish they were British, and the project was officially declared a failure with the separation of 1922. The Japanese islands, on the other hand, were definitively unified by Tokugawa Ieyesu in 1603 after several centuries of a shared literary and religious culture.

The experience of Europe, which we might characterise as ethnie nationalisms and state nationalisms mutually reinforcing each other to create cultural homogeneities, beginning with England and Holland in the sixteenth century, helps us very little here. Instead, we have to see a state nationalism at work in China since very ancient times, operating primarily in a dynastic and elite mode but having the same effect of creating cultural homogeneities. State nationalism (*guojiazhuyi*) is readily understood in contemporary Chinese debates, and distinguished from ethnie nationalism (*minzuzhuyi*) (Harris 1997: 125). We can also perceive an early dose of anti-imperial nationalism in the way Vietnamese, Korean and Japanese literati insisted on asserting their equality with and difference from the Chinese world-empire while emulating its mores. Combined with the objective features of common elite training and written language, these factors produced earlier signs of a modern nationalist consciousness than in Europe itself. The populist nationalism which emerged in the twentieth century, therefore, had a distinctive identity base to build on.

Southeast Asia experienced this time-scale through the Chinese sojourners and settlers among them, as will be examined in chapter 3. Even more important was the Vietnamese state, which used Chinese bureaucratic methods very effectively to resist further expansion of the Chinese state southward into Southeast Asia. Though its people were Southeast Asian in many ways, inhabiting the humid tropics and interacting with diversely plural societies, its government was a variant of the Northeast Asian pattern. Like the Chinese state, its military advances were followed by an expansion of bureaucracy and education which effectively turned many Chams, Khmers and Tai-speakers into Vietnamese. The dividing line between Northeast and Southeast Asian patterns is well demonstrated in Vietnam's troubled relationship with

Cambodia. The Vietnamese general sent to administer Cambodia after the conquest of 1833 complained of the personalist style of authority he found—'Cambodian officials know only how to bribe and be bribed. Offices are sold' (Truong Minh Giang to King Minh-Mang, cited in Chandler 1983: 124). The king responded by sending more Vietnamese scholar-officials and teachers, and insisting that 'Since the Tho people are now registered as our citizens, they should adopt our customs ... in line with the idea of transforming the *Yi* [barbarian] into the *Xia* [Chinese/civilised] culture'.[2]

State-averse—Southeast Asia

If Northeast Asia is at one extreme of global experience of strong states over a long period, much of Southeast Asia is close to the other. Its highlands and islands, in particular, never developed bureaucratic, law-giving states on a significant scale and were wary of the externally supported states in their midst. Societies such as the highland Batak, Minangkabau and Pasemah in Sumatra, the Tagalogs and Visayans in the Philippines, the Shan in upper Burma and many of their fellow Tai-speakers in Laos and northern Vietnam, are unusual in having developed complex civilisations, including writing systems, held together by kinship and ritual rather than the power of a state. As Geertz (1980: 135) noted even of the highly complex polities of pre-colonial Java and Bali, they seemed to have 'an alternative conception of what politics was about'.

From the perception of the solid Chinese state, these seemingly state-less barbarians of the south seemed 'like the birds and beasts, without human morality' (Emperor Shi-zong, 1536, cited in Wade 1994, I: 61). Stamford Raffles would echo this impression from the nineteenth century perspective of the by then solid English nation-state, in complaining that the Sumatran societies he encountered from his base in Bengkulu were: 'peopled by innumerable petty tribes, subject to no general government ... At present the people are as wandering in their habits as the birds of the air' (Sophia Raffles 1835: 142).

Was this a question of being further back in an evolutionary sequence, as Raffles implied, or a preferred adaptation to a specific environment? Before going further, it is necessary to take account of Victor Lieberman's impressive assemblage of data in favour of an evolutionary case (Lieberman 2003). He shows persuasively the trend for greater and

---

[2] I am grateful to Dr Li Tana for this reference and translation of Emperor Minh Mang's edict as rendered in the Nguyen chronicle, *Dai Nam Thuc Luc*, for 1839.

greater concentrations of power in mainland Southeast Asia, from at least twenty-three independent polities around 1340 to only three in 1824—Burma, Siam and Vietnam. He points to remarkable similarities between these cases and France's progress towards ever greater concentration of sovereignty within its region, interrupted by an eighteenth century collapse as in the Southeast Asian cases. He shows that not only Vietnam but also Burma 'frequently promoted majority ethnicity and language ... to strengthen psychological identification with the throne' (Lieberman 2003: 41). Although top-down and relentlessly hierarchic, there were, he asserts, many similarities between the way these states evolved and the state nationalism that developed in Europe at the same time. 'While innocent of the insistence on popular sovereignty, evolving political identities, especially in Burma and Vietnam, shared undeniable similarities with their increasingly coherent European counterparts both before and after 1789' (*Ibid.*: 42).

The argument is persuasive enough in the Burmese case to exclude this entirely from the generalisations made about 'Southeast Asia' by the authors discussed below, most of whom are in practice Indonesia specialists. In environmental terms, the major Southeast Asian dry zone of the mid-Irrawaddy basin, where rains were regular but not year-round, contained substantial areas very suitable for the irrigation of permanent bunded rice-fields. The ease of military movements both on the river and across the basin in the dry season made this a natural area for a substantial state. By contrast, the vast area persistently covered by what Lieberman calls 'fluid, small-scale Tai polities', seems almost equally resistant to the bureaucratic state as does the Archipelago, partly for similar environmental reasons.

For most of Southeast Asia, then, its humid tropical climate was inimical to the development of dense agricultural populations and centrally controlled bureaucratic polities. Where rainfall was heavy around the year (as in the central zone of Southeast Asia including the whole Peninsula, most of Sumatra, west Java and Borneo, the rain-forest was dense, difficult to cut and burn for rice-growing and prone to malaria. The first settled agricultural populations therefore grew in areas where there is a marked dry season—January–April in the northern and central parts of mainland Southeast Asia, and May–September in eastern Java and the islands to its east. For reasons of water control and evasion of malaria, highlands were in general earlier settled for agriculture than the coastal regions. These highland populations, however, clustered in particular irrigable river valleys, separated from each other by mountain barriers. Even here travel by road was difficult, and in the densely forested swampy coastlands it was impossible. More extensive polities were held together by water transport, typically up and down a river navigation system, not by the firmer bonds of roads and marching armies.

Despite these environmental obstacles, there have been kingdoms in Southeast Asia since at least the seventh century of the Common Era. But where these had extensive leverage over people at any distance from the palace it was on the basis of Indian or Chinese ideas, and the wealth and technology that came with international trade. The more indigenous Southeast Asian forms of authority appear to be based on supernatural rather than legal sanctions, ritual rather than military predominance. Rulers readily adapted Indian cosmologies to enhance their supernatural effectiveness. Sophisticated cultures with substantial literary traditions (Javanese, Balinese, Batak, Minangkabau, Bugis, as well as Tai communities away from the port/capital) were held together by something other than the legal, bureaucratic and military complex known elsewhere since Roman, Persian and Han times.

Historians of Southeast Asia have been much concerned recently to elaborate what it is, to use Tony Day's words, 'that looks like a bureaucracy, in early as well as contemporary times, but is not one, according to a Weberian definition' (Day 2002: 288). Geertz may have set this ball rolling with his influential *Negara* in 1980, based on the evidence of nineteenth century Bali. He developed the paradigm of the 'Theatre State',

in which the kings and princes were the impresarios, the priests the directors, and the peasants the supporting cast, stage crew and audience ... Court ceremonialism was the driving force of the court politics; and mass ritual was not a device to shore up the state, but rather the state, even in its final gasp, was a device for the enactment of mass ritual. Power served pomp, not pomp power.

(Geertz 1980: 11)

Both internal and external sources do celebrate warlike kingdoms in Java, Bali, Maluku and Champa, as well as the temple-builders of Angkor and Pagan. Chinese sources and indigenous inscriptions were the major sources for kingdoms before 1500, and both seemed to concur that Southeast Asia was constituted by long-lived 'Kingdoms'. But archaeology, anthropology and a re-reading of these texts have combined to reveal most of these as multi-centred networks of kin and ritual, whose genius should perhaps be seen in their ability to mobilise large bodies of men and women by means that were not at all bureaucratic. As for the inscriptions and later royal chronicles, 'What was high centralization representationally was enormous dispersion institutionally' (Geertz 1980: 132).

If Geertz found the social glue that replaced bureaucracy in theatrical state ritual, Jane Drakard (1999) found it in the charismatic power of the written word. Luc Nagtegal (1996) explained pre-colonial Java and Henk Schulte Nordholt (1993) explained Bali largely in terms of unstable competing networks of kinship and ritual. Merle Ricklefs (1992, 1998) and Margaret Wiener (1995) saw Java and Bali respectively rather as systems of magic and ritual to weave or at least assert coherence and unity.

Although the authorities writing in this vein were overwhelmingly concerned with Indonesia, Tony Day attempted an ambitious synthesis and interpretation on a Southeast Asian scale. His *Fluid Iron* (2002) categorises the different theories about how power was managed and society made to cohere in terms of four themes—kinship; knowledge, especially external and cosmological knowledge; bureaucracy; and terror. The first two are familiar from the recent literature, but bureaucracy requires more explanation, since he holds that 'Even in its most authoritarian and totalitarian forms, the Southeast Asian state is closer to anarchy than to statehood in a Weberian sense' (*Ibid.*: 282). Yet 'bureaucratic polity' arguments remain prominent in the literature of colonial and post-colonial polities. The missing glue the first three categories fail to provide is terror, Day argues, or the capacity arbitrarily to strike your enemies down, whether by supernatural means or more brutal everyday ones.

External powers, European and Chinese, brought different concepts into the region. Whereas the older Indian ideas had been ritual and religious and strengthened the supernatural side of Southeast Asian kingship, Chinese rule brought enough bureaucracy to Vietnam in the first millennium CE to ensure that the independent Viet state from the eleventh century was distinct from its Southeast Asian neighbours. The Portuguese, Spanish and Dutch looked at first little more than a belligerent variant of the Indian traders who had preceded them, in establishing themselves in ports and being more concerned with profitable trade than controlling populations. But both Spanish (in Manila from 1571) and Dutch (in Batavia from 1619) also brought bureaucratic methods of a quite different order, keeping records, establishing and enforcing legal claims and constantly replacing officials in a way that avoided dynastic crises. The Spanish, uniquely in Asia, also brought a muscular counter-reformation ideology which in less than a century placed a layer of Iberian Catholicism and bureaucratic rule from Manila over the stateless diversities of the lowland Philippines.

It was only three centuries later, in the period 1880–1910, that the other twentieth century borders of Southeast Asia were filled out by

Dutch, British and French empires with modern ideas of sovereignty and bureaucracy. All Southeast Asians became aware of the claims and functions of modern statehood; aristocrats were deprived of their arms and their slaves; all were subjected to the monopoly of a single state system of laws, with origins far distant from them. This imposition of a new order was resisted passionately by some, in the name of dynastic pride (Burmese, Vietnamese, Acehnese, Balinese), nascent ethnie nationalism (Vietnamese, Acehnese, Batak, Javanese), or OSH-flavoured Islam (Tausug, Magindanao, Acehnese). Most however adapted quickly to the modern opportunities offered by the broader worlds they now entered. The new states were useful, and above all they were identified as 'modern' by the new educated groups, but they remained for the most part alien and remote—as indeed they were intended to.

Case studies from a state-averse archipelago

It is in this state-averse world that my case studies are situated. Before embarking on them, however, I have some further Southeast Asian distinctions to make in the following chapter. This first discusses five particular markers which have served to consolidate and define identity in modern times. They have been the building blocks of the three types of nationalism, always present but assembled differently in each case. The chapter then makes a four-part distinction of the ways in which colonialism affected Southeast Asian political identities.

Three of the types are further exemplified in the subsequent case studies dealing with the Archipelago. The fourth, labelled 'Expanding an ethnie core', is discussed only in general terms in chapter 2. It needs specific analysis because it has often been thought to be the classic or normative form of nationalism. In these cases, Burma, Siam and Vietnam, ethnie nationalism, pre-colonial state nationalism and anti-imperial nationalism, have reinforced each other to such an extent that few analysts have seen the need to separate them conceptually. The brief discussion in chapter 2 is intended to show that the factors do need to be kept separate, and that conflating them has been at the root of the problems which Burma in particular has faced since independence.

Five case studies follow, examining particular identities and their evolution into different forms of nationalism. The first, paradoxically, is Chinese identity in Southeast Asia, in chapter 3. This is prioritised in part because overseas Chinese nationalism slightly preceded the anti-imperial nationalism of Indonesia and Malaysia (though not the Philippines), so that the different forms of nationalism emerging from the Malay category of chapter 4 emerged in critical dialectic with perceived Chineseness. Only outside China could 'Chinese' represent an ethnie distinct from the state. Chinese ethnie nationalism developed in Southeast Asia around the turn of the twentieth century, and played its part in stimulating both state nationalism in China and ethnie and anti-imperial nationalism in Malaysia and Indonesia.

Indonesia, Malaysia and Brunei each incorporated strong elements of Malayness into their post-independence state nationalism, and even the Philippines flirted with it. Chapter 4 argues that in Malaysia this label was so powerfully fashioned into ethnie nationalism as to constantly endanger the state nationalist project. In Indonesia elements of Malayness were embedded in anti-imperial nationalism, which in turn laid the basis for state nationalism, delegitimising any distinct Malay ethnie. In Brunei nationalism of any kind is stunted by monarchy, and Malayness remains at the level of an official construct.

Aceh follows as the ethnie nationalism most threatening to the Indonesian state. Chapter 5 demonstrates that the strength of this ethnie nationalism, by contrast with the stateless examples that follow, is precisely its memory of state. Acehnese may be less distinctive as a minority than Indonesia's Bataks or Malaysia's Kadazan, but they inherit an unusually strong sense of state resistance to outside control. The Batak and Kadazan cases, in chapters 6 and 7, reveal the different paths of political identity formation and assertion of previously stateless peoples that were possible in Indonesia and Malaysia respectively. The different outcomes are largely set by the gulf between the two state nationalisms with which they contended: post-revolutionary, centralising civic nationalism in Indonesia; evolutionary, federal and ethno-nationalist Malaysia.

Chapter 8 returns to the Southeast Asian level of analysis to draw these case studies together.

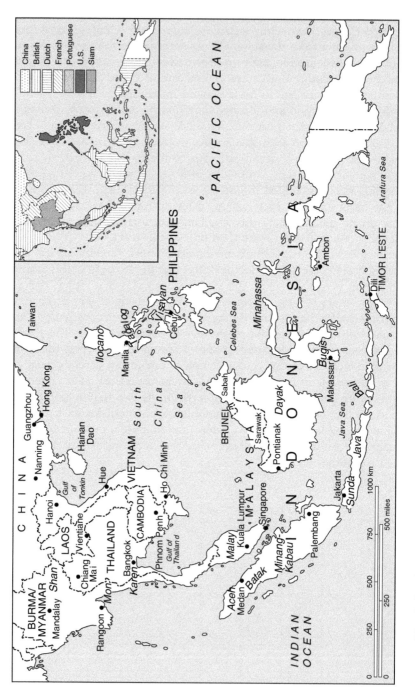

Map 1 Southeast Asia, colonial and contemporary

2 Understanding Southeast Asian nationalisms

Anti-imperial nationalism was strong in twentieth century Southeast Asia partly because there was little of the older state nationalism to balance it. Burmese, Siamese, Vietnamese, Cambodian, Aceh and Lombok kings had generated some degree of commonality with the majority people they ruled, partly by manipulating religious symbols. But unlike the Northeast Asian rulers, they employed abundant foreigners and utilised broader sacred or trade languages (Pali, Sanskrit, Arabic, Malay) often in preference to the vernacular which united them to their people.

The model for anti-imperial nationalism was the Philippines, where three centuries of Spanish rule and shared religion made the imperial unit appear persuasive as early as the 1860s. By the time of José Rizal and his fellow-*ilustrados* in the 1890s, the case they made in Spanish for a Filipino national unit as a focus for passionate loyalty was sufficiently convincing to dominate the anti-Spanish revolution of 1896 and the war of resistance against American occupation that followed. At more populist levels, there were naturally tremors of ethnie nationalism carried by Tagalog and Cebuano, but these never seriously shook the conviction that the boundaries established by colonial fiat were the correct ones.

Indonesian nationalism, as we shall see, initially coexisted with embryonic Javanese, Minangkabau, Batak and Minahasan ethnie nationalisms. But without the stiffening of state nationalism, these were quickly swallowed up in the anti-imperial mood. The watershed moment is usually taken to be a Youth Congress in 1928 (see below), when various ethnic, regional and religious student groups agreed on one fatherland, race/nation and language. The first two represented the classic tool-kit of anti-imperial nationalism in claiming the imperial unit as their own. But in adopting as national language the *lingua franca* of trade, of Islam and of the Dutch administration, Malay, they put themselves in a uniquely advantageous position. Javanese was mother tongue to almost half the Indonesian population, but unknown to most others. Dutch, in which most of the student elite spoke and felt comfortable, would have had to be abandoned eventually. Malay was mother tongue to only a tiny minority of islanders at the time, but understood in all the cities. It gave the anti-imperial nationalists an advantage over both the Filipinos, who had to operate uneasily between a foreign language (Spanish and later English) and a regional one (Tagalog/Pilipino), and the mainland nationalisms, which had to use the language of one dominant ethnie at the expense of minorities.

Change of imperial masters at a critical juncture (Spanish to American in the Philippines, 1898; Japanese to European in the rest of Southeast Asia, 1945) made possible the revolutionary assertion of the new anti-imperial identity in the Philippines, Indonesia, Vietnam and Burma. As in France in 1789, the revolutions sacralised the new identities which had been charted on the map by the old empires. To greater or lesser extent, the alchemy was effected through revolution, making the multi-ethnic imperial identity transform into a passionately felt new community. This provided a huge impetus for the new states in building on the heroic myths of revolution for their state nationalisms.

Through this revolutionary means, the new states partook of some of the supernatural aura of pre-colonial Southeast Asian states. The blood of revolutionary martyrs helped to sacralise the flag, the independence declaration and the sacred sites of the dead. They were for the most part not able to continue or revive an older state nationalism, as in Europe or Northeast Asia, but instead inherited two potent lineages of past states that had ruled them. One was that of the state as a supernatural source of power, awe, fear and belonging. In Indonesia and Burma, where it is strongest, this inheritance was sacralised by revolution to legitimate harsh military suppression of those who challenged the state. The other lineage was the imperial one of the state as an essentially alien but necessary construct, which opened doors to a broader modernity than would otherwise be possible. The absence of an indigenous strong state tradition made the post-colonial states appear fragile or 'soft', in Gunnar Myrdal's (1968) parlance. Nevertheless this combination of matter-of-fact if alien necessity with a real, if fading, supernatural charisma, has gone some way to create genuine new imagined communities, which look set to outlast most of the ethnie nationalisms that revive in democratic environments.

Key identity-markers

Language

Benedict Anderson (1991: 43–5) showed how the development of print in Europe stimulated national consciousness through creating 'unified fields of exchange', a new 'fixity' which could be made to appear antique, and a privileging of 'core' spoken languages closer to the print version, and thereby able to provincialise their more distant cousins. But while Northeast Asian identities had a much longer interaction with print than did European, Southeast Asian identities had a singularly short one. The books that arrived in the region printed first in Chinese characters and, from the sixteenth century, in Latin characters, seemed alien from the Indic and Arabic scripts in use in the region, and did not inspire emulation.

Until the nineteenth century, Christian missionaries were alone in introducing printing to Southeast Asian languages, but did so chiefly in romanised form. The first book was a version of the Doctrina Christiana translated into romanised Tagalog and printed in Manila in 1593. Through the subsequent expansion of doctrinal texts also into Cebuano and Ilocano, Filipino languages did become more fixed and unified among the Christian elite. But since very little else was printed in Philippine languages, literacy in the romanised script led quickly towards Spanish for the elite, and did not generate strong ethnie nationalisms around language.

In Vietnam the Jesuit pioneer Alexandre de Rhodes stimulated the creation of a romanised script, in which Christian texts were printed as well as his 1651 dictionary. In the longer run, once adapted as the standard Vietnamese 'national language' (*quoc ngu*) in the 1920s, this would have profound effects on cultivating ethnie nationalism. But previously its role was marginal 'as a rather crude vehicle for foreign religious and political propaganda' (Marr 1981: 145). At a similar period Dutch missionaries developed romanised Malay as the language of the printed Bible for their formerly Catholic constituency in Batavia, Maluku and Minahassa. Early examples of print romanisations are in fact very various and did nothing to promote standardisation. Only with the so-called Leydekker Bible (New Testament 1731, Old Testament 1733) did printing begin to have this effect for Christian populations. In the nineteenth century, printed romanised Malay built on this tradition to become the vehicle for a new polyethnic urban culture, in the Indies and more hesitantly the Peninsula. But for almost everybody except local urban-born Chinese and Malays for whom it became a mother tongue, romanised Malay remained a second language, a *lingua franca*. Very late, essentially in the 1920s, it began to be a unifying language of urban high and low culture.

Thai and Burmese began to be printed in their indigenous scripts in the second half of the nineteenth century, largely again through the mediation of Christian missionaries. When newspapers followed in the twentieth century they had the standardising effect on nationalism known from Europe. In the Archipelago, however, only Javanese, Sundanese and Arabic-scripted Malay were large enough language pools to sustain a vernacular press in the original script for much of the twentieth century, but these always struggled to survive against the romanised Malay media. For the upland people who were Christianised only after European romanticism had convinced missionaries that they must operate in the vernacular, romanised print did become important in their ethnie nationalisms (see chapters 6 and 7). Most other ethnie in the Archipelago, however, used their language primarily as an oral medium and wrote by preference in Malay, whether in Arabic or romanised script.

In short, the impact of printing was extremely late in fashioning Southeast Asian identities, primarily because of the factor of script. When it eventually came, it served in the island worlds to assist multi-ethnic anti-imperial nationalism (in Spanish, Dutch, English and especially romanised Malay) more than it assisted the vernacular of the ethnies. Because its impact came late and under imperial rather than state nationalist auspices (except in the Thai case), it seemed a very unequal battle between the printing of the multi-ethnic *lingua franca*, and the primarily verbal expressions of the hundreds of language communities, still not reduced and homogenised by printing as had happened in Europe and Northeast Asia.

Religion

Religious identities preceded nationalist ones in Southeast Asia as elsewhere, and may well outlast them. We must distinguish however the world of the mutually exclusive Abrahamic religions, Islam and Christianity, from that still dominated by Indian-derived religions. In the world of Mainland Southeast Asia Buddhism continued to dominate and became popularly grounded through the beloved monkhood (*sangha*), present in every village. Migrants from other parts of the Buddhist or Hindu worlds had no difficulty fitting into this pattern, sometimes retaining aspects of their original religious world (Chinese spirit festivals, Burmese/Shan *nat* cults, Brahmanic rituals) while also joining royally patronised Theravada rituals. Because the king was the great patron of Theravada Buddhism within his domains, religion assisted him in integrating a diversity of people into his polity, but did not require them to conform to a cultural or intellectual norm.

Christianity and Islam, on the other hand, established and often enforced clear boundaries. For Islam the minimal boundaries with the older Southeast Asian belief pattern were the abandonment of pork (formerly the favoured item of feasting) and the adoption of certain norms of modest dress and simple funerals (Reid 1988–93, II: 140–3). For Christianity, the boundaries had to do with monogamy and sexual mores, and some form of contact with the institutional church. Christianity was introduced in heavily politicised form. First the Portuguese used adhesion to Catholic Christianity as a sign of loyalty to their side of their politico-commercial conflict with the Muslim trade network. The Dutch arrived in 1596 in an equally determined anti-Catholic spirit, forcing the Catholic converts in Maluku and Batavia to go along with their form of Calvinism as a sign of being on the Dutch rather than Portuguese side of their own politico-commercial struggle. Since the main threat to the Catholic Philippines was the Dutch Company (VOC) in the seventeenth and eighteenth centuries, the divide between Catholic and Protestant was one of the most clear-cut identity boundaries of the region. Although the anti-imperial nationalism of the Philippines produced its 1896 revolution in an anti-Catholic spirit influenced by masonry and the Enlightenment, the identity on which it drew had been created by the church.

Islam was free from internal boundaries of this kind in Southeast Asia, since the Shafi'i school of Sunni Islam was accepted everywhere. Externally, the contest with the Portuguese in the sixteenth century produced a politicised Islam in Aceh, Demak and Banten in particular, which engendered a counter-identity among the peoples who successfully fought to resist Islamisation by force. This helped create a non-Islamic identity for the Bataks of Sumatra and the Balinese in the sixteenth century, and for the Toraja of Sulawesi in the seventeenth, while the Dayak of Borneo and other non-Muslim peoples had a more porous boundary with coastal Malayo-Muslim culture.

The roles of Islam in creating identities can be distinguished in terms of the interactions between the Arabic script it introduced and the indigenous pattern. Of the peoples who became Muslim in the fifteenth to seventeenth centuries, most adopted the Arabic script as the only means of literary expression, with writing only known in Malay or Arabic itself. These peoples, including those later known as Malay, Acehnese, Minangkabau and Banjarese, thereby established a powerful commonality with each other and with the broader Islamic world. The most developed pre-Islamic literary cultures, on the other hand, the Javanese and Sundanese in Java and the Makasarese and Bugis in Sulawesi, retained their own scripts and literary languages, translating a limited selection of the Arabic and Malay corpus into their vernaculars. For them language represented a formidable boundary that prevented Muslim outsiders from penetrating and shaping their fundamental sense of identity.

For all who became Muslim, however, religion represented the principal option for solidarity beyond the particular speech-group or dynasty. Aceh was the spear-head of one kind of solidarity in the 1560s, when its economic rivalry with Portuguese Melaka in the spice trade drove it into alliance with Ottoman Turkey and various other Muslim ports involved in the spice trade. In his appeal to the Turkish sultan in the 1560s for military help against the Portuguese, the Acehnese sultan repeatedly appealed to the sufferings of 'Muslims' at the hands of 'unbelievers' and asked for help accordingly (Reid 1988–93 II: 147). In practice Southeast Asian Muslim rulers proved almost incapable of acting together. But after the Dutch Company had humbled the most powerful of them, a series of millenarian adventurers appealed with more effect to the solidarity of Muslims (*Ibid.*: 320–4). In the period 1850–1920 Islamic solidarity again became important as the readiest means to express resistance to the rapidly advancing power of the Dutch colonial state. The first mass movement of Indonesia's modern nationalist experience, from 1912, naturally called itself simply 'Islamic Association' (*Sarekat Islam*).

The triumph of anti-imperial nationalism everywhere after 1920 made it appear as though this form of religious solidarity was a thing of the past. Yet Islamic solidarity never disappeared. To some extent it nested harmoniously with the dominant nationalism, but it also coexisted in tension with it. Islam has reappeared as a political identity-marker whenever permitted to do so, and notably during Indonesia's democratic phases of 1950–7 and since 1998. In Malaysia since 1970 it has made huge inroads on Malay ethnie nationalism as the identity-marker of choice for younger Malays. Analytically it should be kept distinct from nationalism, though powerfully interacting with it.

Bounded sovereign space

If the indigenous 'state-averse' Southeast Asians focussed on centres and patronage, the European imperial nationalists introduced a great emphasis on the need for boundaries. As the British envoy Burney told the Siamese court in 1826, they believed that only fixed boundaries between territories would 'prevent all chance of mistake or dispute', and enable the British occupiers of Lower Burma to have more stable and harmonious relations with the Siamese than the Burmese had had (Burney 1971, I: 85–6). Boundary-making, with its presumption of sovereign monopolies within each boundary, even preceded the ships. Spain and Portugal signed the Treaty of Tordessillas in 1494, after Columbus' voyage but before the Portuguese had reached Asia by sea. It drew a North–South line between the lands to be conquered for Spain and those for Portugal, an Atlantic meridian which implied a Pacific anti-meridian allotting most of Asia to Portugal. Other powers were excluded, and they naturally took little account of it.

The boundary-making continued between European nationalists. The powerful trading companies of the Dutch and English did not make grandiloquent claims to territory as the kings of Portugal had done, but they were more effective in seeking the monopolies that were important to them—monopolies of trade and of spice production centres. As early as 1615 the VOC told the rulers of Makassar that their free-trading principles conflicted with VOC claims to monopolise the spice trade of Maluku. The king replied that an earlier generation of Dutchmen had also been ready to die in fighting for the claims of Spain. 'God made the land and the sea; the land he divided among men and the sea he gave in common. It has never been heard that anyone should be forbidden to sail the seas' (cited in Stapel 1922: 14). Nevertheless, after forty more years and a great deal more bloodshed, the VOC was master of the spice islands and able to exclude those it labelled 'smugglers'. Among the losers in this process was the English Company, forced to concede its tenuous access to nutmeg-producing Banda at the Treaty of Breda in 1667, and to settle for what then seemed the meagre compensation of New York.

What might properly be called the third world-wide war, after the Hapsburg versus Ottoman conflict of the sixteenth century and Protestant versus Catholic of the seventeenth, pitted England and France against each other in a series of wars in Europe, North America and Asia between 1744 and 1815. While the two parties had begun by backing rival Indian monarchs in their contest for trade dominance in India, the English ended in control of vast swathes of territory. European state nationalism, greatly stimulated by war and revolution, transformed the nature of rival claims in Asia. Dutch possessions in the Archipelago were occupied first by the pro-French revolutionary general Daendels (1808–11) and then by Stamford Raffles for England (1812–15). The series of treaties which followed Napoleon's final defeat concluded with the Anglo–Dutch London Treaty of 1824. This transformed maritime thoroughfares into international boundaries. The Straits of Malacca and of Singapore, in particular, were decreed to constitute the boundary between Dutch and British claims and ambitions. The territory on either side was by no means controlled by Britain and Holland respectively, but in contrast to local patterns, the boundary came first. Only about a century later were the inhabitants of the islands to realise they were part of one polity with monopoly claims over them, and those of the Peninsula of another—however disguised by continuing local 'sovereignties'.

The boundaries between British and French territorial claims came later, at a time when state nationalism was at its peak, and the Europeans were ceasing to tolerate disorderly corners not responsible to a 'civilised' (read industrial) state. France conquered Vietnam in stages between 1859 and 1885, and advanced up the Mekong through Khmer and Lao regions in the long tributary to both Siam and Vietnam. Britain had done the same with Burma. But neither power could allow the other to occupy the third major state of the region, Siam. In 1893, France forced Siam to yield all its claims on the eastern side of the Mekong, making another former trade artery into a sterile boundary. Britain and France in turn agreed in 1896 that they would uphold the independent sovereignty of Siam, which had been quicker than its neighbours to grasp the need to modernise in a European fashion in order to survive. Siam's modern borders were in place after another round of carefully balanced advances. France took the contested Cambodian provinces of Siemreap and Battambang in 1907, and could not then object to Britain taking responsibility for the sultanates of Kedah, Perlis, Kelantan and Trengganu on the Peninsula in 1909.

In the wilder east, Holland had agreed to divide Timor with Portugal in 1749. In New Guinea, lines on maps were drawn by Dutch, German and British negotiators in the 1880s and 1890s, though it would be long before the interior inhabitants knew anything of them.

These borders were all artificial in their origins, slicing various emergent ethnie in half and turning crucial crossroads and meeting places into remote peripheries of the new states. But in the twentieth century the boundaries impressed themselves on a new school-educated generation as fixed realities featured on the classroom maps. They became icons of the new nationalisms.

Censuses

Southeast Asian kings frequently acknowledged the diversity of their subjects; a few kings, notably of Burma, Siam and Vietnam, also counted their subjects for tax purposes. The colonial innovation was to combine these two exercises, using a periodic census to classify the whole population, taxable or not, into groups. The British were much the most consistent census-takers, managing one every decade in Malaya and Burma between 1900 and the interruption of the (European) war in 1939. They were also the great classifiers, animated by their conviction in the early twentieth century that 'race' was an important scientific category, albeit of peculiar exuberance in Southeast Asia.

In practice census-takers encountered a huge diversity of self-identifications, having to do with place of birth or residence, language, religion and style of dress. This was very much at odds with their everyday understanding of race, which had in Europe become entangled with nationality, and therefore relatively fixed. The Burmese enumerators of 1931 saw no difficulty listing English, Welsh, American, French, Dutch etc as 'races' within the category of 'European and Allied races'. When they transferred this notion of basic self-identification to Burma, however, they found 135 indigenous 'races' (*Census of India* 1931, XI: i). The Malayan census of the same year identified over seventy 'races', fifteen of which were categories of 'Malaysians by race'. Of large categories, only the Chinese 'race' was blurred with the state nationalist category, so that speakers of different southern Chinese languages became 'tribes' in the census (Vlieland 1932).

Yet in having defined so many 'races', in consultations with various colonial officials knowledgeable about local languages and customs, the census-takers realised they were imposing categories on a shifting world. They complained of 'the extreme instability of racial distinctions in Burma' (*Census of India* 1931, XI, ii: 259). Census-takers in Malaya were similarly frustrated, seeking after 1900 to impose the 'scientific' category of race on a population blissfully unaware of it. C.A. Vlieland, in charge of the 1931 census, admitted that this attempt had failed. 'Most Oriental peoples have themselves no clear conception of race, and commonly regard religion as the most important, if not determinant, element.' Conceding that it was impossible to define 'race', but insisting on using the term, he sought some kind of 'judicious blend, for practical ends, of the ideas of geographic and ethnographic origin, political allegiance, and racial and social affinities and sympathies'. In a very English manner he excused this muddle-headedness as merely enshrining the everyday understanding of the question, 'in ordinary non-technical conversation, "What is that man?"'(Vlieland 1932: 73–4).

Yet the census conferred a spurious authority on these arbitrary divisions. The peculiar British confidence in the importance of race continued into the censuses of independent Malaysia, Singapore and Burma. The very people who had 'no clear conception of race' became among the few in the twenty-first century world still convinced by their governments that these categories were basic and ineluctable.

The categories did, however, become steadily more homogenised into large blocks, convinced by the census that they were competing for survival or dominance in a social Darwinian world. As will be considered further in chapter 3, the British in Malaya progressively defined a 'Malay' category as a protected one of political importance. While the 1921 census was still taking seriously the idea of 'race', and classifying as 'Malay' those Sumatran immigrants whose first language was Malay, that of 1931 adopted a political definition, so that only those born in the Peninsula, and thus entitled to 'protection', were classified as 'Malay'. Others in the 'Malaysian' category were specified by their self-identification or place of origin, Javanese, Boyanese and Minangkabau being the most significant (Vlieland 1932: 75–6).

Netherlands Indian officials were similarly bewildered by the variety of identities the population gave themselves. For them the term 'race' did not appear except in the abbreviated English translation of categories. The most important distinction was between the four 'population groups' (*bevolkingsgroepen*), translated as 'racial groups' for the English. These were European, Chinese, 'other Asiatics' and 'natives' (*inlanders*), the last being 95 per cent of the population. Different ethnie, in bewildering variety, were labelled *landaarden* (something like 'countrymen'), only translated for English eyes as 'races and tribes'. The 1930 census, the only comprehensive one, attempted a definition after pointing out the usual difficulties. 'We have taken as criteria for specifying the meaning of *landaard*, as far as possible: a common culture, and for smaller groups in particular also their own inclination, not to mix with other *landaarden*' (*Volkstelling* 1930, I: 13). As in Burma, the extraordinary variety of groups was difficult for the state in practice to 'read' or comprehend, and so they adopted the procedure of 'grouping as far as possible' the different *landaarden*—'so as not to make the work of the tellers too complex and the processing and publication of the data too costly' (*Volkstelling* 1930 IV: 15). As will be explored in the following chapters, these larger groupings had an important effect in forming the competitive ethnie of contemporary Indonesia. More important overall, however, was the profound divide created in every official statistic or publication, between the 'natives' on one side and the foreign population groups on the other. This was a major gift for eventual Indonesian unity, but at the expense of those labelled 'Chinese'.

Names

In the contemporary era of globalisation and mixing, names have become the primary means of retaining identities over many generations. When assimilation was the predominant means of dealing with migrants, altering their names to something more 'normal' was seen as a vital means to hasten the process. The new multi-culturalism abhors such effacement, yet still compromise is common. One name may be used for the majority society, another for the family; or bi-culturalism may be signalled in a hybrid name (Theresa Nguyen; Ibrahim Chen). The dynamics of naming are critical for understanding imagined communities and imagined boundaries, yet they remain strangely understudied (but see Macdonald and Zheng 2009).

Chinese and Arabic names have been particularly resistant to transformation in changed circumstances. In the Chinese case, this derives from the importance of patrilineages and the unchanging nature of the Chinese characters in which they are expressed. The Chinese were far ahead of the rest of the world in feeling that patrilines should be preserved through the use of surnames. Legends place the requirement that all should have a surname (*xing*) to a decree of 2852 BC (Jones 1997: 1). Despite their longevity, Chinese surnames are few, and the characters well known. Conventionally there are said to be a hundred names, though the reality is perhaps two or three times that. However pronounced in different times and places, the character remains, and can lead back to standardisation in the age of a single *pinyin* romanisation. In diasporic situations of great diversity, Chinese have been reluctant to abandon the tight Chinese naming system even when they had no other command of Chinese language. Perhaps because the name appeared central to their residual Chineseness, Southeast Asian governments sometimes brought pressure on them to abandon it.

The same small corpus of Chinese surnames served for Vietnam and Korea, though the pronunciation of the characters varied even more widely than in Chinese dialects. Nothing so radically marked out the distinctiveness of Vietnam from China than the romanisation of names, along with the rest of the language, in the early twentieth century. When all those with one Chinese character (*Ruan* in pinyin) became Nguyen, and with another (*Pan* in pinyin) became Phan, they parted company with the Chinese naming world in a way that could not be rejoined.

Arabic names have been changeless for a different reason. Since the Quran was expressed in the sacred language of Arabic, and was studied and memorised in that language rather than in vernacular translations, the names of the characters within it did not change. The nationalisation of Christian saints' names, whereby a Latin Jacobus became French Jacques, Spanish Iago, German Jacub, English James and Italian Jacopo, was not parallelled in the Muslim world. For those Southeast Asians who adopted an Islamic or Arabic naming system, therefore, there was little in the name (except the slight shift to *bin*, 'son of', as opposed to Arabic *ibn*) to say they had any identity except an Islamic one. The practice of Islamic naming gradually spread to become the majority pattern among Malays, Acehnese and Makassarese by the twentieth century, but was much more restricted among Javanese, most of whom have continued to the present to mark their ethnie in their name.

The dominant Southeast Asian pattern was one of bilateral descent and matrilocality, at the opposite extreme to the Chinese pattern of surnames and patrilineage markers. Nobody except Chinese and Vietnamese had any kind of surname passed down through a paternal line, with the possible exception of the Bataks discussed in chapter 6. Names might change at different life-stages, or even in relation to different people, but there was no idea that one name should be inherited (beyond one generation) and the other personal.

Modern nationalism did however bring a concern to emulate Europeans and Chinese by adopting surnames. Sometimes this was for the perceived advantages of a state, in making its population 'readable', to use James Scott's (1998a) term. The Spanish governor-general who proclaimed the need for Filipinos to adopt a surname in 1850, for example, was concerned at the confusion caused in 'the administration of justice, government, finance, and public order' by lack of surnames to hold people responsible for their families (Governor-General Claveria, cited in Cullinane 1998: 296). A *Catalogo de Apellidos* was circulated giving thousands of acceptable names, the majority of which were in fact indigenous although the elite set a pattern of choosing Spanish ones. This was a remarkably successful state-orchestrated transformation, which made Filipinos the first non-Sinified Southeast Asians with a clear surnaming pattern. It is difficult to avoid the conclusion that this contributed much both to subsequent Filipino identity and to the importance of family politics in the following century.

The founder of western-style Thai nationalism, King Rama VI (Vajiravudh, 1910–25), also decreed in 1913 that surnames must be selected by every male family head, to be passed down in the male line, 'to ensure that government records of births, deaths and marriages would be clear and reliable'. Part of the motive was undoubtedly state convenience of this kind, as with the Philippine governor. But there was clear state nationalism in his comment that 'Now we have surnames it can be said that we have caught up with people who are regarded as civilised' (Vajiravudh, 1913, cited in Vella, 1978: 131).

Lest anyone think he sought to emulate Chinese practice, he argued that the Chinese were still at the stage of divisive clan names, whereas real modern nations had surnames individual to them. He also believed that surnames would provide 'an aid in the maintenance of family tradition. It will also serve as an incentive to every one to uphold not only personal honour but the honour of the family as well' (Vajiravudh 1914, cited in Vella, 1978: 130). Vajiravudh gave names personally to many of the elite, but encouraged even commoners to adopt one. Gradually, therefore, Thais followed Filipinos in adopting a family name, even if they were seldom used in common parlance. In relations with non-Thais, at least, these names served to demarcate the state, making the Thai-ness of the dominant ethnie clearer and minorities who declined to follow more alien. During the 1940s high point of Thai state nationalism, great pressure was put on Chinese and Muslims also to adopt Thai surnames. The degree of success of this process measured the success of Thai state nationalism against its major rivals.

Colonial constructions of states and ethnies

Southeast Asian nationalisms were distinct from those of Europe not simply because they arose in a culturally different context. The modern states which introduced state nationalism in its modern form were alien imperial states. They were able to establish their authority in Southeast Asia in the late nineteenth century in large part because they embodied, to a much greater extent than their local opponents, that homogeneous amalgam of ethnie and state nationalism which proved so successful in the nineteenth century—'the sure and attested way of attaining power and wealth' (McNeill 1985: 56). The policies of these imperial states therefore have an important bearing on the shaping of identities.

Only the Spanish, in the Philippines from 1571 to 1898, extended their state nationalism to their Asian subjects, gradually remoulding them in the direction of Hispanisation. With this exception, the Europeans in Asia did not seek to create communities of belonging between the state and its subjects. Far from it. As they became more modern in their sense of an absolute state, they became more separate from the Asians they lived among, and more determined to remain so. Although it was no part of colonial intentions to generate ethno-nationalisms within the imperial borders, the homogenising effect of colonial rule was bound to produce such a result. By creating common legal, financial, bureaucratic and educational regimes within the domains they ruled, the British, Dutch and French laid a firm basis for anti-imperial nationalism, but they did not take the final step of mobilising populations for war or other common action. That step was left for the indigenous nationalists to take.

The effects of colonial rule or influence on ethnie-formation varied widely. The different styles and motivations of the rival colonisers was one factor, but far more important was the type of Southeast Asian society with which each interacted. We need to distinguish at least four types of interaction, which I will label: (i) expanding an ethnie core;

(ii) protecting fragile monarchies; (iii) from trade empires to revolutionary unities; and (iv) ethnicising the stateless.

Expanding an ethnie core—Burma, Vietnam and Siam

The British conquered Burma, and the French Vietnam, knowing them to be formidable established states proud of their independence. Both had beaten back Chinese attempts to absorb or 'punish' them as recently as the 1760s (Burma) and 1788 (Vietnam). The Burmese rulers claimed to be world-rulers (cakravartin), kings of many kings, as well as frequently boddhisatva (incarnations of the Buddha). In their contests with neighbouring Tai states they had been able to mobilise armies of hundreds of thousands, and to deploy artillery effectively. The Vietnamese were also extremely effective militarily, accustomed to prevailing in their contests with neighbours, as well as with China.

Both states also played the Asian diplomatic game of unequal alliances. They still sent profitable tribute missions to the Middle Kingdom, and were with Siam the only Southeast Asian states to continue doing so into the nineteenth century (Womack 2006; Reid and Zheng 2008). Accepting tributary relations of diverse kinds with their own neighbours, they had no such understanding of sovereign equality as Westphalia had taught the Europeans. Britain and France, however, were not interested in occupying a ritual space comparable with the intangible primacy of China in northern Southeast Asia—they sought control of certain key economic levers, and were unlikely to obtain it without a serious fight.

State nationalism was a reality in Vietnam, in the Northeast Asian pattern sketched above. Despite being divided into hostile states for most of the seventeenth and eighteenth centuries, Dai Viet had created the kind of homogeneities of bureaucracy and print culture which could readily be reassembled by the unifying Nguyen after 1802, on the Chinese model. Although the Viet states had many tributaries, as did China, they understood the boundary between civilised and barbarian, Viet citizen and highland tributary, only the former having direct responsibility for the state. Conquered Cham and Khmer could be assimilated into the settled population by adopting Chinese-style writing and names, but it remained clear where the boundary of the core ethnicity was.

Burma and Siam also had vigorous dynasties, generated out of the same period of turmoil in the second half of the eighteenth century, which had allowed the Nguyen to emerge masters of Vietnam. But they were conscious of being multi-ethnic amalgams. The Siamese king often saw himself as ruler of Thai, Lao, Khmer, Mon and at slightly greater remove, Malay and Chinese. Thai sovereignty had begun in pluralism, with multiple rulers in Nan, Chiang Mai, Sipsongpanna and Sukhothai alternatively hostile and tributary to each other, as also to Burma or China. Much of the economic strength of nineteenth century Siam was due to Chinese traders and cash-croppers. Siamese skills learned in co-opting Chinese traders proved useful in dealing with Europeans in the nineteenth century.

The Burmans, with their capital more than a thousand kilometres from the port, were less inclined to accept symbiotic relationships with non-Burmans, and more inclined to repression and cultural assimilation. After brutally crushing a series of revolts from the embittered Mon of the southern Irrawaddy basin, the Burmese state encouraged the migration of Burmans to the Mon area, and the forcible assimilation in language and dress of Mons who remained. Lieberman calculates that in consequence the Irrawaddy basin became 90 per cent Burman by 1830, having been only 60 per cent so in 1400 (Lieberman 2003: 206). Outside this basin the strongest Burmese kings might have favoured reducing other ethnie to a kind of servitude, but assimilation was impossible both physically and in terms of the ideology of a world-ruler over scores of discrete 'peoples' (*Ibid.*: 200–1). Fr Sangermano (1818: 42–3) discussed nine different 'nations' within the Burmese empire, 'all of whom speak a peculiar language, and have customs different from the Burmese'. These were sometimes fierce competitors, sometimes tributaries, sometimes ruthlessly conquered subjects.

In conquering the two stronger states, Burma and Vietnam, but leaving Siam as a buffer, the Europeans gave the Chakri kings an additional benefit. By detaching most of their tributary periphery, they made it much easier for a more compact kingdom to transform itself into a modern nation-state. King Chulalongkorn and his able interior minister Prince Damrong knew that they had to emulate the colonial powers in establishing a monopoly of force and a unified government within the borders to which they had been reduced. Because they had none of the ambivalence of the colonial governments about absorbing the peripheries into a national identity which was essentially Thai, the Thai leadership can be considered the most successful in developing a strong state nationalism which went far to transform its population into a majority ethnie with only a modest periphery of 'minorities' (Bunnag 1977; Thongchai 1991).

The British and French claimed to have inherited the vaguer tributary relations of various peripheral communities towards Mandalay and Hue respectively. They created a border of modern sovereignty with the Manchu empire which excluded the possibility of further tribute to Beijing. Within the maximal borders they thereby established (for themselves and for China), they built a wholly modern monopoly of power, and uniformity of financial, educational, commercial and administrative systems. Yet the form under which this steel frame of authority was exercised still appeared bewilderingly complex, reflecting the different local accommodations to the mosaic of indigenous structures. Indochina was divided into four protectorates each under a different mixture of indigenous and French authority, and the colony of Cochin-China in the Vietnamese south. One third of Burma constituted the 'scheduled areas' of the north, where Shan, Chin and Kachin princes continued to rule under British tutelage. Even in 'Burma Proper' where a parliamentary system was established, Karen and Rakhine (of Arakan) had somewhat different constitutional positions from Mon and Burman. Anti-imperial nationalists of the dominant ethnie naturally believed this superficial diversity was a sham and a feudal anachronism, only kept alive by colonial intrigue. The other ethnie, though touched in different degrees by anti-imperial nationalism, could accept the administrative novelties of a distant ruler more readily than a return to domination by Burmans. The tension between the ambitions of the dominant ethnie and those who discovered themselves 'minorities' within new states would dominate the twentieth century and continue into the twenty-first.

The effect of this type of imperial interaction was to create expectations in the nationalisms they produced which would be very difficult to fulfil. The colonial boundaries were of course sacralised as the 'correct' boundaries for anti-imperial nationalism. But in Burma, Burman ethnie nationalism became fatally entangled with state nationalism after independence, with a constant state of unwinnable war against minority ethnie nationalisms. Vietnam was very fortunate that the anti-imperial nationalism of the Indo-Chinese communist party was unable to take control of the whole colony in 1945, and eventually renamed itself the Vietnamese Workers' Party in 1951. The French were able to steer Laos and Cambodia to a fragile independence in 1954 (Goscha 1999). The wars of Indo-China up until 1980 were nevertheless bedevilled by Vietnamese attempts to lead the anti-imperial nationalisms of Laos and Cambodia in the 'Indo-Chinese Revolution' of which they had dreamed since 1930, and problems remain between these variants of nationalism.

Protecting fragile monarchies—Malaya, Cambodia, Laos

The British sphere in Malaya, and the French in the Mekong basin, were the outcome of purely economic objectives along real or imagined trade routes to China. The British sought trading bases in the Malacca Straits area for the collection of tropical trade goods for China; the French hoped the Mekong would provide direct access to the fabled China market. No strong states posed major obstacles in these two zones. A number of petty port-states in the Peninsula had been partly tributary to Siam, partly to the old Malay dynasty of Riau (tributary to the Dutch since 1784), but overall very little populated because of the area's unsuitability for rice agriculture. As long-standing crossroads of trade these states had a tradition of cosmopolitanism, with traders from India, China, the Archipelago and the Gulf of Thailand all meeting in ports of which the *lingua franca* and most of the dominant dynasties were Malay. The Mekong region was also a 'water frontier' (Cooke and Li 2004), where Khmer sovereigns had a tenuous hold over Chinese, Malay, Cham and European traders, periodically invoking Vietnamese and Thai intervention against their rivals.

Having arrived for reasons to do with trade well beyond these regions, the British and French gained influence almost accidentally. Economic vested interests would come later in the twentieth century, but these did not begin by being strategic or economic prizes in themselves. The Europeans found a multiplicity of weak and divided princes, some of whom were eager to invoke their help against others, and so they quickly found themselves in the place of 'protectors' of endangered states. They preserved and enriched the monarchs they chose to back, but met their own expanding economic needs by encouraging outsiders to exploit resources—Chinese, Indians and Europeans in Malaya; Chinese, Vietnamese and Europeans in the Mekong countries.

In the twentieth century, as nationalist and Marxist pressures mounted, the colonial ideology shifted significantly from the protection of the rulers to the protection of their subjects. While the initial populations had been very heterogeneous, this protective system required that the objects of this colonial protection be homogenised as charming but indolent 'natives' of their territories, all peasants, fishermen or officials of the court, inherently loyal to the monarchs recreated by colonial intervention. The more developed the economy of the 'protected' area became, the more this population was seen to need 'protection' against more dynamic and modern migrants. Among such populations and their aristocratic elites, anti-imperial nationalism developed less robustly than ethnie nationalism. Populist commoners had difficulty wresting leadership from these elites, but when they did so, it was in the name of pressing the state to assist this weak and vulnerable 'native' population more effectively than had the princes against outsiders believed to be more dynamic.

The Malayan case will be discussed in greater detail in chapter 3, in the context of unravelling the multiple meanings of 'Malay'. In order to suggest that it can be seen as part of a typology as well as uniquely *sui generis*, however, it will be helpful to consider here a few features of the Khmer and Lao 'fragile protected monarchies'.

The vigorous new Thai state refounded after the Burmese conquest by King Taksin at Thonburi (1767), and by Rama I at its present Bangkok site (1782), wasted no time in expanding to the east. By 1779, military expeditions had established Siamese influence over all the Mekong territories. The three Lao kingdoms (Vientiane, Luang Prabang and Champassak) were subjected as never before, and their palladium, the emerald Buddha, was removed from Vientiane to Bangkok. A rebellion by the Vientiane King Anuvong in 1826 represented a final attempt at using Lao ethnie nationalism, on both sides of the Mekong, to reconstitute the seventeenth century Lansang kingdom. It was punished by the total destruction of Vientiane and removal of its remaining population across the Mekong where it could be better controlled.

For its part Cambodia began the century unusually subject to Siam, its kings crowned in Bangkok and their relatives held in the Thai capital as hostages for their loyalty. Siamese-connected officials were in key positions, especially in the westernmost Khmer provinces of Battambang and Siemreap, site of the Angkor ruins symbolically important to both monarchies. These provinces were effectively detached from Cambodia under a local dynasty responding to Bangkok rather than Phnom Penh. The Khmer court itself, riven by factionalism and irked by Thai paternalism, widened its options by sending tribute also to the Vietnamese court at Hue. In 1833, a Siamese army invaded, closely followed by a stronger Vietnamese army, each backing rival princes and intent on maintaining its influence. In the period 1833–40, the Vietnamese King Minh Mang applied his vigorous version of neo-Confucian state nationalism to Cambodia, attempting to 'civilise' and incorporate the central Khmer territory as had been done earlier with Cham territories and the Mekong delta. When this king died in 1840, however, his successors conceded that the challenge was too great, and accepted a kind of dual Viet/Thai suzerainty over Cambodia from 1848.

When the French in 1863 offered King Norodom protection, after they had conquered the adjacent portion of Vietnam, it was an already familiar pattern. Even when in 1884 they imposed a sterner requirement that he accept 'all the ... reforms that the French government shall judge, in the future, to be useful', it gave Cambodia a better chance of survival than Vietnamese rule had done. The princes of Laos, facing gradual absorption into an ever more centralised Siam, were equally ready to sign on as 'protected' in the 1890s. Even more than Cambodia,

Laos was a country that had to be reinvented by the French on the east bank of the Mekong, after its elites had effectively lost their battle for autonomy from Siam. Under French protection the monarchies of the Mekong were institutionally secure for the first time in centuries, and protected from the sort of succession conflicts which had in the past ensured the survival of the toughest. Like their Malay counterparts they were encouraged to focus their energies in the areas of state ritual, symbolism, culture and religion. Some 220,000 Vietnamese migrants (2.7 per cent of population in Laos, 6.3 per cent in Cambodia) and 110,000 Chinese (0.3 per cent in Laos, 3.5 per cent in Cambodia) filled the middle positions of the administration and the economy respectively (Naval Intelligence 1943: 212). In Cambodia, rice production was stimulated by the French, and a stable peasantry grew rapidly in numbers. As with its Malay counterpart, the educated Khmer elite was tiny and predominately aristocratic. Such nationalism as developed before the Japanese occupation was directed against Vietnamese domination of the administration and Chinese of commerce, not against colonialism or the French *per se*. Anti-imperial nationalism remained very weak as a unifying force or a basis for civic nationalism.

From trade empires to revolutionary unities—Philippines, Indonesia

The Spanish empire in the Philippines, and the Dutch one in the Indonesian Archipelago, were also constructed for essentially commercial reasons, with the added element of imperially sponsored Christianisation in the Philippines. The Dutch had to fight gruesome and costly battles, but they chose their targets carefully for commercial purposes, generally seeking to fight for rather than against the strongest inland powers with which they had no quarrel. By the late nineteenth century when the British and French were fighting Burmese and Vietnamese monarchies, the Dutch and Spanish were already well established in their respective heartlands and engaged in fighting desperate Muslims in what they already identified as their peripheries—Aceh and Sulu respectively. The hitherto independent sultanate of Aceh believed itself comparable to the Burmese and Vietnamese monarchies, and put up a similar fight (see chapter 4), but from the perspective of Java Aceh had become a messy borderland that had to be made to conform with an established colonial pattern. Java and Luzon already represented secure if multi-ethnic bases of a (colonial) state. In these archipelagos the core of the future state was effectively the three-century experience of colonialism interacting with indigenous structures in a central island. No single ethnie was placed strongly enough to be a core. Tagalogs and Javanese were closest, and attempts to make Tagalog the basis of the national language shared some of the problems of Burmese. But the effective *lingua franca* of Filipino nationalism was Spanish, followed in the twentieth century by English, while Dutch and Malay played this role in Indonesia. A much more creative task was needed in the two archipelagos for anti-imperial nationalists to develop the substance of new communities of belonging, to match the colonial boundaries.

European colonial authorities knew that they were dealing with peoples of various languages and cultures, but in the high colonial period of racial hierarchy (roughly 1870–1940) these distinctions paled before the status of 'natives' (Dutch, *inlander*) as the indigenous base of the racial pyramid. As the generic name for these indigenous subjects both Spanish and Dutch used the same term 'Indians'—Spanish *Indio*, Dutch *Indiër*. The novel idea that there was a collective unity among the subjects of Dutch-ruled and Spanish-ruled archipelagos respectively, other than that of religion, began with the colonisers. It spread to the colonised as a category of humiliation, or as nationalism gathered strength, of oppression. As it did so a new term was necessary, which did not carry the negative or alien associations of 'native' or 'Indian'.

The Philippines was luckier, paradoxically, in having the name of a Spanish king applied to it in the sixteenth century. By the nineteenth century, it was uncontroversial as the name of the colony. 'Filipino' was then used as the term for locally born Spaniards, but this was gradually accepted also by Chinese *Mestizos* and elite *Indios* in search of an inclusive local identity. There was opposition from ethnie terms such as Tagalog, used by Pedro Paterno in his ethno-nationalist *La antigua civilización tagálog* (1887). Influenced by Paterno's idyllic view of pre-Spanish Tagalog society, the revolutionary populist Andres Bonifacio addressed his manifesto of 1896 to 'the Tagalogs' (Ileto 1979: 102–5). As a broader category of belonging, 'Malay' was also appealing, especially to the nationalist hero José Rizal (see chapter 4). But in the transition to a new American administration and its different set of idioms at the beginning of the twentieth century, 'Filipino' became firmly established as the object of nationalist striving. Although, as in Indonesia, those designated as 'Chinese' often fell outside its parameters, it had little of ethnie nationalism about it, and should be considered the Southeast Asian anti-imperial nationalism which can most confidently be described as 'civic' in spirit.

In the Dutch-ruled Archipelago, the earliest nationalists in quest of pan-Archipelago unity had to use a Malay equivalent of 'Indian'—*orang Hindia*—to describe themselves. Only with the first generation of nationalist students in Holland was the esoteric term 'Indonesia' embraced. This Greek term ('islands of India') had been occasionally used in European linguistic and ethnographic circles since the nineteenth century, and became more current around the First World War years as a more scientific term than the racialised 'Malay' for what we today call the Austronesian language group. A Latin version of the same term, Insulinde, had probably been rendered less appealing to majority nationalists by its adoption by one of the earliest colony-wide nationalist parties (1907), primarily Eurasian in membership. In 1924, the students changed the name of their association from 'Indian' to 'Indonesian', and began a nationalist journal with the rousing title *Indonesia Merdeka*. This novel term spread very quickly through the colony. In 1928, representatives of various youth and student groups in the colony subscribed to an oath of imagined unity later celebrated as the defining moment of Indonesian identity—'One fatherland, Indonesia; one *bangsa* [nation or race], *bangsa* Indonesia; one language, *bahasa* Indonesia.'

Indonesia's revolutionary experience came a half-century later than that of the Philippines, in the aftermath of the Japanese occupation, in 1945–9. It was even more effective than its Philippine antecedent in transforming the unitary nationalist ideals from the discourse of a small group of intellectuals to the sacred foundational ideas of a new state. Even ethnies with strong and recent memories of proudly independent states, like Aceh and Bali, were passionately caught up in the unitary ideal as a means of overthrowing Dutch rule. Ideas of separatism, federalism or asymmetrical relationship with the new state were initially put on the back-burner as luxuries, and eventually redefined as treachery to the struggling post-revolutionary state. As revolutionary populism faded after the fall of its mouthpiece, Sukarno, in 1965–6, the unitary idea was kept sacred and central by the military-based regime of General Suharto. Only in the democratic space after his fall in 1998 have such questions again been vigorously discussed, with East Timor, Aceh and West Papua forcing the issue. The Aceh case will be taken as paradigmatic of these questions, in chapter 4 below.

Ethnicising the stateless

While I have characterised 'state-averse' as an historical feature of Southeast Asia (minus Vietnam and the Irrawaddy basin), there was a wide variety of experiences with states both of the cosmic temple-building and the trade-oriented type. At one end of the spectrum were the hill peoples in general, along with boat people or 'sea-gypsies' of small-island clusters, and the inhabitants of some other small islands of the east. These were examples of 'untamed' peoples who had disappeared centuries earlier in Europe and China proper. They were aware of rulers with some claims to statehood controlling river-mouths or other strategic trade arteries, because it was necessary to trade with them for essential items such as salt, fish paste, metalware and weapons. In many cases these exchanges were characterised as tribute, but most were complementary trade relations. Their life-style was in some cases nomadic, but more frequently based on the shifting cultivation of hill rice, a labour-efficient but land-expensive means of annually changing the fields to be cultivated from the forest.

Such societies consciously rejected assimilation into the states they knew. This always reflected a prizing of their relatively mobile mode of production, and often a difference in religion and of customary laws regulating land-holding and marriage. Most had had to fight at some time to protect their free status. At least one substantial group of South Sumatra highlanders explicitly claimed the status of free men *(orang mardika)*, who paid no tax and owed no obligations to the *raja* of the river-mouths, nor to the Dutch and British (Collins 1979: 90–2). The Bataks of North Sumatra appear to have deliberately built up an exaggerated reputation as ferocious cannibals to ensure that they were left in peace by coastal rulers (Hirosue 1996).

By definition these societies had a low sense of ethnie nationalism; they perceived themselves as extremely various, with different dialects and customs in each river valley, and a common sense of themselves only in relation to extremes of outside pressure. They faced a crisis of identity when for the first time at the beginning of the twentieth century they were brought, by force or persuasion, within the fixed boundaries of a modern (colonial) state, with strong ideas of sovereign rights over them. Before this incorporation, imperial authority had been limited to coastal ports, from which vantage hill peoples seemed no more than a primitive periphery. Europeans adopted from lowlanders some generic terms which perceived these people only as highlanders, countryfolk, pagans and savages—Montagnards, Karen, Orang Ulu, Dusun, Ifugao, Alfur, Toraja, Dayak or Batak. In general, the claims of lowland kings to hegemony over these peoples had been supported by colonial power, and taken over by that power when it supplanted monarchs.

Even the most ambitious Southeast Asian state could at best assimilate captive or adventurous individuals from these communities. Lieberman (2003: 208) put it in physical terms: 'illiterate Chins, Kachins, Karens, Palaungs, and so forth escaped Burman political control entirely by virtue of their poverty, inaccessibility, and the fragility of their supra-village organisations'. In the Archipelago I argue that this was also partly choice, but a choice no longer available once incorporated into colonial states after 1900.

Within the multi-ethnic European-ruled state, such people had need of broader ethnie labels, which the classifying work of European missionaries, ethnographers, linguists and census-takers hastened to provide. By this stage missionaries were convinced of the necessity of preaching in vernaculars, but practical necessities forced them to homogenise local dialects into a manageable number of languages for translation and printing of bibles and prayers. European officials also learned only a few languages, or more frequently used indigenous translators and mediators who imposed their dialects upon a wider group. The demands for political representation, when it came, also called for broad categories. Gradually, therefore, the colonial experience welded the variegated mosaic of stateless peoples into larger groups, some of whom became ethnies. Chapters 6 and 7 consider two of these cases, the Batak and the Kadazan/Dusun, in order to understand what this meant for the nationalist potential of such groups.

Dutch and English census-takers in the twentieth century began with relative diversity, reflecting the immense diversity of ways in which people identified themselves, particularly in stateless societies. The Burmese census listed forty-five distinct 'races' under the stateless Kuki-Chin heading, seventeen under the Karen, and eleven under the Palaung and Wa, the smallest of which had less than a thousand members. For practical purposes the state could only comprehend and deal with them on the basis of these groups. During the colonial period the Mon and Tai (Shan) categories, both Theravada and long acquainted with states, tended to be absorbed into Burman, diminishing from 3.1 per cent and 8.5 per cent respectively in 1901 to 2.3 per cent and 7.1 per cent in 1931. The other categories protected by the 'scheduled areas' status, on the other hand, held relatively stable or in the Karen case even increased (8.7 to 9.3 per cent). In the censuses after independence the fifteen indigenous groups of the colonial scheme were reduced to eight, and a reverse trend tended to increase all the lowland Theravada categories (Burman, Mon and Shan), which now had the benefit of states within the Union of Burma system. The once stateless highlanders fared less well, Karens dropping to 6.2 per cent in 1983 (*Ibid.*: i: 224; *Burma 1983 Population Census*: 1: 21).

The Batak and the Kadazan/Dusun, discussed in chapters 6 and 7, are among the more coherent and effective of the once stateless groups now making their way in independent modern states. It should be remembered that dozens of other language groups have been wholly absorbed within the past century, either into the dominant national ethnie or into a regionally dominant one. The survivors are those which adapted relatively quickly to the new opportunities for education, entrepreneurship and political mobilisation that the colonial states offered. A few of them became favoured sons of colonial regimes, rewarded for perceived loyalty by being better represented in colonial armies, and wary of the dominant nationalism. Most, however, were supportive of the independent successor states, seeing in the national leadership the same kind of protection against local rivals or oppressors they had enjoyed under colonial regimes, without the paternalism. They had no other memory of state to resort to than this one, and the demands for statehood from some Karen, Ambonese and Papuans should be noted as exceptions to be explained, and by no means the norm.

3   Chinese as a Southeast Asian 'other'

A chapter on Chinese political identity in Southeast Asia may seem anomalous. Insofar as nationalism was 'Chinese' in Southeast Asia it was fixated on the fate of the Chinese state rather than a local identity. Yet Chinese, like the less numerous but more aggressive Europeans, carried to Southeast Asia a stronger sense of state-centred identity than was common in Southeast Asia, and developed particularly robust forms of supra-local community in market towns all over the region. Once a more balanced gender ratio and regular contact with China enabled them to reproduce that community in Southeast Asia, from the seventeenth century, they became 'essential outsiders' (Chirot and Reid 1997), creating commercial and information networks essential to the birth of many nationalisms. The Chinese relationship to Southeast Asian nationalisms was crucial.

'Chinese' as a Southeast Asian concept

Labels have great power to unite and to divide, particularly when believed to be unproblematic and natural. One of the most divisive such labels in the long term has been 'China', which in Southeast Asian languages is both noun and adjective. Like many ethnonyms, this usage appears to have been fixed by outsiders, and pre-eminently in Southeast Asian encounters. The subjects of the Middle or Flowery Kingdom themselves had little need of it. It was in Southeast Asia that such subjects became detached from the imperial framework and began to be defined as if they were an ethnie. Encountering a great variety of other peoples defined by religion, language, political allegiance or place, they found the need to define themselves also in terms that resembled the ethnic. In the sixteenth and seventeenth centuries, the subsequently dominant Europeans in turn encountered this particular form of politico-civilisational boundary and reified it in their own ways.

Inside the world of Chinese characters in Northeast Asia, when a need arose to distinguish the 'civilised' subjects of the empire from the barbarian outer tributaries, the most frequent resort was the name of a dynasty. This could be the one currently ruling, or an admired past dynasty, usually Tang or Ming. Only in relatively modern times do such terms as *hua* ('flowery') or *zhongguo* ('middle kingdom') make it possible to detach Chineseness internally from particular dynasties.

Outside that world, something like 'China' has been part of international discourse for a long time, though until the sixteenth century always competing with other terms. This description of the eastern empire is most frequently presumed to have derived from the Qin Dynasty of Shi Huangdi in 221–206 BC, the first to unify what is today north-central China in a bureaucratic empire. The term was not much used by Chinese themselves in subsequent periods, the Qin being much less admired a dynasty than Han or Tang. It does appear to have spread around Southeast Asia and the Indian Ocean quite early as a designation for the Chinese empire, however. The ancient Indian *Arthasastra* referred to *Cinabhumi* as the source of a kind of silk known as *Cinapatta* (Kangle 1969: 74). In early Islam *Sin* represented a shadowy but powerful land in the farthest east, as in the well-known *hadith*: 'Seek knowledge even unto *Sin*' (Yule and Burnell 1979: 196–7). Even Ptolemy, in Egypt, referred to the *Sinae* races of the furthest east, though the term was less common in Europe than overland-derived terms such as 'Cathay'.

Southeast Asian languages followed this Indian Ocean pattern— Malay and Indonesian *Cina*, Thai *Chin*, Khmer *Chen*, Burmese *Sina*, Tagalog *Tsina*. From the fifteenth century the written sources were consistent about using this nomenclature, though it occurs much earlier. A 947 Sanskrit inscription in Cambodia described King Yasovarman's realm as extending to Champa and to 'China' (Lavy 2004: 437; Coedes, 1968: 114). Marco Polo, who used 'Manzi' to designate China, noted that there was an island near China which called its ocean 'the China Sea—that is the sea adjoining Manzi, because in the language of the islanders "China" means Manzi' (Marco Polo, 1292: 220). The Javanese *Nagarakertagama* or *Desawarnana* of 1365, also listed 'China', alongside Annam, Cambodia, Champa and three Indian locations, as places from which pilgrims came to Java in search of sacred knowledge (Pigeaud 1960, IV: 98; Robson 1995: 85).

It was the intense involvement with the early Ming Empire from 1368, and notably the Zheng He expeditions of 1405–33, which established the imperial reality of 'China' in insular Southeast Asian consciousness, and fixed the term. This was virtually the only time when the Chinese presence in Southeast Asia was an imperial one, and it is understandable therefore that maritime Southeast Asians (unlike Chinese) came to use a single term for the empire, the various spoken languages, the written language and a disparate group of traders with connections to that empire and that written language.[1] Earlier Javanese references to the Mongol invasion of the 1290s generally use terms such as Tartar or Mongol (Berg 1927: 77), or ignore the foreign origin of these forces in concentrating on the Javanese contest which gave rise to the Majapahit kingdom. The *Hikayat Raja-Raja Pasai*, a Malay chronicle which ends with Majapahit's conquest of Pasai in the mid-fourteenth century, ignores both the term and the reality of 'China'. From the fifteenth century, however, the term appears fixed.

'China' in Southeast Asian writing

'China' in fact appeared frequently as a distant and powerful empire in pre-colonial texts not only of the contiguous states, Dai Viet and Burma, but also of those whose contact with China was by sea. Since many such maritime states originated in the interaction with Ming China during the long fifteenth century, the 'Ming factor' could not be ignored (Wade and Sun 2009). Yet even the states known from Chinese sources to have gained their initial comparative advantage by riding that Ming factor and sending their first rulers to China with the imperial fleets, like Melaka and Brunei, do not acknowledge that link directly in their chronicles. The hundreds of tribute missions sent in this period, the thousands of Chinese who settled in the Southeast Asian ports as refugees or defectors, and the role of a Quanzhou diaspora in spreading Islam, are scarcely mentioned. Instead the royal chronicles of the major Muslim states tend to incorporate a less plausible but more culturally acceptable story of a Chinese princess, *puteri Cina*, sent by the Chinese emperor to marry the local king and thereby confirm his status.

Melaka, the epitome of the Southeast Asian emporium which became established as a reliable base and trade gateway for the Zheng He fleets of the early 1400s, sent all its first three rulers for investiture in China. According to the earliest version of the Malay chronicle tradition, relayed to Tomé Pires soon after the Portuguese conquest in 1511, the greatest of Melaka's kings, Sultan Mansur (1459–77), was 'always a true vassal of the kings of the Chinese and of the kings of Java and of Siam'. His incompetent successor Mahmud, who lost Melaka to the Portuguese,

---

[1] In this as in other respects there may be two Southeast Asias—states contiguous with China and those whose relations with the Middle Kingdom were by sea. In Vietnam the plurality of what others called 'China' was often recognised. Trinh Hoai Duc (1765–1825) noted that in Saigon at the beginning of the nineteenth century, 'the languages of Fujian, Quandong, Zhaozhou, Hainam, West [Khmer, or Portugese?] and Siam are used as means of communication'. I am grateful to Choi Byoong Wook for this reference.

arrogantly rejected his tribute to Siam and Java but sent it only to China, 'saying why should Melaka be obedient to the kings who were obedient to China?' (Pires 1515: 248, 253). The Melaka chronicle set down in writing a century later, however, was at pains to deny any inferiority in the relations of Melaka with China. Its principal reference to China is a lengthy story of the 'king of China' (the same rank as Melaka) sending his daughter to marry the great Sultan Mansur. The chronicle acknowledges that a letter was sent to China presenting homage (*sembah*) to its king, but only as the gratitude of a son-in-law for the gift of the Chinese princess. When the envoys brought this letter to Beijing, the 'king of China' was stricken with a disease, which a wise man interpreted as being caused by his sin in having accepted tribute from Melaka. The Chinese ruler repented and sent a mission to Melaka to request the water in which Sultan Mansur's feet had been washed, which successfully cured his ailment. He then solemnly declared 'all my descendants, never demand homage from the Raja of Melaka but only an agreement of friendship' (Winstedt 1938: 116–19; English in Brown 1952: 89–91).

The 'Great Chronicle' of Java, *Babad Tanah Jawa*, has the founder of its Islamic dynasty, Raden Patah, born from the last Majapahit king and a Chinese princess. This appears to be a device to explain why in the wake of the same massive Ming intervention a half-Chinese port ruler from Palembang could become the legitimate Javanese king. Because his first wife objected to the competition, King Brawijaya of Majapahit gave away his already-pregnant Chinese princess wife to the Muslim ruler of Palembang. The child thus born, Raden Patah, although deriving from the Chinese and Muslim stronghold of Palembang, was presented by the Mataram chronicler as 'really' a son of the last Majapahit ruler and thus appropriately destined to bring about the fall of Majapahit and the rise of Muslim Mataram (Olthof 1987: 20–4).

Various legends current in Java and Bali describe the exploits of Zheng He (known as *Sanbao gong* or *Sam Po Kong*), or of his assistants who opted to stay in the Archipelago—his pilot known as Dampu Awang, or in Bali even his cook known as Cong Po (Salmon and Siddharta 2000: 89–93). The Brunei royal tradition, the most indebted of all to Chinese origins if we follow Chinese sources, has the ruler marry the daughter of the Chinese general Ong Sum Ping. Various non-Muslim indigenous legends of northern Borneo go further in claiming descent from the soldiers of an invading Chinese army, and linking the two most important toponyms in Sabah, Mount Kinabalu and the Kinabatangan River, to Chinese intervention (*Kina* = China in Dusunic languages:) (Tan 1992: 100–8). The Malay-language chronicles of Banjarmasin and Patani, two states with no official relations with China but many Chinese traders and craftsmen in their midst, explained their indebtedness to Chinese civilisation through stories of craftsmen being sent from China to make particular bronze artefacts—cannons in Patani and statues in Banjarmasin (*Hikayat Patani* II 1970: 152–4, 224–6; *Hikajat Bandjar* 1968: 254–63).

If Southeast Asian courts spoke by the fifteenth century as if there was a single place and a single people called 'China', it was different in the imperial court itself. As the model of the 'enduring states' discussed above, the empire was certainly unique among pre-modern polities in the strength of its centralised structures and literary uniformity. Although a variety of different languages and cultures continued to exist, especially in the south and southwest, more Chinese would have been aware of being part of one civilisation and subject to one dynasty than any other pre-modern group. But this civilisation presented itself not as Chinese but as universal. Imperial theory was that this was the only civilisation, even if unpleasant encounters with a succession of powerful barbarians forced official spokesmen to admit, and many more to cover up with silence, the fact that it was in reality a **particular** civilisation they were defending (Duara 1995: 56–60).

The position of Dai Viet, aspiring to (Chinese) civilisation but rejecting the bureaucratic authority of the empire, put this culturalism theory sharply to the test. On the one hand the ideal relationship was set out in one imperial letter to Dai Viet:

I am the Emperor, and having received Heaven's great mandate, I rule the Chinese [*hua*] and the *yi*. The one language/culture provides a norm for the 10,000 places, while cultural influence educates beyond the four quarters. Of all who are contained under heaven or supported by earth, there is none who does not submit in heart. (Tian-shun Emperor 1466, in Wade 1994, I: 63)

On the other, those not fully subject to imperial bureaucracy would always remain barbarian in imperial eyes. 'Although Annam follows the Court's calendar and brings tribute to the Court, its people are, in the end, still foreign *yi*' (Xiao-zong Emperor 1495, in *Ibid.*: 64).

Europeans and the Chinese 'other' in Southeast Asia

Once we enter the exceptionally plural world of maritime Southeast Asia, where interaction was by sea rather than by land, Chinese traded and settled as minorities and Chineseness could only be seen as one ethnie distinct from others. In 1567 the Ming government finally accepted the necessity of trade with Southeast Asia, and from this date Chinese communities in the trading emporia of the south were constantly refreshed by annual fleets from Canton and Fujian. From this point, in particular, Southeast Asians appeared to be unanimous that these traders were 'Chinese' (*Cina*), with no need for sub-division.

The term itself appears to take fixed form in the sixteenth century, first among Southeast Asians and then Europeans. The Portuguese came to the region in 1509 using the term *Chijs* for the trading people of whom they had heard, but once established in Melaka and elsewhere they adopted the Malay usage whereby the same term (*China*, and for the people *Chinos*) served for the great empire and for its mercantile sons in Southeast Asia (Barros 1563: II, vi: 36–8, 56–7; III, ii: 186–204). There was one rival word on the eastern route of Chinese commerce through the Philippines to eastern Indonesia. This was *sangley*, probably derived from a Hokkien term for businessman, and the commonest description of Chinese traders in Philippine and South Sulawesi languages in the Ming period (Cense 1979: 659). Even here the term 'China' was also prominent from the sixteenth century, especially to describe the country, and it gradually drove out the other term.

In most Southeast Asian sources there appeared to be only one kind of Chinese, despite the fact that the people so designated spoke a variety of languages. The existence of two different *syahbandar* (port officials) for Chinese merchants (presumably those from Fujian and Guangdong respectively) in Cambodia of the 1630s (Gaelen 1636, in Muller 1917: 63) is the only evidence I have found outside Vietnam of Southeast Asians regarding Chinese as inherently plural. The weight of references on the other side, to 'China' as a singular category, is overwhelming.

It can be argued that it was Chinese, even more than Europeans, who introduced Southeast Asians to distinctive otherness as opposed to their own continuum of shifting and overlapping identities. The Chinese arrived earlier and in greater numbers, and from the sixteenth century they implanted the tangible signs of ethnie corporate life. Prior to the Ming change of heart in 1567, when it had been illegal for Chinese sojourners to return home and they may have faced execution, no such clear-cut Chinese otherness developed. There was little incentive to retain Chinese language, dress and hairstyles in order to be acceptable on return to China, and the contrary pressures to intermarriage, bi-culturalism or assimilation were high. The tribute records of the fifteenth century are full of envoys from Java and Siam who carried both a local title and a Chinese name, and who clearly profited from being bi-cultural brokers between two civilisations. When they spoke to the first generation of Portuguese in the early 1500s, many Javanese and Malay traders took pride in their descent from China on the male side (Reid 1996: 21–37; 2006b).

After 1567, however, permanent 'Chinatowns' developed in the trading cities of Southeast Asia. A rich Chinese ritual and organisational life developed around the temple and the sequence of annual ceremonies for New Year and for the souls of the dead—*Qingming* in April, *Yulanpen* in August–September (Raben 1996: 240). Most were speakers of some Min dialect (Hokkien), and all shared a ritual system centred on lineage and the commemoration of ancestors, as well as similar technologies and financial practices. When described in the great port and sultanate of Banten (Java) by the first Dutch travellers to arrive in 1596, the Chinese were already very distinctive:

The Chinese live at Banten in a separate quarter [outside the walled city], that is surrounded by a strong palisade reinforced by a moat, where they have the finest houses which there are in the city. They are a very subtle people, in all their dealings very eager to make money, and thereby they keep a good table. When they first come from China, they do as I have explained for other merchants and buy a wife, who serves them until they want to return to China. They then sell her again, taking the children with them if the union has produced any. (Lodewycksz 1598: 121–2)

Already they had their own temples, opera troupes and vigorous ritual life, their own currency of copper cash which played a vital role in the commerce of the city, and means of subsistence including the pigs that ensured the majority Muslim population of the city kept its distance. A colourful English account of the same city suggested considerable tension between the two communities, so that the Javanese 'do much rejoice when they see a Chinese go to execution (as also the Chinese do when they see a Javanese go to his death)' (Scott 1606: 121).

Such Chinatowns developed after 1567 in ports such as Hoi An in Vietnam, Ayutthaya in Siam, Patani in the Peninsula, and Aceh and Brunei as well as Banten in the Archipelago. The largest such communities in the seventeenth century contained as many as 3,000 Chinese in the trading season. In these and other independent states there was still an incentive for the more ambitious Chinese traders to adopt the local religion and 'become' Malay, Thai, Javanese or Acehnese. Only in that way could they enter the ruling oligarchy of merchant-officials. By the seventeenth century in all Muslim-majority countries, this was an explicit step from one identity to another from which there was no going back. It was often marked by public rituals, and it required the abandonment of pork, a change of dress and the cutting of the long Ming-style hair, for 'if once they cut their hair, they may never return to their country again' (Scott 1606: 176). The 'shorn Chinese' of the seventeenth century, equivalent to the Malay terms *peranakan* or *Cina peranakan*, were new Muslims who had changed religion, identity and loyalty.

Under European rule in Spanish Manila (from 1571), Dutch Batavia (1619), Melaka (1640), Makasar (1669) and other such ports, and eventually British Penang (1786) and Singapore (1819), the ruling class was an impervious racial one and there was very little incentive to change identity. After much initial hostility and competition, the European officials established a remarkable symbiosis with Chinese merchants and craftsmen, who became a classic 'middleman minority' filling the commercial space between ruler and ruled (Zenner 1991; Reid 1997).

European concepts of racial distinctiveness had a powerful influence in the longer term. The Dutch and British in particular showed little interest in Christianising the Chinese under their authority, still less in seeing them assimilate into the majority Muslim community. So long as a few wealthy resident Chinese learned enough Dutch, English or Malay to communicate with the rulers and manage most of the economy for them, they were content for the pattern of Chinese separateness to continue, with distinct quarters of the city under their own Chinese administrative and judicial arrangements. While bi-culturalism was essential at least on the part of the elite, the colonial system discouraged ambivalence and boundary crossing. Chinese should remain Chinese (Reid 1988–93, II: 311–19; Hoadley 1988: 503–17).

The dependence of Europeans on Chinese enterprise produced very mixed emotions of admiration, fear and scorn. Europeans immediately equated the Chinese of the region to Jews in Europe—uncannily successful in commerce, inscrutable in ritual, but marginal and powerless 'essential outsiders' or pariah entrepreneurs (Lodewycksz 1598: 26; Reid 1997). To instance one of many such stereotypes, Scott remarked of the Chinese in Banten that they 'live crouching under them, but rob them of their wealth and send it for China (Scott 1606: 174).

European ambivalence about Chinese in Southeast Asia continued through the nineteenth century, as liberals and conservatives divided as to how they regarded both Jews and Chinese, and some paternalistic reformers sought to blame Chinese middlemen rather than Dutch rule for the poverty of the Javanese. Among Southeast Asians themselves there is evidence of hostility towards Chinese, though more frequent evidence of violence at their expense as a relatively defenceless wealthy minority (Reid 1997). Only in the twentieth century did competing nationalisms and the competition for middle-class roles give rise to systematic resentment and discrimination against Chinese. The 'Jews of the East' analogy was first used by a Southeast Asian to excoriate the Chinese in 1914, when no less than the Thai king, Rama VI, the first Thai ruler to have all his education in England, published an anonymous pamphlet denouncing the 'yellow peril' (Landon 1941: 34–43). Nevertheless the roots of such sinister stereotypes were very deep.

Diasporic identities in the colonial era

During the century before 1740, the European-ruled ports of Batavia and Manila were the greatest magnets for Chinese trade in Southeast Asia, with more than half the big junks sailing to the South Seas from Xiamen (Amoy) every year heading for those two ports. As many as 200 Chinese would stay behind from each of the dozens of junks arriving each year. In both cities thousands of Chinese (15,000 in Batavia by 1739; Raben 1996: 91–3, 133–9) formed the lifeblood of the city, and levies on the Chinese through opium, spirit and gaming taxes formed a large part of its revenue. The Dutch perfected a system of tax farming in their Asian cities, whereby the leading Chinese residents bid for the right to operate certain monopolies and the levying of port duties. These tax-farmers were frequently also the Chinese captains, tasked by the Dutch with keeping order and administering justice within the community. A few bi-cultural magnates, therefore, came to control the destinies of the Chinese communities.

In 1740 an appalling pogrom (the only one in Batavia's history) took place against the Batavia Chinese, with paranoid Dutch soldiers and residents killing the majority of this flourishing population and driving the rest out of the city. Manila had had a history of more frequent irruptions of anti-Chinese violence, and in 1755 Chinese who had not shown their loyalty by becoming Catholic were excluded from the Philippines. A specifically Chinese identity was for the following century less attractive in the Dutch settlements and virtually impossible in the Spanish. Chinese in Java were more inclined to assimilate into the indigenous states, in the Philippines to avoid Manila in favour of ports such as Sulu, and in general to increase their dealings with Asian rather than colonial ports. These setbacks, together with the declining centrality of Batavia and Manila in Asian trade, directed the increasing flow of Chinese traders and migrants thereafter to a variety of other centres still under Asian rule. Saigon, Ha Tien, Trengganu, Brunei, Pontianak and Sulu were beneficiaries of this Chinese enterprise in the succeeding century, roughly 1740–1840, but the greatest winner was Bangkok. The new Thai capital (1782) quickly became the leading port for Chinese shipping outside China. With about eighty ocean-going Chinese junks based there, and sixty more visiting each year from China, Bangkok probably replaced Batavia by the end of the eighteenth century as the busiest port between Calcutta and Canton (Crawfurd 1820 III: 182–4; Reid 1993).

Some of the migration of the period following the fall of the Ming Dynasty in 1644 had an unprecedentedly political character. An alternative Chinese polity based on maritime trade had arisen in Taiwan and the ports of Fujian as the Ming collapsed and the Manchus struggled to establish their control. This regime under the ship-owning Zheng family was nominally Ming loyalist, but in practice it represented a new kind of Chinese authority based on partnership between wealthy shipowners, for the most part Hokkien (Wang 1994: 37–47). As the Manchus gradually succeeded in re-establishing control over first the Fujian coast and finally Taiwan in 1683, some of these big shipowners took refuge in Southeast Asia. One such group of fifty junks loosely served the Vietnamese cause in the then unruly frontier of the Mekong delta. By 1700 a Cantonese adventurer, Mac Cuu, had established an autonomous Ming-style port-state at Ha Tien, playing off Cambodian, Siamese and Vietnamese claims over this borderland. Throughout the Manchu (Qing) period in China, the justifications for any form of Chinese political authority tended to be anti-Manchu, and notably so among the secret societies (*hui*) which periodically galvanised Chinese settlers into armed action.

In the middle of the eighteenth century, however, the Manchus relaxed their restrictions on international trade. In 1754 they declared that any Chinese with valid reasons would be entitled to return home and have his property protected (Ng 1991: 373–400). Traders, miners, planters, shipbuilders, craftsmen, mariners and adventurers flowed southward in unprecedented numbers. They particularly occupied the hitherto scarcely populated central zone of Southeast Asia, from the Gulf of Thailand in the north to West Borneo, Bangka and South Sumatra in the south, embracing the whole Malayan Peninsula. They mined gold in West Borneo and Kelantan, and tin in Bangka, Phuket, and by the 1840s the Malay states of the Peninsula. They planted pepper in Brunei, Cambodia and Southeast Siam, gambier in Riau-Johor, sugar in Siam and Vietnam.

Although a conventional nationalist view is that large and unassimilable Chinese minorities were foisted on Southeast Asia under colonial influence after 1870, the reality is that Chinese were as large a proportion of the Southeast Asian population in the early 1800s as under colonial domination in the early 1900s, and considerably more influential. Newbold's estimate of 'nearly a million' Chinese in Southeast Asia as a whole around 1830 would represent about 3 per cent of the population (Newbold 1839, I: 9). The three million counted in the better documented 1930s were a significantly smaller percentage. What is true is that the largest communities of the early 1800s were in Siam and West Borneo under Asian rule, and the Philippines where Chinese *Mestizos* were soon to be reclassified as Filipinos. The huge influx of the high colonial period made Malaysia and Singapore the leading concentrations of Chinese after 1870 (Mackie 1996: xxii–xxiv).

Singapore replaced Bangkok as the leading centre for Chinese shipping in Southeast Asia within a few decades of its founding in 1819. In a commercial sense it thereby became the new centre for the dispersion of Chinese migrants, and for those aspects of the import and export trade that flowed through Singapore. Chinese newspapers and Chinese education were better maintained in the British colony than was possible in the Dutch Indies or Siam. As reform movements and the beginnings of overseas Chinese nationalism affected the *Nanyang* Chinese from the 1890s, therefore, Singapore was a major centre for their dissemination. The presence of Chinese as a middleman minority everywhere, the networks of trade and information, and the role of Singapore as a communication hub for them, made the Chinese more aware of a Southeast Asian (or as they put it, *Nanyang* or 'South Seas') identity than either Europeans or majority communities in the region. The quest for a political identity **as** Southeast Asian Chinese, however, had to cope with other diversities.

Creole identities and urban print culture

The story of three nineteenth century Sino-Southeast Asian creoles in the Philippines, Malaya and Java, has been well told by Skinner (1996). He argues for the use of the linguistic term creole for the blend of Hokkien Chinese and indigenous elements which stabilised in the eighteenth century and came to dominate the commercial life of the three colonies in the nineteenth. In each case the language they used was a creole based on the dominant indigenous *lingua franca*, Malay and Tagalog, while influenced by Hokkien both in grammar and vocabulary.

As he points out, European colonial control changed the process whereby Chinese migrants had eventually assimilated into societies ultimately regarded as indigenous through Islamisation. Once European Christians who offered no female marriage partners occupied the high status roles, the incentive to assimilation in this way was removed. In the Philippines there was almost a century (1756–1850) when immigration from China was forbidden and Chinese already there had to become Catholic and marry locally. By 1877, shortly after Chinese immigration recommenced, there were 290,000 in the creole category of 'Chinese *Mestizo*', over 5 per cent of the Philippine population, as against only 23,000 'Chinese'. Melaka (Malacca) in Dutch hands for most of the period 1641–1824 was a sleepy place attracting few new Chinese migrants, and the original Chinese migrants intermarried with women brought there (predominately as slaves) from the Archipelago, producing a stable creole society. This was the base for the *baba* society or 'Straits Chinese' of the Straits Settlements (British Singapore, Melaka and Penang) in the nineteenth century, socially and economically dominating the newcomers until mid-century. At their peak (in absolute terms, though already declining as a percentage of Chinese) around 1891, the *baba* numbered about 16,000 in Singapore, 8,000 in Melaka and 23,000 in Penang.

In Java, Chinese immigration was never interrupted, and there was more of a gradual spectrum between one extreme of culturally Chinese and the other of creolised speakers of the mixed languages of the cities. There was a consistent policy by the Dutch to treat these 'Chinese' as a single legal and administrative category distinct from the native majority, controlled by Chinese officers who were of the creole group. Chinese-speaking Chinese remained a distinct minority, marginal in all matters except trade with China. In 1900 there were still only 24,000 China-born Chinese in Java, as against 250,000 of the creole group. The latter were dominant enough simply to be called Chinese in Dutch discourse, though when a distinction from the China-born became necessary in the twentieth century, the creoles were called by the old seventeenth century term *peranakan*. Now however, the *peranakan* were seldom Muslim. Like the *baba* in the Straits Settlements, they had few incentives to become either Christian (which gave no advantages as in the Philippines) or Muslim, and retained the festivals and ancestor rituals of popular practice in the Fujian homeland (Skinner 1996: 52–8).

The creole languages that became the mother tongue of *peranakan* and *baba* were very similar. As summarised by Skinner on the basis of Shellabear, 'the lexicon was perhaps two thirds Malay and one fifth Hokkien Chinese, the remainder being Dutch, Portuguese, English, Tamil and assorted Indonesian languages' (Skinner 1996: 60–1). Both in the Peninsula and in Java this Malay creole became the most important *lingua franca* of trade, as well as mother tongue of many city-dwellers. The first Malay newspapers from the mid-nineteenth century depended heavily on these Sino-Southeast Asians as both producers and consumers. The romanised Malay that became first the urban *lingua franca* and eventually the national language of both Indonesia and Malaysia drew heavily on this eclectic print tradition, though more so in Indonesia than Malaysia.

Commercial elites, however, needed the language of the ruling classes—English, Spanish or Dutch for the colonial high culture, and written Chinese for dealing with China and retaining some elements of its tradition. On the one hand local-born Chinese residents of the colonies were the first Asians to seize the opportunities of mission or government schools, and to produce the early Europe-educated graduates in the 1880s and 1890s. The *ilustrados* of the late nineteenth century Philippines were the largest such group to benefit from European education, and the only one large enough to generate a veritable nationalist movement (Wickberg 1965: 134–45; Mojares 2006).

The fate of these creoles in the twentieth century age of nationalism is instructive. The Spanish-educated elite of the Chinese *Mestizos* of the Philippines were among the creators of Filipino national identity. Excluded by race from the ruling Spanish elite, they nevertheless shared enough linguistic and religious (anti-clerical Catholicism) ground with the majority population to reinvent 'Filipino' as an inclusive category. The Chinese *Mestizo* category thus merged into a Filipino one at the end of the nineteenth century.

The *peranakan* of Java too have a reasonable claim to being the first Indonesians, as the largest element in the nineteenth century of that urban Malay-speaking culture which eventually became Indonesian national culture. But the Indonesian national identity was imagined a generation later than the Filipino one, following rather than preceding the peak of Chinese nationalist enthusiasm in 1911. Idealistic young people searching for a dignified modern identity had grasped at the 'Overseas Chinese' one, since the 'Indonesian' alternative was not yet available to them. Had Dutch education and Indonesian nationalism begun in the late nineteenth century when Spanish education and Filipino nationalism did, Chinese-descended creoles would probably have been the torch-bearers in both places. Instead, the earliest populist variant of Indonesian nationalism, organised through Islamic associations such as Sarekat Islam in the second decade of the twentieth century, assumed an anti-Chinese character, sparked in part by the Chinese nationalism which had begun to stir Chinese Indonesians just a few years earlier. The pressures of Chinese nationalism, of the much increased flow of migrants from China in the period 1890–1930, including women, and of differential education systems, combined with this suspicion on the Indonesian nationalist side to prevent the *peranakan* following the Filipino model.

Nevertheless Indonesian, as an identity and a language, retained many of the open and inclusive features which had marked the 'low Malay' or 'market Malay' creole of the Chinese. As a second language for most Indonesians, it was 'owned' by nobody, and continued throughout the twentieth century to borrow relatively liberally from European, Sanskrit and Javanese lexicons. It could not become identified predominately with Islam, since Christianity and Chinese religion had also long been expressed in Malay, the Malay Bible translated by Leydekker (1733) having represented 'high Malay' for Ambonese, Menadonese and Eurasians for centuries. At several points (the 1920s, 1950s and 1970s) it looked as though the 'Chinese' quality of the *peranakan* might be forgotten in the surge towards inclusive Indonesian-ness. Yet resistance on both sides ensured that a large measure of outsider status remained.

In Malaysia and Singapore, finally, demography was wholly against the *baba* in their struggle against a more powerful set of forces. Already in 1891 they were outnumbered 3.5 to 1 in the Straits Settlements, and more acutely so in Malaya as a whole. Following the establishment of Hong Kong as an open city in 1840, and of various Treaty Ports thereafter, the majority of the migrants who flooded southward were from Guandung or the port of Xiamen (Amoy) in south Fujian. Cantonese and Hakka became the predominate languages of the newcomers on the mining frontier in Malaya, and Teochiu on the agricultural frontiers of Johor and the Indonesian islands of Riau south of Singapore. They were not easy for the Hokkien, Malay and English speaking 'Straits Chinese' establishment to control. A multi-racial anti-imperial nationalism based on imperial boundaries was hardly thought of before the 1940s, and remained a weak growth throughout the century (see chapter 4). Such a 'Malayan nationalism' would have been the natural vehicle for *baba*, and insofar as it did have life in the 1945–8 period it was they who supported it. Overseas Chinese nationalism (below) gave additional prestige to Mandarin as its vehicle, and to redefining Sino-Southeast Asians as an inescapable part of a Chinese race. Through a powerful system of Chinese schools, newspapers and clan associations, pressure was put on the *baba* to have their children learn Chinese and categorise themselves as simply Chinese or Malaysian Chinese (Salmon 1996; Skinner 1996). Education policies of Malaysia and Singapore have in different ways militated against hybridity and overarching civic nationalism. In Malaysia a separate Chinese school system enrolled 85 per cent of Chinese children in the 1990s, as much from lack of confidence in the Malay-medium national system as from a passion to re-sinify a new generation by educating them in Mandarin. The latter, however, was the result. Singapore, by contrast, opted for a single national school system in English, and by the 1970s was phasing out Chinese-medium education which had culminated in Nanyang University. Instead, Lee Kuan Yew in the 1980s imposed a bi-lingual policy whereby children with 'Chinese' on their identity cards (relentlessly following the father's line in hybrid cases) are also required to learn Mandarin to fluency. As he put it, 'Mandarin is emotionally acceptable as our mother tongue. It also unites the different dialect groups. It reminds us that we are part of an ancient civilization with an unbroken history of 5,000 years. This is a deep and strong psychic force' (cited Kwok 1998: 216).

The creoles which emerged from earlier male-only migration from Fujian, in other words, have not fared well in the age of race-based nationalism. Only the Chinese *peranakan* category in Indonesia has survived, and its survival owes more to outsiderness—the economic role it occupies in business and the entrenched racial resentment this provokes—than to any remaining cultural distinctiveness from the majority society. Nevertheless these creoles, surviving for shorter or longer periods, have played an exceptionally important role in forging Southeast Asia's modern identities.

Overseas Chinese ethnie nationalism

The revolutions in communication, telegraph, steamship and railways, which tied the world more closely together in the late nineteenth century, also made Chinese in homeland and diaspora much more aware of each other. Having for centuries dismissed its emigrants as disloyal and unfilial, the Chinese government in 1893 finally opened its doors fully to overseas Chinese and began to woo their money and talents. This was largely through the initiative of China's consul in Singapore, one of the most active of the representatives Beijing had appointed in Southeast Asia since 1877 (Yen 1995: 31–42). While Sino-Southeast Asian elites began to enjoy honours from the imperial court in return for their contributions, anti-Qing reformers gained a wider and more enthusiastic following.

Japan's 1895 victory over China galvanised Southeast Asian Chinese even more than it did those in the Middle Kingdom, to clamour for reform of the empire that made them ashamed. When in 1899 full legal equality with Europeans was extended to Japanese residents in the Netherlands Indies, but not to the much more numerous Chinese, the outrage at state humiliation (OSH) factor was felt personally. Spencerian ideas of a struggle for survival of the 'races' of mankind had spread from Meiji Japan to interact with the racial schemes of Chinese reformers like Liang Qichao and the youthful Zou Rong (Dikötter 1992: 61–119). 'The reason why our sacred Han race, descendents of the Yellow Emperor, should support revolutionary independence arises precisely from the question of whether our race will go under and be exterminated' (Zou 1903, as cited Pan 1998: 103; also Wang 2000: 66–9 and 131). Southeast Asian Chinese devoured these ideas avidly. Re-defining the issue in terms of race rather than state gave them an obvious role to play. There was still no name in China for this 'race' except Han or yellow, but it had immediate resonance among the diaspora who were daily reminded that they were *Cina* in the languages of others.

This was also the time the old hierarchic order of *Kapitan Cina* and tax farmers began to dissolve. The twentieth century order was more open and competitive, but also more sharply racialised. The Europeans at the top of colonial society now thought themselves not just different from 'natives', but superior by education and achievement. Ambitious *peranakan* excluded from this conservative hierarchy had sometimes sought to escape from its constraints by seeking to be reclassified as 'natives', but the racialised hierarchy of education and achievement determined them to seek rather equality with Europeans (Ho 2006: 184–5). Like Jews in Europe after the French Revolution, Sino-Southeast Asians became 'emancipated' into the modern struggle of urban root-lessness, each potential elite seeking a new community in the dawning age of mass-based politics.

Not surprisingly, therefore, the radical reformers who struggled for a hearing in Beijing were embraced by many in the *Nanyang*. The reformers Liang Qichao and Kang Yuwei took refuge in Singapore after the constitutional monarchy movement failed in 1898, while the revolutionary Sun Yat Sen made frequent visits to the *Nanyang* (eight to Singapore alone in 1900–11) to raise support for his party. A branch of his Revolutionary League was formed in Singapore in 1906, while its successor the Kuomintang (KMT) spread to many parts of the region after the victory of the revolution in 1911. Sun was later to declare the overseas Chinese 'the mother of the revolution', because his wealthiest backers were the successful merchants of Southeast Asia (Yen 1995: 74–7; Wang 1981: 146). He moved quickly to endorse a law of *jus sanguinis*, making all overseas Chinese automatic citizens of his new Republic.

The excitement which accompanied the Chinese revolution did not affect all Sino-Southeast Asians, but it did draw the enthusiasm of just the kind of young idealists who might in other circumstances have supported anti-imperial nationalism in the colonies. In Indonesia and Thailand there was a watershed in 1910–11 as Chinese organisations grew more assertive, while the struggling indigenous bourgeoisies parted company with them. In Thailand a strike by Chinese workers in 1910 brought Bangkok to its knees, encouraging the beginnings of a distinct anti-Chinese strain in Thai nationalism (Skinner 1957: 155–63). In Java some earlier cooperation between Chinese and Javanese workers gave way in the period 1911–18 to a series of conflicts and anti-Chinese riots in the towns of Java. Dutch officials blamed the effect of Sun's revolution in leading Chinese to demand the same deference as Europeans.

The revolution of 1911 did represent for some young Chinese-Indonesians a route to national dignity as the equal of Europeans and Japanese. They began to dress like Europeans and see themselves as distinct from the Indonesian majority. A structural analysis would consider the transition to a more open and competitive economy at that time, and the determination of both Chinese and a weaker Muslim entrepreneurial class to take some of its opportunities. The timing of this extraordinary birth period was critical. The first party to launch the idea of a colony-wide, anti-imperial nationalism, the Indische Partij, began in 1911 with Eurasians and elite Javanese, but very few Sino-Indonesians (Elson 2008: 17–20). Had this happened, as in the Philippines, just *before* the Chinese revolution, the outcome would have been very different. The first mass-based Indonesian organisation, Sarekat Islam, was founded in 1911 by batik merchants and manufacturers in competition with Chinese suppliers. Sarekat Islam spread like wildfire in the ensuing decade, implanting the idea that the new national community it envisaged was inspired by Islam and excluded Chinese (Shiraishi 1997: 187–94).

By the 1930s there was still no 'Indonesian' or even Dutch nationality to belong to, but several rival national ideas in the air. On the other hand there was a colonial elite and its institutions, where people of Chinese, indigenous and European background mixed on the basis of Dutch and Malay language. Though not using the label, the dominant Sino-Indonesian figures of that time were in practice as 'Indonesian' as anybody in that period. They spoke Indonesian and Dutch rather than local languages or Chinese, they were born in the ethnically mixed cities of the colony, and they identified with the Netherlands Indies as a whole rather than with a local nationalism such as that of Java, Minahassa or Minangkabau. Twang Peck Yang has shown that the 'Chinese' business leaders of the late colonial period were almost exclusively local-born *peranakan* who identified locally and spoke no Chinese—in marked contrast to European business leadership, which was strongly oriented to a Dutch or German fatherland. The Sino-Indonesian business elite invested much in Indonesia, a little in Singapore, but very little in China, with which it had nothing in common but that awkward label (Twang 1998: 38–52). The politically stable (if repressive) conditions of late colonialism, in other words, favoured a business leadership which was also stable and locally rooted.

In Malaya and British Borneo Chinese ethnie nationalism focussed on China was the only serious political movement until the very last years of the pre-war old order. Arnold Toynbee was profoundly wrong but symptomatic of the times when he declared 'When I touched at the Straits Settlements on my way out east I realized that British Malaya was destined, by 'peaceful penetration', to become a new Chinese province' (Toynbee 1931: 259). The Malayan Communist Party (MCP) was formed to rival the KMT in 1934, and while it sought more actively to recruit non-Chinese for anti-imperial nationalism, the reality was that membership was overwhelmingly Chinese and preoccupied by the China–Japan conflict. One of the favourite weapons of Chinese nationalist mobilisation was the boycott, directed occasionally against Europeans but with increasing frequency against Japanese. Early boycotts of Japanese goods in Penang and Singapore occurred in 1908, 1915 and 1919, but were dwarfed by the outrage against Japanese aggression expressed in 1928 and 1937. There was widespread boycott action throughout the cities of Southeast Asia, enforced by clandestine militant brigades who resorted to threats and sometimes violence (Yen 1995: 146). Since this deprived poor consumers of cheap Japanese textiles and other goods, the boycott movement tended to drive a further wedge between Chinese and majority communities. It also led Japanese exporters to seek out non-Chinese distributors, further deepening the perceived competition between established Chinese commercial networks and a nascent Muslim middle class.

The Japanese invasion of Southeast Asia in 1941–2 was naturally received profoundly differently by Chinese and majority nationalists. The Japanese military knew that Chinese organisations had been at the heart of anti-Japanese mobilisation and boycotts, and many of them had bitter memories of Chinese hostility from previous China campaigns since 1937. They quickly rounded up thousands of Chinese leaders, activists and members of KMT and MCP in Singapore and Malaya. By March 1942 they had executed at least 6,000 even by Japanese estimates, and up to 40,000 by those of Chinese (Cheah 1980: 78–80). A few leaders such as Tan Kah Kee managed to flee to the greater anonymity of Sumatra; others joined the guerrilla resistance in the Malayan jungle mobilised by the communists but assisted by the British. Chinese leaders who agreed to cooperate, like the veteran Straits Chinese intellectual Lim Boon Keng, were forced to collect $50 million as 'atonement' for pre-war anti-Japanese activity. In the worst single Japanese massacre in Indonesia, of about 1,500 members of the Pontianak urban elite in 1943, the majority were also Chinese (Purdey 2006: 7). As a whole, therefore, Chinese communities were embittered about the Japanese occupation and those who collaborated with it. Nevertheless their 'Chineseness' was probably accentuated by Japanese dismissiveness towards any Chinese who did not read Chinese (Japanese *kanji*) characters, the banning of Dutch in Indonesia and the closure of Dutch and English schools.

By comparison the nascent Malay ethnie nationalists organised in the Young Malays' Union (KMM) sought contacts with the Japanese fifth-column organiser, Major Fujiwara, as did many Indonesian nationalists outside Java. On both sides of the Melaka Straits nationalist activists totally marginalised by the Dutch regime were given unprecedented opportunities to address an audience through Japanese propaganda organisations (McCoy 1980). Many Malay and Indonesian officials had undreamed of increases in responsibility through the internment of Europeans. Sukarno in Java, and some comparable figures in the other Indonesian islands, owed their high visibility and post-war prominence to the opportunities given them by the Japanese. Unquestionably, there-fore, the Pacific War, and the two rapid regime changes at its beginning and end, widened and embittered the gap between Chinese nationalism and its local equivalents.

While the Japanese occupation was a disaster for the Westernised *peranakan* elites, its autarchic and often arbitrary economic policies gave remarkable opportunities to ambitious newcomers who took the risks involved in smuggling and bribing authorities. Some of the new men of the independence era made their start in these dangerous times. The Indonesian revolutionary period of 1945–50 provided more opportun-ities to risk-takers. While revolutionaries or those acting in their name wrought havoc on established Chinese capital in this period, the embat-tled Republic could not have survived without the help of a new Chinese business element. Despite the rhetoric of anti-capitalism and extreme nationalism, the strong men of the revolution usually had a Chinese entrepreneur at their elbow to provide the essential supplies and finances. These were almost invariably 'outsider' Chinese-speaking *totok*, epitomised by the China-born Hok-chiu Liem Sioe Liong who formed an early partnership with the young army officer Suharto. These new men had no property to protect under the Dutch order, but took a chance by connecting with the Republic's young military leaders, which served them well in the long term (Twang 1998: 178–81).

Chinese as 'outsiders' in independent Southeast Asia

The social hierarchies of Southeast Asian colonial societies fitted rather well the theory of the **status gap**, developed primarily to explain why a Jewish entrepreneurial minority was essential in Eastern European societies divided sharply between aristocrats and peasants. 'Outsider' entrepreneurs are necessary, argued Irwin Rinder, when 'the yawning social void which occurs when superior and subordinate portions of a society are not bridged by continuous, intermediate degrees of status'

(Rinder 1959: 253). Status-conscious Dutch colonials and Javanese aristocrats both sought to maintain a social distance from the masses, and encouraged an outsider group of Chinese to fill the intermediary roles. Chinese were a kind of 'essential outsiders' in the plural societies of the colonial era (Chirot and Reid 1997). This role, however, had existed before colonialism and continued to a surprising degree after it. The effect of high colonial racial categories was to heighten and consolidate the boundaries and remove the incentive to intermarriage and hybridity at the top of the social hierarchy.

Independence removed the status gap, and the colonial habit of classifying by race. Officially the new Indonesian nation-state adopted a policy of assimilation, discouraging, and after 1966 prohibiting, public expressions of Chinese language or culture. The Indonesian censuses dropped colonial-style questions about ethnicity, and officially all citizens became equal. Race was implicit in the attitudes of both parties, but not explicit as in the racially bounded polities of Malaysia and Singapore. The Sukarno regime sought to incorporate Chinese like every other ethnicity into a diverse national community, with a few left-leaning *peranakan* politicians in most cabinets of that period.

Independence and its heightened expectations, however, immediately increased the conflict over economic issues. In the Philippines the anti-Chinese legislation of the 1950s was directed against the disproportionate role of Chinese who did not have Philippine citizenship, but in Indonesia discriminatory measures included even citizens who were 'non-indigenous'. Particularly in the democratic period 1950–9 successive governments courted popularity by putting curbs on Chinese business in their access to licences and foreign exchange. Since Dutch business was also expropriated through a series of bitter conflicts in the 1950s, the economy would have stalled had Sino-Indonesian entrepreneurs not been able to work around these regulations. While some did move their capital out of Indonesia (frequently to Singapore), others managed to flourish by taking non-Chinese partners, exploiting loopholes or bribing compliant officials. While such measures were probably necessary, they did nothing to counter the attraction of Marxism as an explanation for Indonesian weakness. Business was widely seen in this period as greedy, devious and above all alien, because associated with the Chinese other. The widespread takeover of Dutch enterprises by government or military in this period had no significant domestic opponents.

Sukarno's turbulent Guided Democracy period began badly for Chinese business. A regulation of November 1959 institutionalised a number of local anti-Chinese initiatives by banning aliens from residing in rural areas. Mainly targeted were some 25,000 Chinese retail outlets which maintained distribution networks around the Archipelago. Over 100,000 Chinese left Indonesia the following year, mainly for China. The leftward current of Indonesian politics thereafter briefly offered one possibility for a kind of resolution of the Chinese dilemma—integration as one of Indonesia's *suku* in a secularised socialist Indonesia. This was the path advocated by one of the leading Chinese associations, Baperki, which moved close to the centre of Indonesian politics in this period through a close association with Sukarno. But in the anti-communist blood-letting that followed the Untung coup against the Army leadership on 1 September 1965, Baperki was branded as pro-communist. Its leader, Siau Giok Tjhan, had been compromised by being unwittingly named a member of the plotters' 'revolutionary council'. The Baperki University was burned, its branches were banned or closed voluntarily, and many of its activists suffered death or imprisonment along with hundreds of thousands of members and supporters of the communist party. It was out of this trauma that Suharto's peculiar hostility to Chineseness arose (Heidhues 1974: 82–6; Coppel 1983).

Malaysia's Chinese were very differently placed, with almost 40 per cent of the population of Malaya (including Singapore) at the end of the war, an insurgent army that had held out against the Japanese in the jungle, and some sympathy from the British who reoccupied Malaya without opposition after the Japanese surrender. The Malayan Union scheme developed by British post-war planners to provide the basis for a modern Malayan nation-state with a single citizenship was the best chance the community ever had for an equal place in the post-war order. But the Chinese community was far too divided to support this scheme effectively, with many focussed on China and others embarked on a proto-revolutionary path of strikes and disruptions. Instead the Malay ethnie nationalism described in the following chapter was able to occupy centre stage, forcing the British to abandon the Malayan Union in favour of an arrangement which left Malay sovereignty intact through very complex federal arrangements.

The communists began an armed insurrection in 1948, returning to jungle camps they had used against the Japanese. Although the communist revolution was in the name of Malaya, its failure to gain more than token support from other communities, and its excessive dependence on the Chinese Communist Party, made Chinese seem still more alien. The anti-communist Malayan Chinese Association partnered the United Malays National Organisation (UMNO) successfully in 1951 to fight elections, a partnership that enabled Malaya to claim its independence in 1957 and to annex Sarawak and Sabah into the Malaysian fold in

1963. The partnership kept the communal peace, to a far greater extent than in Indonesia, within a context of regular orderly elections and a very robust economy. Yet it remained a flawed citizenship, in which rights depended on race.

Suharto and the outsider insiders

The thirty-two-year regime of Suharto (1966–98) reintroduced a kind of economic and political stability that might have been expected to remove the business advantages of 'outsider' status and to produce a more integrated business culture as had been happening in the 1920s and 1930s. The virtual cessation of immigration after 1930, and the success of Indonesian as a unifying national language, should have made this easier. Yet an extraordinary ambivalence marked the Suharto regime in respect of Chinese, which proved to have some very sinister results. This regime began in a revived mood of great hostility to all things Chinese, presumably based on its sharp reaction against Sukarno's closeness to Beijing and a virulent anti-communism which provided the legitimation for Suharto's rise to power. While anti-communism marked the whole New Order regime, a degree of paranoia about Chinese influence appears to have been specific to Suharto, often handicapping the foreign ministry in pursuing a flexible policy in Indonesia's national interest. New regulations in 1967 banned Chinese newspapers, indeed Chinese writing in any form, Chinese social organisations and schools and the public celebration of Chinese religion and customs. A name-changing campaign persuaded most of those previously using Chinese names that they might escape the worst discrimination if they changed to Indonesian-sounding ones. This was immediately frustrated by the adding to identity cards of an extra zero, making Chinese ancestry clear to every official. In an atmosphere tolerant towards corruption, it became established practice throughout the bureaucracy to expect those of Chinese descent to pay under the counter for government services they received. Chinese were excluded from the bureaucracy, the army and political life, and only a small number were admitted to state universities (Suryadinata, 1992: 145–64; Godley and Lloyd 2001).

But the opening to foreign investment and rapid economic growth gave unprecedented opportunities to Sino-Indonesian business, whose efficiency, capital and networks were absolutely indispensable to the new economic climate. Those who flourished most were the famous crony capitalists, notably Liem Sioe Liong and Bob Hasan, both of whom were already heavily involved in smuggling and other questionable business of the Diponegoro Division in Central Java in the 1950s. They were mostly from the diminishing band of China-born (*totok*) outsiders, who had built links with particular Suharto-related military units before 1965. Hasan was the exception as a *peranakan* born in Semarang, but nevertheless had been an insignificant 'outsider' until ingratiating himself with General Gatot Subroto, Suharto's predecessor as Diponegoro commander. But even these rent-seeking conglomerates with their palace connections could only do well because of their links with a broader base of efficient and predominately Sino-Indonesian small business.

As has been documented in relation to the timber industry, Suharto began by dealing with Sino-Indonesian loggers in consequence of their expertise as partners of foreign concessionaries. When he squeezed out the foreign firms after 1980 the handful of Chinese-Indonesian cronies (Bob Hasan, Prajogo Pangestu, Liem Sioe Liong) became absolutely central. Their vast extra-budgetary revenues from timber concessions gave Suharto a weapon he could use both to enrich himself and his family, and to pursue uneconomic pet projects such as the national petrochemical industry (Chandra Asri), Habibie's aircraft factories, Taman Mini and transmigration, without a head-on clash with the technocratic ministers in charge of the budget. Precisely because of their outsider status and lack of *entrée* into the bureaucracy, these cronies posed no threat and had minimal capacity to resist the first family's demands.

Thus the Indonesian Chinese were included not only for their business expertise, international connections, and pre-existing business links with the armed forces, but also for their lack of status as an independent political force. By the end of the Suharto regime, it was calculated that the top fifteen tax-payers in Indonesia included thirteen Chinese Indonesians and two sons of Suharto (Purdey 2006: 22). Of course, resentment against rich Chinese became a feature of every discontent, increasing the marginality of the Chinese should they ever lose the protection of Suharto, and thus increasing their dependence on Suharto (Ascher 1998: 55; Suryadinata 1992: 142). The catalogue of anti-Chinese riots continued, but gained in frequency in the 1990s—1945; 1947; 1959–60; 1963; 1965–7; 1973; 1980; 1994; 1996–8.

On the positive side of Suharto's rule, economic growth and the liberalisation of the economy gradually diluted the majority prejudice against private enterprise and money-making activity. An indigenous middle class at last emerged, increasingly merging with Sino-Indonesian entrepreneurs despite some intense areas of competition (Robison 1986). Ruth McVey (1992: 25) has pointed to a change in attitude of the regime itself during the 1980s, as it began to see that it had become so involved with Chinese business that the periodic outbreaks of anti-Chinese popular violence were not so much an outlet for diversionary scapegoating as another way of attacking the regime itself. This is evocative of Hannah Arendt's point about anti-Semitism in nineteenth-century Europe: 'each class of society which came into a conflict with the state as such became anti-semitic because the only social group which seemed to represent the state were the Jews' (Arendt 1968: 25).

In the 1990s, as Suharto's grip on power weakened and contests about his children and the succession mounted, several contestants stoked the fire of Islamic and racist resentment as never before. Suharto's extremely ambitious son-in-law, General Prabowo, was one of those in the inner circle who encouraged extremist Muslim groups to see the most promi-nent Chinese-Indonesian tycoons as part of a conspiracy of Christians, Chinese and Jews to overthrow Suharto (Hefner 2000: 202–4). This kind of irresponsibility in the palace inner circle undoubtedly encouraged the increased wave of violence against Chinese property and Christian churches which accelerated from 1996, as it encouraged military ambivalence about curbing them (Purdey 2006: 38–105). The financial crisis which hit Indonesia in 1997 provided more grist for conspiracy theorists, and the attacks increased to a peak in early 1998.

Two May riots

On 13 and 14 May 1998, Indonesia experienced one of the crises of its modern history as urban mobs turned on their countrymen of Chinese descent, killing hundreds (though most deaths were non-Chinese looters trapped in burning buildings), pack-raping at least 180 women and destroying millions of dollars worth of property. The violence was a factor in the fall of President Suharto and the turbulent transition to democracy that followed. Indonesia began a profound crisis of transition the outcome of which is far from clear.

Exactly twenty-nine years before that, on May 13 1969, mobs of urban Malays turned on their fellow countrymen of Chinese descent, dragging them from their cars, burning their shops, killing around 170 and causing massive property damage. Although Chinese were in no position to fight back, the overwhelmingly Malay security forces arrested more than twice as many Chinese as Malays during the three days of chaos (National Operations Council 1969: Reid 1969c). This trauma proved the major crisis of independent Malaysia, permanently shifting the political ground and the relations between Malaysia's communities. Both these May riots shocked the nations and the world because they occurred at the very centre of two flourishing new nations, before the international media (see figures 3.1 and 3.2). In both cases the

Figures 3.1 and 3.2 Aftermath of May riots in Kuala Lumpur, 1969 (3.1, top) and Jakarta, 1998 (3.2, bottom)

immediate reaction of the ruling group was to blame the victims and talk of ways to reduce the wealth gap between Chinese and others.

The result for Malaysia was a loss of innocence of Tunku Abdul Rahman's once easy-going multi-racial country. The stakes of ethnic management were suddenly dramatically raised. The New Economic Policy (NEP) was devised amidst a change of leadership from the discredited Tunku Abdul Rahman to Tun Abdul Razak. By engineering a shift from agriculture to employment-heavy urban manufacturing, it provided a path to the city for Peninsula Malays and proved economically more successful than anyone imagined. In a generally booming economy, the ownership of shares in '*bumiputra*' hands increased from 1.5 per cent of the total to 15.6 per cent between 1969 and 1982, at the expense of rapidly diminishing British ownership (Jomo 1997: 244–5). But by entrenching a pattern of racial preference for Malays in education, government employment, contracts and licences, the NEP created expectations and attitudes favouring a permanent racial division in society. It also tended to embitter the groups which had access to neither economic nor political influence, notably Indians and the indigenous peoples of Borneo.

In both cases, resentment against the overwhelming dominance of the Chinese entrepreneurial minority in private business was an underlying reality. In both cases, though Chinese were known to control much urban capital, the majority communities were known to control the means of violence, both at street level and in the security forces. Attacking Chinese property, therefore, was both a means of reminding Chinese of their vulnerability, and a relatively safe way of venting rage against the government or 'the system'. The politics of the two cases were, however, very different.

In Malaysia, there was a real racial contest for power through the electoral system as soon as it was established in the first (1955) election. The issues were the usual ones—education, language use, affirmative action and symbolic issues about what kind of country this was. The party system which developed already before independence was an alliance between the aristocratic-led Malay Party and big business-led Chinese party, with a me-too Indian party thrown in for balance. The Alliance (from 1970s National Front) ruled and rules from the ethnic middle, putting Malay candidates up in predominately Malay rural seats against Islamic opposition, and Chinese or Indian candidates in urban seats against a more leftish opposition always claiming to be multi-racial but dominated by Chinese. When the Alliance leaned too much to the Malay side it lost the 'Chinese' seats, and when it leaned the other way or was worsted in the battle over symbolic Muslim issues it lost 'Malay' seats. The two key parties then bargained again over policies and the distribution of power.

Once Malaysia was formed in 1963, with Singapore initially in, the dominance of Peninsula Malays was no longer secure, though it has gradually become so through expulsion of Singapore (1965) and then gradual demographic change. 1969 was the first election after Singapore was expelled, and a somewhat tired Alliance lost ground to opposition parties on both sides. Although state governments went to the Malay/ Muslim opposition on the heavily Malay east coast, the changes in urban Selangor were more portentous, since the Malay establishment party seemed about to be defeated by a Chinese-dominated one. This was therefore seen as a change in the racial balance of power, to which the violence was a direct response.

The May 1998 anti-Chinese riots and killings in Jakarta, and to a lesser extent in Surakarta and elsewhere, were of a very different type. They were not a weapon in a bitter racial contest for power, as in Kuala Lumpur in 1969, Fiji in 1997 and 2000, or the various ethnic cleansings of the Balkans. The Chinese were less than two per cent of the Indonesian population (as against 35 per cent in Malaysia 1969); they were for the most part very Indonesian in language and culture; and they had been rendered into a classic case of 'pariah' or 'outsider' entrepreneurs totally excluded from any political leverage except through back-door use of their money. Attacks on the Chinese were used by some to send a warning to various opponents in the elite political game, as it intensified in the early months of 1998.

The crisis of the late 1990s was a testing time for the young Indonesian polity that can be compared with the crisis of the great depression of the 1930s for Europe. A conference in 1994 comparing the historic paths of Southeast Asian Chinese and central European Jewry had concluded that the resentment factor appeared to be remarkably contained in Southeast Asia given the much greater financial muscle of Chinese there than Jews had ever had in Europe. But it cautioned that this benign picture could change if the then booming economies should fail (Chirot and Reid 1997: 22, 27, 64–5). In the event Indonesia's financial melt-down was estimated to have caused a 14 per cent gross domestic product (GDP) loss in 1998 alone. The impact overall was almost comparable to the 24 per cent GDP loss suffered by Germany over the whole depression period 1929–33. The parallel goes further: the boom which preceded 1998 had brought Indonesia to roughly the gross national product (GNP) levels reached by Germany in the 1890s or Italy in the

1920s (derived from Maddison 2001: 264, 298). By 1997 the degree of urbanisation in Indonesia (about 35 per cent) was comparable to that which Europe as a whole had reached in 1925.

In Indonesia's 1998 depression there were millions of angry semi-educated unemployed in the cities. Such an economic crisis undermines confidence in the global financial system, and in the beneficence of ruling elites. Demagogues such as Hitler and Mussolini become plausible to far wider circles when they claim that the problems are all caused by racial, national or class enemies manipulating the system. Looked at with the advantage of hindsight, it was this political undermining of confidence which was the most fatal consequence of the 1930s, not the terrible but temporary suffering induced by the depression itself.

In this perspective, the outcome of the crisis in Indonesia was by no means severe for the Sino-Indonesian minority and downright favourable for democracy. There was a great deal of interethnic and interreligious violence in the period 1997–2001 (see chapter 6) but, just as in 1965–6, Chinese as a largely middle-class community were not the major victims of it. Again as in 1965–6, however, their victimhood was particularly public, particularly political, and particularly damaging for the country. The anti-Chinese violence occurred in the capital, targeted wealthy elites at least as much as little people, and had the result of bringing to reality some of the anti-Chinese rhetoric. Even the most committed Indonesians among the Chinese minority felt threatened and alienated, at least 30,000 left the country in the three months following the violence, and those who could move capital offshore did so, further deepening the economic crisis (*FEER*, 30 July 1998).

On the other hand, whereas the Kuala Lumpur violence had the long-term result of reducing Chinese rights and bargaining power within the Malaysian system, the Jakarta riots had on balance the opposite effect. The bravery and dedication of some women's and Christian groups to document and publicise the rapes of 1998 produced an unprecedented wave of shock and sympathy from Indonesia's political public. For the first time many Indonesians were ready to acknowledge that their everyday disparagement of Chinese was indeed racism, with serious potential for danger. Some demanded that the 'pariah' status of Sino-Indonesians be removed once and for all.

Discrimination continued in the public service and police, as part of the ingrained habit of demanding bribes differentially from those with more wealth and less power. Yet the speed of reversal of the heavy-handed assimilationist measures of Suharto was remarkable. China's rapid rise as an economic partner of Indonesia complemented the popular shift. In 1990 Suharto had finally accepted the inevitable and restored diplomatic relations with the People's Republic which had been suspended after his rise in 1967. In the post-Suharto era trade with China boomed, with about 25 per cent growth every year, and by 2007 China was Indonesia's fifth most important source of both trade and investment (*Jakarta Post*, 18 June 2008).

Presidents Habibie and Wahid moved quickly after Suharto's fall to remove the most egregious official reminders of Chinese pariah status, such as the different coding of identity cards and the customs forms announcing a ban on drugs, firearms and anything printed in Chinese. Whereas all public manifestations of Chinese identity or culture had been banned under Suharto, the firecrackers, lion dances and Chinese newspapers were everywhere in the new century. During the Suharto period a whole generation had grown up knowing nothing of Chinese public rituals, and much of that loss was permanent. Chinese New Year (*Imlek* in Indonesia), however, made a spectacular return. Permitted by President Wahid in 2000, it was subsequently declared a national holiday from 2003. Sino-Indonesians who wished to reclaim Chineseness had to relearn the essential rituals. The virtual destruction of Indonesia's Chinese language capacity in the Suharto years was increasingly recognised as a handicap, and Chinese language classes mushroomed both in the official education system and privately.

Democracy and difference

Southeast Asians have made their transition from imperial to democratic order in hardly more than a half-century. Looking back on this period in comparison with the longer history of Europe, outbreaks of violence and intolerance should be less surprising than the capacity of different ethnie to adjust to democratic politics without either ethnic cleansing or fragmentation of imperial boundaries. Pre-modern monarchies, empires, and autocracies generally allowed or encouraged their peoples to remain distinct, united only by the personal power at the top. Democratisation not only involved lifting the lid on all sorts of buried hatreds, as in the ex-Soviet Union and Yugoslavia, but also allowed politicians to exploit these hatreds cynically to win votes. Programmatic anti-Semitism developed in Europe only in the last quarter of the nineteenth century, as franchises were widened to include the whole population in elections. The worst ethnic crimes were committed by governments which had been popularly elected.

Hannah Arendt was one of the more acute observers of the apparent paradox that anti-Semitism reached its height only after a considerable degree of democratisation and cultural assimilation. As she put this dilemma,

Equality of condition, though it is certainly a basic requirement for justice, is nevertheless among the greatest and most uncertain ventures of modern mankind. The more equal conditions are, the less explanation there is for the differences that actually exist between people; and thus all the more unequal do individuals and groups become ... The great challenge to the modern period, and its peculiar danger, has been that in it man for the first time confronted man without the protection of differing circumstances and conditions. And it has been precisely this new concept of equality that has made modern race relations so difficult, for there we deal with natural differences which by no possible and conceivable change of condition can become less conspicuous. It is because equality demands that I recognize each ... individual as my equal, that the conflicts between different groups, which for reasons of their own are reluctant to grant each other this basic equality, take on such terribly cruel forms. (Arendt 1968: 54)

Daniel Chirot reminds us that the changes brought about a century ago in Europe by mass migration to the cities, privatisation of communal land, rationalisation of the law and the development of a new middle class 'neither quite in the elite nor, any longer, a part of the peasant masses', both unsettled old identities and provided possibilities for a modern nationalism which could redefine ancient neighbours as outsiders. The political environment conducive to the rise of anti-Semitism in Austria and Germany was marked by a reaction against the liberal and progressive German culture (read today's globalisation), which helps explain why it was precisely the most assimilated, successful and cosmopolitan Jews who most provoked anti-Semitism. 'Not only were they successful competitors in the economic and cultural marketplace, but they were also interpreted as insidious agents of antinationalism who poisoned the purity of the nation by introducing foreign—that is liberal and antinationalist—ideas and practices' (Chirot and Reid 1997: 8–9).

The European contrast is helpful at least in moderating our expectations for the Southeast Asian transition. Both Indonesia and Malaysia lurched back and forth between authoritarian and liberal formats in their different ways, but in the years after 1998 both have appeared to be maturing as more open democracies. Malaysia remains relatively peaceful if fundamentally divided in racial and religious terms, and developments since Dr Mahathir's resignation as prime minister have offered promise of eventually overcoming that divide. Indonesia's democratisation since 1998, discussed more fully in the following two chapters, survived both the anti-Chinese riots of 1998 and the much more bloody confrontations (generally along religious lines) in Maluku and Sulawesi.

The progress since 1998 in accepting 'outsider' Chinese into the political and moral community of Indonesia is particularly impressive. There are grounds for thinking that *peranakan* Indonesians may be on the way to integration in the manner of their counterparts in Thailand and the Philippines, albeit as members of religious minorities. If so, Indonesia will have managed its democratic transition less wounded than central European societies were by theirs. Just as the harsh measures of the Thai nationalist regimes of the 1930s and 1940s against distinctive Chinese symbols, particularly Chinese names, made it easier for the subsequent generation to be accepted, Suharto's assimilationist measures may prove an advantage for the subsequent generations. Sino-Indonesians are once again (as in the nineteenth century) the most 'Indonesian' of Indonesian ethnies, with one of the highest proportions using the Indonesian language at home.

Indonesia's wonderfully diverse social fabric has been and remains the greatest potential asset in negotiating the crisis. Pluralism is inescapable as long as Indonesia remains a vast Archipelagic country, and this established pluralism even within a very assertive nationalism is the best guarantee that narrow ethnonationalism of a Balkan type can be avoided. It was only the culture of the mainly urban Chinese-Indonesian minority, along with those of the hunter-gatherers and shifting cultivators at the other end of the spectrum, that were singled out as somehow unacceptable within that diversity. The 'outsider' status of the Sino-Indonesian minority can be overcome within the current democratic climate if their culture and symbols cease to be seen as outside the moral community, and the economy becomes more open and predictable. Overt economic discrimination against the minority has been shown to be counterproductive, creating the kind of distorted economy that requires further covert special deals with 'outsiders'.

Two further reforms would speed the process of normalising the *peranakan* Chinese as a legitimate part of Indonesia. One would be a suitable label to replace the tyranny of the term 'Chinese' in English or 'Cina' in Indonesian. That term is used to cover too many contradictory things, including a minority which is patently Indonesian in every respect, as well as a foreign language, culture and polity often seen as a threat. The burden of the term was well illustrated by the 2000 census, where a question about ethnicity was included for the first time since the 1930 census. Just over 2 per cent of the population had responded as Chinese in 1930, and this proportion was universally believed to have grown over the subsequent three decades through population stabilisation and larger families. Yet only 1.14 per cent responded as Chinese in the 2000 census, and even fewer in the first-published summaries that failed to list small communities (Terry Hull personal communication; Suryadinata *et al.* 2003: 75–9). Even allowing for emigration, a large number must have preferred to forget the 'Chinese' side of their ancestry. Sino-Indonesians would be well served by following the path of Sino-Filipinos in inventing a hybrid term (*Chinoy*) to underline the distinctiveness of a hybrid but Indonesian (Filipino) identity.

The other obvious path to integration is to join the state nationalist formula through which Indonesian ethnie link themselves to the national myth. The Sino-Indonesian absence from this system is a powerful symbolic exclusion from the definition of the nation. The officially sanctioned means to establish the legitimacy of a group within the national community, and its education system, is to make the case for the canonisation of a particular national hero (*pahlawan*) of ethnic Chinese background. There is no shortage of candidates for such an honour. By the usual criterion, leading a last stand against the advancing Dutch colonisers, the leader of the Chinese-Javanese forces in the 'Chinese war' of 1740–3, Tan Singko alias Singseh, is well qualified. So are the elected leaders of the Lan-fang *kongsi* of Monterado, north of Pontianak (West Kalimantan), who defied Dutch claims over them for many years until finally defeated in 1854. But in an era of reform it is time to look for national role models among those who more positively built the national culture, such as the *peranakan* writers and publishers who developed a Malay-language press and modern popular literature in the last decades of the nineteenth century.

4   Malay (*Melayu*) and its descendants: multiple meanings of a porous category

Melayu is an ancient term, which has served multiple roles in its long career. It entered European languages in the sixteenth and early seventeenth centuries as Malay (or French *Malais*; Portuguese *Malayo*), and the different European and Malay meanings of the term affected each other markedly thereafter. As the trade language of Srivijaya and later Melaka, the language eventually called Malay was used as a *lingua franca* in commercial centres over a wide area of maritime Southeast Asia and even beyond. It was therefore adopted by English speakers in particular as a broader racial or regional term. When researchers discovered the vast family of languages today known as Austronesian, and stretching halfway around the world from Madagascar to Easter Island, this too was first labelled 'Malay' from its best-known language. This broadening eventually played back into indigenous nationalist usage. The language was harnessed as the basis of the 'core culture' of Malaysia, Indonesia and Brunei, though differentially in the three countries, while a racial use of the term served to build Filipino nationalism. The term played other roles in the definition of minority ethnies in Singapore, Thailand, Cambodia, Sri Lanka and South Africa.

Together with the 'China' discussed in the previous chapter, this term is the most widespread, ambiguous and portentous of Southeast Asian labels.

Melayu origins

The term *Melayu* goes back at least as far as Ptolemy, the second-century (CE) Egyptian geographer. Like some later Arab and Chinese writers, he thought it to be a place in or near the island we call Sumatra. In Tang period Chinese sources it is associated with the kingdom of Srivijaya, but particularly the Jambi area which was a secondary or later centre of that kingdom (Andaya 2001; Reid 2001: 297–8). Melayu is indeed better represented in the non-Chinese sources than Srivijaya itself. Nevertheless it was late in establishing itself as the name for a people in any sense. Before the sixteenth century the commonest term used by foreigners to designate the whole Archipelago or its people was *Jawa* or *Yava*. Only in 1730 did the term Melayu (*wu-lai-yu*) first appear in a Chinese source, to indicate the same broad cultural area as Jawa had previously done (Wang Gungwu 1981: 108–17). This is about the same time as the earliest European uses of generic terms such as 'Malay Archipelago'.

The earlier Malay-language sources themselves make surprisingly little use of Melayu as an identity-marker. The Melaka chronicle uses it for the name of a small river said to flow from the sacred hill (Bukit Siguntang) of Palembang into the Musi River. In modern times, however, the only river named Melayu waters the sacred temple complex at Jambi, not Palembang. Other than this the chronicle used the term Melayu sparingly, in most cases as an adjective for custom (*adat Melayu*), or for kings (*raja-raja Melayu*), specifically the line of Melaka kings descended from Bukit Siguntang. The earlier part of this Melaka chronicle designates its subjects as the Melaka people (*orang Melaka*). Only after Melaka is firmly established as a Muslim kingdom does the term *orang Melayu* also begin to appear, especially in describing the cultural preferences of the Melakans as against these foreigners. By the end of the Melaka sultanate in 1511, it appears, Melayu had become a way of referring to the minority of the Melaka population who had lived there long enough to accept its religion of Sunni Islam, to speak Malay as a first language and to identify with the Sultan as his loyal people (Matheson 1979; Reid 2001: 298).

When the Portuguese arrived in the region after 1500 they initially adopted the same view, that *Malayos* were essentially the ruling group of Melaka, one restricted ethnie among many in the city. Tomé Pires (1944: 265) explained how the Melaka sultanate itself classified visitors to Melaka into four groups with a separate harbour-master (*syahbandar*) for each one. Malays were not mentioned in the list of categories, which were primarily defined by the direction from which they came to the city. Thus South Indians were in one group with people from north Sumatra and Burma (Pegu), and Chinese of various kinds with those from Ryukyu. Gujaratis from the wealthy ports of northwest India were the only ethnie strong enough to have a *syahbandar* to themselves, while Austronesian speakers were spread among all the other three. The Portuguese did, however, describe *Malayos* as traders in other places such as China and Maluku. Until they were forced into diaspora by the Portuguese conquest of Melaka (1511), this term appeared to mean people from the ruling group in Melaka, most closely associated with its sultan. When collecting a Malay word-list from the eastern islands, only a decade after the fall of Melaka, the Magellan expedition translated *cara Melayu* (lit. 'Malay ways') as 'the ways of Melaka' (Pigafetta 1969: 88). For Portuguese writers of the sixteenth century, these *Malayos* with their origins in Melaka were one of several Archipelago-based maritime traders active in the Java Sea and South China Sea. To the others they gave labels Jawa, Jawi and Luzon. All four labels were intermediate between place and ethnie. All appear to have emerged from the inter-action between the Srivijaya heritage, the indigenous populations, and Chinese and Muslim seafarers in the late fourteenth and fifteenth centuries. All would eventually assimilate into a diasporic 'Malay' ethnie, relatively open to newcomers. To understand this process requires a more careful look at the crucial fifteenth–sixteenth century period of ethnogenesis.

Hybrid identities of the long fifteenth century

Melaka was one of several port-states of the fifteenth century that owed its prosperity to a special relationship with China during a period when this was particularly critical. This exceptional period may be said to have begun with the Yuan or Mongol period when foreign world conquerors ruled China (1276–1368) and to have ended when the native Ming Dynasty abandoned active state relations with Southeast Asia in the 1430s following the exceptionalism of its first three rulers.

The first Mongol ruler not only sent massive land-based expeditions into Vietnam and Burma, but also unprecedented naval expeditions to Japan, and most importantly for our purpose, to Java in the 1290s. Defectors and captives from this massive fleet, along with the chiefly Muslim traders of the Indian Ocean trade route to China's port of Quanzhou, inaugurated a particularly hybrid period in the trading ports of Southeast Asia. As foreigners the Yuan valued the loyalty and cosmo-politanism of their Muslim subjects, and gave a particularly favoured position to the Muslim commercial group in Quanzhou. This group was itself very plural, including Persians, Arabs and maritime peoples with origins in Southeast Asia.

As the Mongol hold began to weaken, however, some of the powerful Muslims of Quanzhou overplayed their hand. In 1357 the Persian sol-diers of the Quanzhou military garrison rebelled and took control of South Fujian. When they were eventually defeated in 1366, a witch-hunt began against cosmopolitan Muslims which continued in the early years of the Ming Dynasty. Only in 1407 did the Yung-lo Emperor command that violence against the Muslims should stop, since he had need of them in the vast expeditions he sent southward under the Muslim eunuch Zheng He (So 2000: 108–125; Ke 2001: 315–17).

Thousands of more-or-less Sinified Muslim merchant families opted to take their ships to Southeast Asian ports with which they were already familiar. Many others, Cantonese as well as Fujianese, appear to have taken their ships south to avoid the very strict ban on private seaborne trading introduced by the Ming. The Gulf of Siam, Singapore, Palembang, the ports of northern Java, Brunei and Manila appear to have been the chief beneficiaries. Quanzhou ceased to be a major international port in the fifteenth century, but these new Southeast Asian ports were among those to take its place (Reid 2006b).

The influx of this cosmopolitan group of traders, taken together with the collapse of Sirivijaya's hold over the Archipelago trade to China and the recovery of the spice trade to Europe after the Black Death, brought about major realignments in Southeast Asia. The last Srivijaya tribute mission recorded was in 1309. New research shows how multi-ethnic Siam (Ayutthaya) and Singapore took advantage of these skilled 'Chinese' traders to fill the gap (Baker 2003; Miksic and Low 2004; Reid 2006b). By the early 1400s, however, Melaka had replaced Singapore by successfully playing the Ming card to gain access to the China market in succession to Srivijaya. Ayutthaya, some Javanese ports, and Brunei had also negotiated the Ming transition successfully, emerging in Chinese records as the important players in the game of trading with China through elaborate tribute missions. Those who failed to gain acceptance as tributaries, sometimes precisely because they had large 'Chinese' communities seen as disloyal 'pirates' by the frequent emissaries of the early Ming rulers, had to operate indirect or clandestine trade, such as that via Ryukyu. In this category was the charismatic centre of Malay kingship itself, Palembang, which in Chinese records of the early 1400s had become the principal centre in the Archipelago of Chinese 'pirates' whom Zheng He punished just as he rewarded Melaka (Ma Huan 1433; Kobata and Matsuda 1969: 131–3; Wade and Sun 2008).

The consequence of this rearrangement of Southeast Asian commerce was the rise in the fifteenth century of a number of hybrid coastal cities in which Chinese or Sino-Southeast Asian traders played a major role. The ruling groups in Melaka and Brunei, and in the Java port-states of Demak, Japara, Grisek and Surabaya, will have been hybridised 'new' communities, who adopted Islam if they were not Muslim already, and whose languages became primarily Malay and Javanese respectively, as their links with China ended in the mid-fifteenth century. Some of them probably had dynastic connections with the old ruling houses of

Sirivijaya and Melayu on the one hand, and Majapahit on the other, but both polities valued these connections and developed elaborate myths to confirm them.

The Ming court's short-lived involvement in Southeast Asia quickly petered out once the capital moved from Nanjing back to its long-term base in Beijing in 1421. Large and frequent tribute missions were discouraged in the second half of the fifteenth century, and the Archipelago ports stopped sending them. Large-scale migrations or defections from China proper ceased between about 1430 and 1570. The deep-ocean 'Eastern route' which linked the Philippines and eastern Indonesia with Fujian ports fell into disuse, and the new Sino-Southeast Asian commercial elites of Brunei and Manila reoriented their China trade through Melaka and Siam, both better able to trade with China by smuggling in the guise of coasting trade. The first Portuguese reports on Southeast Asia in the years after 1509 show that the large Chinese communities of a century earlier were no longer visible to them, having presumably assimilated completely into the new merchant-aristocrats they show dominating the trade of the Java Sea (Reid 1996: 21–37).

Portuguese writers claimed that two of the commercially oriented *ethnie* they encountered in and around Melaka themselves traced their origins to Chinese migrations of a century or more earlier. These were the Javanese (*Jaoa*) of the northern Java coast, and the *Jawi* of coastal Sumatra. The coastal Javanese were 'the most civilized people of these parts, who according to what they say themselves came from China' (Barros 1563, Dec. II, Livro ix: 352). This information fits well with the growing consensus among historians that the origins of the ruling families of Demak, Japara and Gresik were very mixed, with the Chinese element now the best documented (de Graaf and Pigeaud 1974: 34–41; 1984; Reid 1996; 2006b).

The *Jawi*, on whom Barros reported in similar terms, are an even more ambiguous category not usually associated with Chinese. *Jawi* was used by Arabs as the adjectival and individual form of the broader category *Jawa*, to designate Southeast Asian Muslims for whom the *lingua franca* was Malay. The earliest known writers in Malay, in the sixteenth and seventeenth century, called the written language not *Melayu* but *Jawi* (Marsden 1812, II: xii–xv; Roolvink 1975; Laffan 2005). If it was associated with any particular place at that stage it was Sumatra. Raffles' view was that the original meaning was something like creole or *mestizo*, referring both to people and language (Raffles 1835 I: 40–1). I share Michael Laffan's view that while Jawi for distant Arabs was a broad category of Southeast Asians with whom they shared a bond in Islam, in the region itself it was likely to have begun as a term for relatively new converts or migrants into the mixed world of commercial, Malay-speaking Southeast Asian Islam. It was not an ethnic but a cultural and linguistic term. Given the known importance of Chinese migrants in Palembang's transition to Islam, and the importance of Chinese ceramics and artifacts at fourteenth century sites such as Singapore and Kota China near Medan (Miksic 1979), Barros' view can be accepted with the meaning that Chinese were an important element in their mixed ethnic origins.

The other two categories the Portuguese understood to have dominated the trade between Melaka and China before 1511, 'Malays' (from Melaka) and 'Luzons' (from Brunei and Manila), were not described as having mixed or 'Chinese' origins, but similar conclusions can be inferred. Managing the China trade was difficult if not impossible for those unfamiliar with Chinese dialects, written Chinese and the habits of local officials and brokers. The 'Luzons' who played a role in both the Manila–Melaka and Melaka–China trade around 1500 are easiest to understand as successors of those who managed the Brunei–Manila–China trade directly eighty years earlier. When the Spanish encountered this group of Muslim traders in the Philippines after 1565 they simply called them 'Moros' (Moors, or Muslims). However one early report from Mindanao conceded that 'boats from Borneo [Brunei] and Luzon are called Chinese junks in these islands, and even the Moros themselves are called Chinese, but in fact Chinese junks do not reach here' (cited Scott 1982: 37).

We have defined the 'Malays' in Malay understanding of the time as the ruling group in Melaka, and that group itself was of very mixed origins, undoubtedly including Chinese in the early part of the fifteenth century, and coastal Javanese at its end. Javanese traders were the largest population group in the city at that time, the shipowners of the city appeared to be led by Malay-ised Javanese, the Melaka chronicle itself assumed substantial knowledge of Javanese, and the Malay culture hero Hang Tuah was made to say in the epic about him that 'the Melaka people seem to be bastardised Malays [*Melayu kacokan*], mixed with Javanese from Majapahit' (*Hikayat Hang Tuah* 1971: 175).

After the fall of Melaka to the Portuguese in 1511 the term Melayu continued to mean a line of kings, and a style of language and manners developed in Melaka. The Melaka connections grew more tenuous with time, however. *Melayu* continued to coexist with the more Sumatra-centred *Jawi* as a descriptor of language and Malay-speaking Islamic identities as late as the nineteenth century. Neither was truly an ethnie label. As the interaction between Europeans and Javanese established Java as the name for the island and for its dominant language and people, this term gradually narrowed. Well before Melayu/Malay, it clearly came to represent an ethnie. Outside Java, one continued to find commercial quarters of major trading cities which might be known either as Kampung Melayu or Kampung Jawa virtually interchangeably, representing in either case the Malay-speaking commercial diaspora in areas where Malay was not the vernacular. The 'Luzon' label was still used by Mendes Pinto in the mid-sixteenth century, but disappeared thereafter, to become Malay in its diasporic identity, or 'Moro' in the Philippines.

As explained in the previous chapter, the legalisation of trade to the south by the Ming Empire in 1567 established a continuous direct traffic between all parts of maritime Southeast Asia and Southern China. The label 'China' therefore compacted to refer only to those who were obviously different from the majority societies, and not Muslim. As tension mounted between these recent migrants and well-established local elites, the claiming of Chinese heritage was no longer attractive to these assimilated elites. Some long-established 'Chinese' who had resisted adopting Islam may have reassimilated to the migrant communities, but most integrated fully into local categories, in particular the commercial and maritime categories eventually known only as 'Malay'.

Malay as diaspora

One of the concepts of Melayu that continued through the eighteenth and nineteenth centuries was the lineage of kings that originated from Melaka or from Minangkabau before that. It had necessarily become plural as the particular charisma of one successful sultanate diffused to its many rival descendants, from Deli and Langkat in northeast Sumatra to Pontianak and Brunei in Borneo by way of the mini-states of the Peninsula and eastern Sumatra. Much of the 'classical' Malay court literature that has survived in modern collections was composed or copied in the nineteenth century, preserving the preoccupation of an earlier time to assert the legitimacy and sacred *daulat* (sovereignty) of Malay kings. But by the mid-nineteenth century, especially as represented in the work of the greatest of these court writers, Raja Ali Haji of Riau, there was a growing concern to establish principles of Malayness which were bigger than the frequently unworthy individual king. Malay kings must behave justly; Malay subjects must be loyal; if either rulers or subjects submit to lust and passion (*nafsu*), the judgement of God will bring the kingdom down, as was already happening to one ancient court after another. For the Bugis-descended Raja Ali Haji there was no Malay ethnie in the positive sense, but rather a negative, anti-Bugis, parochial

Malay faction (*kaum Melayu*) on the one hand, and a glorious tradition of kingship (*raja Melayu*) on the other, no longer dependent on any one lineage (Ali Haji 1979: 12–17 and 101–3).

The more dynamic understanding of Melayu, however, was as a commercial diaspora. The merchants who had given Melaka its life spread almost throughout Southeast Asia in their quest for entrepots sympathetic to their trade. Their diaspora helped give new life to a range of port-states like Aceh, Patani, Palembang, Banten, Brunei, Makasar and Banjarmasin, and even Cambodia and Siam. In Melaka they had been identified with origins all over maritime Asia, and many were assimilating to the extent of speaking Malay and practising Islam. When dispersed around the Archipelago these traders became a 'Malay' diaspora held together by language, by Islam, and by a commercial tradition epitomised in a maritime law code sympathetic to shippers. It was a wonderfully eclectic and absorptive category, well designed to serve the commercial needs of the multi-lingual world of island Southeast Asia (Ho 2006: 175–82).

The Malay entrepreneurs recorded in Makassar chronicles as entitled to the kind of autonomy and guarantees of property that traders everywhere require, were reported to originate from 'Johor, Patani, Pahang, Minangkabau and Champa', while Indian Muslims later also played a prominent role in the community. As if prophetically aware of the stereotype into which British colonialism would caste Malays two centuries later, the *Melayu* community who had helped spread Islam in the island of Sumbawa refused to be rewarded with rice-fields, for 'we are sailors and traders, not peasants', and asked instead for exemption from port duties (cited Reid 1988–93, II: 128).

Through the seventeenth century Peninsula and Malacca Straits area, Melayu retained its Melaka meanings as a line of kings descended from Srivijaya and Melaka or Pagarruyung (Minangkabau). In the areas penetrated by Bugis influence in the eighteenth century, Riau-Lingga, Perak and Selangor in particular, this meaning was strengthened and at times given shades of ethnie nationalism by the competition with the Bugis. Elsewhere it was essentially a trade diaspora. This second sense was open to new recruits from any ethnic background, but it nevertheless evolved in the direction of a distinct ethnie (*orang Melayu*). Ence Amin, writer for the Makassar court and author of the *Syair Perang Mengkasar*, declared himself to be 'a Malay of Makassar descent' (*nisab Mengkasar anak Melayu*) and took pride in his fellow Malays' heroism in defending Makassar against the Dutch (Skinner 1963: 19–20). Jeremias van Vliet in his detailed description and history of Siam around 1640 mentions Malay only in this sense, as one of the minorities at the capital which contributed to Siamese armies. By contrast Siamese sources do not mention Malayness as a factor in Patani or its rebellion against Siam (van Vliet 2005). Establishing themselves in the heart of the Archipelago at the beginning of the seventeenth century, the Dutch immediately began making distinctions between the different peoples they worked with as soldiers, subjects, rivals and traders. Batavia in particular was a crucible of ethnic labelling. Apart from the Europeans of different types, the key trade diasporas the Dutch recognised in their ports were Chinese, Moor (Indian Muslim), Malay, Javanese and Bugis. In Batavia the most important trading communities were administered through a headman or *kapitan*. When a '*Kapitan Melayu*' was appointed in Batavia in 1644, and later also in Makassar after its Dutch conquest in 1699, large-scale traders from Patani (itself very multi-ethnic) took on these leadership roles. These were highly valued merchants and intermediaries. The first *Kapitan Melayu* of Batavia, Encik Amat, was sent as a Dutch envoy to Mataram four times, and often arranged the protocol for the reception of Asian dignitaries in Batavia. When the fourth generation of this distinguished family to be *Kapitan Melayu* was caught swindling his fellow Malays in 1732, and exiled to Sri Lanka, he was found to have 329,000 *rixdaalders* in property and hundreds of slaves (Raben 1996: 207–10). He must have been one of the richest men in not only Batavia but all Southeast Asia.

This Malay community of Batavia was wealthy but not particularly large in the seventeenth century. It never exceeded 4,000 before 1750, in a city of nearly 100,000. In the middle of the eighteenth century the numbers dropped to below 2000, but towards the end of the century rose rapidly to 12,000—by then embracing all the Malay-speaking Muslims who came to Batavia from Sumatra, Borneo and the Peninsula (Raben 1996). A similar pattern of decline followed by rapid expansion in the late eighteenth century is evident in studies of the ethnicity of ship captains in Dutch ports. Those labelled as 'Malay' in Dutch shipping lists rose rapidly towards the end of the eighteenth century, to become the most often-reported ship captains moving around the Java Sea (Reid 2001: 302).

Two important shifts may explain these changes. Firstly there was an apparent expansion in the meanings of the label. The seventeenth century Dutch understanding was a narrow one restricted to the relatively wealthy group of ship-owners and operators who formed the initial diaspora from Melaka and related ports. This group necessarily declined in relative numbers and importance as Chinese and Bugis diasporas grew in commercial strength. In the 1780s, however, a broader use of the label began to be applied by Dutch harbour-masters, perhaps influenced by indigenous use itself. One clear change of this sort followed immediately after the Dutch–Bugis War which ended with the Dutch capture of Riau in 1784. This caused such enmity between Dutch and Bugis that vessels calling at Dutch ports must have decided that 'Malay' was a safer label. Secondly, the larger number of 'Malay' vessels at the end of the eighteenth century coincided with a reduction in their size. As the Chinese and Europeans expanded their shipping at the top end of the business, local craft found the competition there tough, but increasing opportunities available for small vessels on feeder routes.

In the earlier stage, before 1770, the Malay trade diaspora had some interesting similarities with the Chinese one. Both Malay and Chinese ship captains used the title *Encik,* and they used a similar range of boat types. The average size of their vessels was about the same, around 26 tons, well above the average for all vessels and double the size of the average Javanese vessel. From the 1780s, however, the stereotype of the 'Malay *perahu*' came to be the modern one of a small vessel filling the lower end of the trading networks. The gap with Chinese vessel sizes grew ever wider. And in Dutch eyes, the importance of distinguishing between different ethnic categories among these small boat-owners was reduced. Increasingly all vessels based in Sumatra, the Peninsula or Borneo were seen as 'Malay'.

At least in European eyes, a change was taking place in the late eighteenth and early nineteenth century, making 'Malay' an ethnic marker for substantial populations of traders, fishermen and agriculturalists. William Marsden (1811: 40) deplored the trend that was taking place in the 1780s 'to call the inhabitants of the islands indiscriminately as Malays'. As with so many ethnonyms, the pattern appears to have been for outsiders to push the term in this broader essentialising direction, and for insiders who interacted with them to carry this meaning back to peoples who had previously made do with local identities.

Prior to this shift, settled cultivators were few in both the lower Peninsula and lowland Sumatra. The main populations of cultivators who would later be classified Malay were in Kelantan and Patani, and appear to have called themselves by these place names or even more local ones. Their Siamese overlords distinguished them where necessary as *Khek.* In Sumatra, around 90 per cent of the population south of Aceh was in the highlands, and identified themselves by the lake (Toba, Ranau, Kerinci), river valley or locality around which they lived. When Muslim traders, rulers and diplomats of the hybrid lowland centres later thought of as 'Malay' needed very broad labels to distinguish themselves from Arabs, Europeans, Chinese and other outsiders they would use terms such as *Jawi* or 'people below the winds'. As Marsden noted of the Malay-language letter-writing pattern, of which he was an intimate part in the 1770s and 1780s, 'the term "malayu" as applied to themselves or other eastern people, very rarely occurs' (Marsden 1812 II: ix).

British renderings of 'Malay'

English writers led the trend to broaden the term Malay from its older meanings as royal lineage, trade diaspora, or language into a term for widespread regions and peoples. While other Europeans continued to call the Peninsula by its best-known ancient city, 'Malacca', the English began to see it as 'Malay' or 'Malayan' in the eighteenth century (Hamilton 1930 II: 41). As the British became more concerned with the Peninsula after the founding of Georgetown at Pulau Pinang in 1786, they rejected both the notion that it was Siamese and the dominance of the sleepy port of Melaka, then in Dutch hands. Raffles and Crawfurd frequently labelled the Peninsula Malay or Malayan, and such usages became normal once the London Treaty of 1824 restricted British activity to this Peninsula.

There is no doubt that Thomas Stamford Raffles' view of the Malays had a great effect on the imagining of English-speakers. He should probably be regarded as the most popular mediator into English orientalism, and ultimately thereby its Southeast Asian reflection, of the German Enlightenment ideas of racial classification discussed below. Through John Leyden he picked up Blumenbach's idea of a great 'Malay race' or nation embracing a large if unspecified part of the Archipelago. This European understanding, unlike the indigenous Melayu, would not be limited to the traditional Malay sultans or even their supporters, but one of the great natural divisions of the world's people. Together with the other influential English writers of the period, Marsden and Crawfurd, Raffles sought to mediate this German classification to the empirical data as they knew it in Southeast Asia. Marsden (1966: 40–1) sought to formulate a clear definition of Malay based on what he understood as indigenous (albeit Sumatra-centred) usage: 'every Mussulman speaking the Malayan as his proper language, and either belonging to, or claiming descent from, the ancient kingdom of Minangkabau'.

But Raffles was at the romantic edge of this Enlightenment Quest, seeking in the rustic Javanese or highland Sumatran the noble vestige of once-great civilisations. Soon after arriving in Penang in 1805 as assistant secretary and commencing his study of the Malay language, Raffles became intimate with Dr John Leyden, a learned Scottish surgeon of almost his own youthfulness and romantic disposition, who had been influenced by Sir Walter Scott before leaving Edinburgh. Together they formed their vision of the Malays as one of the language-based 'nations' into which Johann Gottfried Herder in Germany, and Scott in the English Romantic movement, had seen the world divided. Influenced by Leyden's slightly earlier essay on 'the Indo-Chinese nations', Raffles' first literary essay, sent to the Asiatic Society in Bengal from Penang in 1809, insisted on a similar vision for Malays: 'I cannot but consider the *Maláyu* nation as one people, speaking one language, though spread over so wide a space, and preserving their character and customs, in all the maritime states lying between the Sulu Seas and the Southern Oceans' (Raffles 1818: 103; cf Raffles 1835 I: 28–49). Having been forced to abandon his dream of an English vocation to uplift and extend the once-great Javanese people, Raffles transferred this romantic vision to the Malays. From his new post at Bengkulu he mounted an expedition to the old Minangkabau capital of Pagarruyung, which he declared 'the source of that power, the origin of that nation, so extensively scattered over the Eastern Archipelago'. Eagerly he explained to his patron how 'Sumatra, under British influence, [would] again rise into great political importance' by reviving the prestige of the ancient kingdom (Raffles 1835 I: 426, 433).

His most influential single act for subsequent understanding of Malay identity was to rename and publish the major Melaka royal chronicle, discovered and translated by his late friend John Leyden. The text had called itself 'the Arrangements of all the Rajas' (*Peraturan segala raja-raja* or in Arabic *Sulalatu's-Salatina*) and been conceived to record a line of kings, their ceremonial, and a guide to their behaviour (Winstedt 1938: 42). In having it printed for the first time in 1821, Raffles gave it both an English name, 'Malay Annals', and a Malay one (using a hitherto rare Arabic term), *Sejarah Melayu*, both suggesting that it was the story of a people, not of a line of kings. These names stuck. In his introduction to the translation Raffles declared the Malays to be a race, a then newly fashionable term, and hoped that the stories in the chronicle would shed 'a glimmering of light' on their past (Raffles 1821: v).

Following Raffles' initial publication of the English translation, the subsequent printing in the original Malay of this text hitherto known only to scholars was also under British auspices. Munshi Abdullah, the Malay tutor of British missionaries, edited the text which was published by the Singapore Institution in 1842. As Malay schooling was subsequently developed in British-ruled and British-protected areas on the Peninsula, the 'Malay Annals' were frequently reprinted for use in schools.

To move from this emergent ethnie term to conceptualising a particular place where it belonged was not easy, given its diverse earlier histories. Even in English there was a wide conceptual cleavage between the colony of the Straits Settlements (the port-cities of Singapore, Melaka and Penang), multi-cultural and unquestionably British-ruled, and the 'Malay States' of the Peninsula Mainland. The British in 1874 began their intervention beyond the Straits Settlements by establishing 'protectorates' over selected Malay river-chiefs, in return for their following British advice in everything except 'Malay religion and custom'. This remained the legitimation for the creation of modern infrastructure in Malaya, and for the economic development which saw (and required) a vast influx of migrants from southern China, India, Indonesia and Southern Siam. Whereas the economic motives of these immigrants were initially very similar, those who remained in the long term were encouraged to conform to one of three stereotypes—agrarian, traditional Malay; commercial, clannish Chinese; or the Indian servant of colonial interests in the bureaucracy and estates. The first of these, the 'real Malay' (as opposed to a variety of urban, modernising Muslims the British distrusted), was seen as particularly in need of protection by government against the rampant capitalism which all other communities in Malaya were encouraged to practise. He was rural, loyal to his ruler, conservative and relaxed to the point of laziness. An influential Malayan governor of this period devoted one of his novels to showing the catastrophic results of Malays becoming infected with western ideas (Clifford 1926).

'British Malaya' versus *Tanah Melayu*

The concepts Malay and Melayu were both much older than any name for the lower end of the Peninsula itself, the identity of which became increasingly problematic in the nation-state-dominated twentieth century. In official constitutional law it had no identity. There were the directly ruled British colonies of Singapore, Melaka and Penang, collectively constituted the Crown Colony of the Straits Settlements in 1867, and the four 'Federated Malay States' (FMS) which in 1896 agreed to British urgings to share a nascent bureaucracy in Kuala Lumpur, even though formally still sovereign. The five other Malay states had somewhat more leverage when they came under British tutelage—Kedah, Perlis, Kelantan and Trengganu when they were transferred from Siamese suzerainty in 1909, and Johor when it finally accepted a British Resident comparable to those in other states in 1914. These had no wish to join the federation, and the British in the more protective atmosphere of the new century did not wish to force them. They became known collectively as the 'Unfederated Malay States' (UFMS). Within 'British Malaya' there were therefore ten sovereignties, and at least seven distinct bureaucracies, even if the utilities of a modern economy all worked on a uniform basis.

As Britain took ever greater responsibility for managing the whole of the southern Peninsula, a plural society was created in which Europeans and Chinese were encouraged to develop its resources, produce the exports and pay the taxes which made the area one of the wealthiest economies in Asia by the 1920s. As well as dominating the Straits Settlements demographically, Chinese formed 42 per cent of the FMS in 1931, and Indians 22 per cent. Malay rulers provided the legitimation for the lucrative development onto the Mainland of the Peninsula. Their 'protection' was taken increasingly seriously by many officials alarmed by Chinese nationalism and communism in the Peninsula, and by Indonesian nationalism across the Straits. Yet they stood largely outside the British-managed economic and legal systems.

The adjective 'Malayan', which in the nineteenth century had pertained to the ambivalent term Malay, as in the *Malayan Miscellanies* published in the British Sumatran settlement of Bengkulu as early as 1820–2, gradually came in the twentieth century to pertain to a place—the British-managed south of the Peninsula. At least for some, the English noun for this adjective was now not 'Malay' but the novel construct, 'Malaya'. Sir Frank Swettenham, who as commissioner for the Federated Malay States orchestrated the first conference of the (federated) Malay rulers in 1897, was one of its champions. He scattered the word 'Malaya' through the self-congratulatory proceedings of that conference. His own book, *British Malaya* (1906) was the first to use Malaya as if it were the name of a country, and he was swiftly followed by others (Wright and Cartwright 1908).

Those who knew Malay tradition were more cautious, knowing what shallow roots the new polity had. R. O. Winstedt, concerned as inspector of Malay schools to root Malays in a distinct 'Melayu' tradition, nevertheless eventually called one book he wrote for an English public, *Malaya*. He had to explain what it meant—'The word "Malaya" is an English hybrid applied only to British possessions and protectorates, and especially perhaps to the Peninsula, so that British Malaya is pleonastic' (Winstedt 1923: 1). As if to overemphasise the alien Britishness of the term, he claimed it should properly also cover the Borneo territories, and even Cocos and Christmas islands. Nevertheless a term was needed and 'Malaya' gradually established itself in the 1920s. In the same year as Winstedt's book, 1923, the venerable *Journal of the Straits Branch of the*

Royal Asiatic Society changed its regional adjective from 'Straits' to 'Malayan', while a British-based 'Association of British Malaya' brought out its journal *British Malaya* from 1926.

For those of all communities who were educated in multi-ethnic English-medium schools, 'Malaya' did seem to describe the place they lived. The more 'Malay' was rendered as an ethnic term, the more an alternative term was needed to describe the intensely multi-ethnic land which people of many races were beginning to call home. Sports teams and international delegations began to call themselves Malayan. Among Chinese, the Malayan branch of the KMT and its offshoot, the Malayan Communist Party, carried the 'Malaya' concept into politics. A few English-educated Malays also accepted the term. In 1930, an Arab-owned Malay newspaper was established in Singapore with the title *Warta Malaya* (Malayan News), edited by the English-educated Johor official, Onn bin Jaafar (Harper 1999: 30).

But this hybrid word found no firm place in Malay speech, and it must be said that the colonial officials responsible for Malay education showed no desire that it should. The term could only be rendered in Malay by a leap to *Tanah Melayu*—'the land of the Malays'—an uncomfortable antithesis of 'British Malaya'. The evolution of this term followed English usage in gradually becoming more associated with the Peninsula as British interests congealed there. The *Hikayat Hang Tuah* is the only pre-modern Malay text to use the term *Tanah Melayu*, meaning by it sometimes Melaka alone and sometimes a broader area where there were Malay kings (Matheson 1979: 361). The only way to refer to the Peninsula as such in pre-nineteenth century Malay was in relation to its Johor extremity, *Ujung Tanah* (Land's End). Yet in the early nineteenth century both Marsden and Crawfurd indicate that *Tanah Melayu* had already taken hold as the label for the southern part of the Peninsula (Marsden 1811: 327; Crawfurd 1820 II: 371–3). Both found this appellation puzzling since they wanted to see a single origin-place for 'the Malay race', and were equally convinced that it was to be found not in the Peninsula but in Minangkabau. Crawfurd concluded that Malays become self-conscious only in Melaka, so that 'It was from the colony, and not the parent stock, that the Malayan name and nation were so widely disseminated' (Crawfurd 1820 II: 376).

The evolution of Malay-language textbooks at British hands demonstrates the changing ways in which educational administrators handled the conflict between polyglot 'British Malaya' and the protected 'Land of the Malays'. In marked contrast with the nervousness of colonial administrators in Vietnam, Burma or Indonesia about the nationalism of the core ethnie, British Malayan officials encouraged the construction of a separate 'Melayu' history and identity to be localised in the Peninsula. The first Malay textbook for the very basic Malay elementary schools provided first in the Straits Settlements already sanctioned the *Tanah Melayu* definition, though it was initially explicitly plural and not limited to the Peninsula. The title of the book published by the government printer in 1875 literally translates as 'An account to tell stories about the Malay lands [*Tanah-Tanah Melayu*] and Sumatra and so forth' (*Hikayat* 1875, in Proudfoot 1993: 506). It went through several editions still with this cumbrous title, but in 1892 was retitled in a singular way *Hikayat Tanah Melayu*—'An account (or history) of the land of the Malays'. This was kept in print up until the time the prolific historian, R. O. Winstedt, in 1918 provided a more modern definition of Malay identity that was racial-cultural as well as geographic—'A book of Malay history' (Winstedt and Hasan 1918). This was followed by a more ambitious book in three volumes, 'History of the Malay World' (Hasan 1925–30).

These textbooks well reflected the pattern of Malay education encouraged by Winstedt and his learned predecessor, R. J. Wilkinson. Wilkinson, mainly responsible for founding in 1900 the Malay College in Melaka to train teachers for the vernacular government primary schools, encouraged its students to study the classical Malay literature which he had helped recover (Khoo 1979: 302). He was convinced that the forgotten classics would rescue the Malay language from the Indonesia-oriented modernising urban literati—'the Anglomaniac with his piebald diction and the pan-Islamic pundit with his long Arabic words' (cited Maier 1988: 119). Despite its greater wealth than its neighbours, British Malaya spent less public money on education, leaving the Chinese and Indian populations to support their own schools or missionary ones. Vernacular Malay schools were established to provide basic literacy to the 'protected' Malay population, though only 12 per cent of them benefited from it in 1920. Wilkinson and Winstedt reflected a government bias to keeping the 'protected' population in need of protection by essentialising them as a traditional population of peasants loyal to their sultans. As a British High Commissioner of the Federated States pointed out in 1919, 'It will not only be a disaster to, but a violation of the whole spirit and tradition of, the Malay race if the result of our vernacular education is to lure the whole of the youth from the kampung to the town' (cited Roff 1967: 138).

The education provided drew heavily on the chronicle which Raffles had popularised to promote the older meanings of *Melayu* as a tradition of kingship descended from Melaka (Roff 1967: 28n and 135). Malays were educated to be a people loyal to their sultans and to a classic tradition, even though many of those attending such schools were from diverse migrant and entrepreneurial backgrounds. As Henk Maier characterised it, this most idealistic of British scholar-officials still held that 'the gap between East and West should be confirmed rather than bridged. And the seeds of the necessary regeneration of the Malay people should be sought primarily in the past, when everything had been so much better' (Maier 1988: 119).

The most influential Malayan administrators professed great liking for this gentlemanly but non-competitive Malay stereotype. By contrast the negative elements of a rampant capitalist order tended to be attributed to another stereotype, that of 'the Chinese' inherently dedicated to making money by any means possible. The dominant element of the Malayan Civil Service took the view that its role was to protect the stereotyped Malay identity, not to change it. Sir Hugh Clifford, the most sentimentally paternal of the governors, insisted as late as 1927, when effective power was wholly in British hands, that there must be no change in the Islamic monarchies which Britain was sworn to protect. 'No mandate has ever been extended to us by Rajas, Chiefs, or people to vary the system of government which has existed in these territories from time immemorial' (Sir Hugh Clifford, cited Omar 1993: 5). In this view Malays should have the kind of education 'to breed a vigorous and self-respecting agricultural peasantry such as must form the backbone of every nation' (Federal Council 1920, cited Roff 1967: 138–9). Malay reservations were created in 1913, in which agricultural land could only be alienated to people defined as racially Malay, irrespective of their place of birth. In 1917–18 regulations were passed to oblige rice-growing land to continue to be used for that purpose, in the hope of discouraging Malays from becoming commercially oriented rubber-growers rather than sturdy self-sufficient peasants (Roff 1967: 121–5).

The tenuousness of the ethnie concept until the 1930s should be emphasised. It had to compete not only against specific diaspora ethnicities (Mandailing, Bugis, Aceh, Banjar, Rawas, Jawi Pekan, etc), but among Malay-speakers with loyalties to particular rulers, and among English-speakers with the continuing idea that all speakers of Austronesian languages were in some sense 'Malay'.

Malay as race

As indicated above, the European concept 'Malay' took leave of the indigenous *Melayu* in the late eighteenth century. This was especially the work of the German pioneer of comparative ethnology, Johann Friedrich Blumenbach (1752–1840). His *De generis humani varietate nativa* (On the natural varieties of mankind) of 1775 carried into the study of man some of the scientific principles of classification pioneered by Linnaeus and later developed by Darwin. With its five-fold division of mankind into white Caucasians, yellow Mongoloids, brown Malays, black Ethiopians and red Americans, this was destined to have far-reaching consequences. Though he based this initial scheme on a typology of skull, hair and skin colour, his later work at Göttingen was influenced by the beginnings of Malayo-Polynesian comparative language studies, and by more subtle understandings of the vast variety within and between his initial categories.

Among Blumenbach's students at Göttingen was Alexander von Humboldt (1769–1859), a prodigy in the synthesis of scholarship and direct observation, whose erudition was informed by extensive travels in Latin America and Central Asia. His linguistically gifted brother Wilhelm took up the study of Southeast Asian languages, pioneering the understanding of the influence of Sanskrit on Javanese. He is also responsible for popularising the term 'Malayo-Polynesian' through extensive comparison of languages from Malagasy to Tahiti (W. von Humboldt 1836–9; Fox 2004: 4). Through his influence Alexander became convinced that comparative linguistics, 'one of the most brilliant results of modern studies in the last sixty or seventy years', would be more helpful in understanding 'the relationships of different portions of the human race' (A. von Humboldt 1847–8, II: 108–9). Here too the vast extent of the Malay family was one of his prime examples. But in his encyclopedic lectures summarising the natural world, *Kosmos*, he firmly parted company from his teacher, insisting 'By maintaining the unity of the human species, we at the same time repel the cheerless assumption of superior and inferior races of men' (A. von Humboldt 1847–8, I: 355). He closed his first volume of this universal schema by quoting his late brother: 'If there is one idea which contributes more than any other to the ... perfectibility of the whole human species—it is the idea of our common humanity' (A. von Humboldt 1847–8, I: 356).

The first generation of Southeast Asian anti-colonial nationalists, the Spanish-educated *ilustrados* of the late-nineteenth century Philippines, discovered this liberating strain of German thought when studying in Europe. Their principal link to it was the Austrian Ferdinand Blumentritt (1853–1913), who continued the tradition of comparative ethnography by a detailed study of the Philippines. It divided Philippine society into four racial groups in order of antiquity, the Negritos, Malays, Chinese and 'whites'. Overwhelmingly dominant were the Malays, who through three different 'invasions' of the islands had come to form the fifty-one contemporary Malay ethnic groups (Blumentritt 1882).

José Rizal (1861–96), the brilliant leader of the *ilustrado* generation of the 1880s, discovered Blumentritt soon after this book appeared, as an ally in his attempts to uphold the dignity of his people against the racism of a number of colonial authorities. Rizal was particularly grateful for Blumentritt's help in demolishing a woman writer who had claimed the people of the islands to be 'inferior to the European physically and mentally, and incapable of ever possessing any culture'. In the spirit of the Humboldt brothers, Blumentritt pointed to the achievements of the great Malay language family and the absurdity of judging races by physical characteristics. Through his extensive correspondence with Blumentritt, Rizal became convinced that his people were 'the six million oppressed Malays', and he himself a 'Tagalog Malay' (Salazar 1998: 115–17). It was Blumentritt who pointed Rizal towards the forgotten Spanish text of Antonio de Morga, which Rizal set himself to republishing as a window on the Philippine Malays of pre-colonial times (Rizal 1961). Rizal began learning Malay and corresponding also with the foremost Leiden scholar of the Malayo-Polynesian language family, Hendrik Kern (Rizal–Blumentritt, 1961: 12, 349–50, 500–2).

In his later polemical writing in Spain, Rizal insisted that 'The Filipinos, like all Malays, do not succumb before the foreigner', as shown by the demographic increase despite colonial rule in the Philippines, Java and the Moluccas (cited Salazar 1998: 119). One of his organisations, the Paris-based Indios Bravos, agreed on a secret agenda to liberate first the Philippines, and then Borneo, Indonesia and Malaya (Salazar 1998: 120). Blumentritt was famously to refer to Rizal after his execution as 'the greatest Malay who ever lived', and two subsequent Filipino biographers took this up by labelling him 'The Great Malayan' (Quirino 1940), and 'Pride of the Malay Race' (Palma 1949).

Sanctified by Rizal, and spelled out further by Apolinario Mabini, the sense of being part of a larger Malay race continued under the American occupation of the Philippines, even if the eventual agreement to call the population Filipino made 'Malay' less essential as a marker. The pan-Malay vision achieved its most passionate expression in the 1930s, at the hands of Wenceslao Vinzons, a law student at the University of the Philippines. In his capacity as president of the student union he set up in 1932 a 'Malay Association' with a Dutch-influenced Malay name— *Perhempoenan Orang Melayoe*—with the support of Manila-based students from Indonesia, Malaya and Polynesia as well as Filipinos. 'A miniature league of Malayan brotherhood', this held secret rituals in Malay, and sought 'to promote the study of the history, civilizations and culture of the Malay race' (cited Salazar 1998: 126–7). In 1934 this graduated to a national organisation called Young Philippines, drawing in such prominent nationalists as Manuel Roxas, Jose P. Laurel, Jr., Diosdado Macapagal and Carlos P. Romulo. Self-consciously launched as a step in 'the development of the Malay race', this sought the 'establishment of a confederation of free Malayan Republics' in Southeast Asia (cited Salazar 1998: 127–8).

Vinzons' own promising political career was cut off when executed by the Japanese in 1942, but the ideas he championed remained important in the post-war Philippines. At one bizarre extreme was the eccentric racism of Ahmed Ibn Parfahn, who claimed as Malays the great achievers from Alexander the Great to Jesus and Mohammad, and insisted that the new Pan-Malayan movement must aim at 'blood purification. No race can be strong while adulterated with half-breeds' (Parfahn 1957/1967, cited Salazar 1998: 227–8). Mainstream political thought had no such ideas, but continued to see Filipinos as part of a greater Malay 'race' and often dressed attempts at better relations with Malaysia and Indonesia as Malay solidarity. In particular one of Vinzons' pre-war pan-Malay visionaries, Macapagal, as President of the Republic (1961–5) engineered the Manila accord of 1963 whereby Malaya, Indonesia and the Philippines agreed 'to take initial steps' to the establishment of a pact known as Maphilindo. For Macapagal this was a dream of a 'reunion of brothers', designed to remove the colonial barriers built 'to divide the peoples of the Malay race' (cited Salazar 1998: 132). He then recalled his apprenticeship under Vinzons, when the activists of the 1930s 'also envisioned MAPHILINDO under our rallying cry Malaysia Irredenta' (cited Ismail Hussein 1998: xiii). Nowhere else was this dream so strong, and Maphilindo came to an early end.

In Malaya the concept of a Malay race had meanwhile developed more prominently, but in a very different direction. For racially conscious Englishmen sent to administer Malaya in the early years of the twentieth century, the protection of a 'Malay race' was a more attractive justification for colonial rule than the protection of 'Malay rulers' that had been the original pretext. Charles Hirschman points out that while the early colonial censuses, in 1871 and 1881, listed Malays, Boyanese, Achinese, Javanese, Bugis, Manilamen, Siamese, and so on as separate groups, the 1891 census demarcated the three racial categories of modern Malaysia—Chinese, 'Tamils and other natives of India' and 'Malays and other natives of the Archipelago', each elaborately sub-divided.

The 1901 census for the first time sought to impose a 'scientific' demarcation of race, as separate from birthplace or citizenship. Its report advised that 'the word "nationality" should be changed for that of "race" whenever it occurs. It is a wider and more exhaustive expression than "nationality" and gives rise to no such ambiguous questions in classifying people' (cited Hirschman 1987: 561). This attempt proved untenable in any consistent biological sense. The growing strength of ethnie nationalism in the Peninsula eschewed biology in favour of religion, culture and politics. And yet the genie of race was out of the bottle. The pseudo-scientific European idea of competing biological strains had merged with the indigenous concepts of identity (*bangsa*, *minzu*) among English-educated Malayans, sharpening the boundaries of what had been fluid categories. The census and the official system of registration had contributed most to this through its insistence on a tripartite division by 'race' of Malays, Chinese and Indians.

And yet the contradictions in this process were apparent to its practitioners. The director of the 1931 census dwelt on this at length.

The term 'Race' is used, for the purpose of the Malayan census, in a peculiar sense, which requires explanation ... the word 'Race' is used, for lack of a more appropriate term, to cover a complex set of ideas, of which race, in the strict or scientific sense, is only one small element. It would be of little use to the administrator or the merchant to attempt a classification of the population by race in the ethnographic sense, to say nothing of the fact that any such tentative classification would be highly controversial ... It is, in fact, impossible to define the sense in which the term 'Race' is used for census purposes; it is, in reality, a judicious blend, for practical ends, of the ideas of geographic and ethnographic origin, political allegiance, and racial and social affinities and sympathies ... most Oriental peoples have themselves no clear conception of race, and commonly regard religion as the most important, if not the determinant, element. The Malay, for example, habitually regards adherence to Islam in much the same light as a European regards a racial distinction, and will speak of a Muhammadan Indian and a Hindu (even if the two are of precisely similar origin), as though the distinction between them were similar in nature and magnitude to that between a Frenchman and a German. (Vlieland 1932: 73–4)

From a contemporary perspective, we might say that the European conviction of the importance of racial boundaries, then at its peak, had not yet poisoned the Malayan imaginary. But it had certainly begun its work.

Previous censuses had used the term 'Malay' in two different senses— as the broad category we today call Austronesian, as well as a narrower sense of Muslim Malay-speakers from the Peninsula and Sumatra, arguing that 'linguistically, ethically and ethnologically the Malays of British Malaya and the Malays of Jambi, Kampar, Siak, Minangkabau and other districts of Sumatra are one race' (cited Vlieland 1932: 75). In 1931, responding to the request of Netherlands Indian authorities to distinguish its subjects who had migrated to the Peninsula, the Malayan census used the term 'Malaysian' for 'all indigenous peoples of the Malay Peninsula and Archipelago', and restricted 'Malay' to mean 'those Malaysians (excluding Aboriginals) who belong to British Malaya'. 'Belong' here was taken to exclude not only those born in Indonesia but their Malaya-born children who were not specifically identified as 'Malay'. By this measure only about half the 'Malaysians' of Singapore, Johor and Selangor were 'Malays', though a large majority elsewhere (Vlieland 1932: 75–6).

Despite the tendency of ethnie nationalism to see religion as the more important badge of identity, 'race' remained the means to identify people in independent Malaya/Malaysia and Singapore, and the Malay term *bangsa* was gradually reinterpreted in this direction, as discussed below. For the most part *bangsa Melayu* was interpreted in the sense of the 1931 census, as restricted to inhabitants of Malaya/Malaysia. But rising ethnie nationalism in the 1930s caused increasing debates about the boundaries of the race, the prominent figures of Arab or Indian descent favouring a more religious definition, while many younger activists agitated for a more truly racial definition which might include immigrant Sumatrans but exclude Indian and Arab *peranakan* (local-born creole) (Roff 1967: 244–5; Omar 1993: 16–18; Harper 1999: 32–3).

The more Europe-derived racial sense of a vast family of peoples of diverse languages and religions was sustained primarily in the Philippines, but periodically raised echoes of 'Greater Malay' enthusiasm in Malaysia. As its principal ideologue, Professor Ismail Hussein pointed out various 'Malay' peoples had mingled in the Peninsula to form a self-definition as Malays which was classic in its breadth. 'Their position was also threatened by other racial groups. Hence the feeling and consciousness of being 'Malay' developed very well there.' (Ismail Hussein 1998: xiv). Dr Mahathir's support for these pan-Malay ideas made it possible for a series of seminars on the 'Malay World' to be held, starting with Melaka in 1982. Meetings followed in Sri Lanka, the Champa area of Vietnam, South Africa, Yunnan, Mindanao and Madagascar, and a secretariat for *Melayu Antarabangsa* (international Malay-ness) was set up with government support in 1996 (Ismail Hussein 1998: xiv). Yet the very different ideological positioning of Indonesia on this issue made the largest centre of Austronesian cultures a notable absentee at the table.

Bangsa Melayu as ethnie nationalism

Two generations of being referred to and educated as if they were a distinct race, however, had a predictable impact. Identity took shape around *bangsa Melayu*, a term which goes back at least to Munshi

Abdullah but was more widely internalised from the 1920s as the equivalent of 'Malay race' in English. Like 'race', *bangsa* derived from common descent, but its Sanskrit origins refer to lineage or even caste. In the old texts someone who has no *bangsa* is of low birth. For the young graduates of the Malay teachers' colleges who wrote in the growing Malay press of the 1930s, *bangsa Melayu* became the primary locus of political passion. It was defined by what they perceived as two overwhelming facts—they were the 'natives' with primary claim on the country; and they were the weakest group in it. They concluded that the *bangsa* required unity and solidarity to make stronger demands of the British.

This pattern of a 'protected' Malay peasantry loyal to his sultan made little sense, however, in the urban world of the nineteenth century Straits Settlements. In the competitive and multi-racial environment of these cities, European ideas of first nationality and later race carried much weight. In the person of Munshi Abdullah, the prolific Malay writer and teacher for a succession of Europeans in the Straits, it is possible to observe the evolution of a new sense of Malay identity in close proximity to Europeans and Chinese. Despite the mixed descent he shared with many residents of the Straits, Abdullah considered himself a Malay. Malay was his preferred language, and he was accepted as an authority on Malay culture and language. But he had no time for the lineage of Malay rajas that had hitherto been the key definition of Malay-ness. In his urban perspective, much influenced by the progress and sense of community of other groups in Singapore, the Malay kings were the greatest threat to the well being of what he called *bangsa Melayu*—the Malay race or people. Writing in the 1840s, he was perhaps the first Malay writer for whom, as Milner puts it, 'the race was the primary community'—although in the view of many later Malay nationalists he was not properly part of it (Milner 1995: 51).

This developing Straits idea of Malayness as an essentially racial category, with its own ethnic origin and genealogy, its own language, its own relatively broad boundaries against other ethnicities, was the newest of the three versions of Malay in the nineteenth century. In the Straits Settlements there were undoubtedly many Abdullahs, for whom Malay-ness was a new identity acquired in the ethnically competitive world of these port-states. Austronesian Muslims seemed to be outnumbered and outcompeted by Chinese, Europeans and Indians in these ports. Although of various origins, they were too small a minority to carry much weight separately as Bugis, Aceh, Java or Mandailing, and in any case they intermarried with each other in the ports. The English rulers of the Straits used 'Malay' as the collective term to refer to them, and to a considerable extent it became internalised. When the first Malay-language daily newspaper appeared in the Straits Settlements, in 1907, it was named not after a place but after a language and potential ethnie—*Utusan Melayu*.[1]

Malay ethnie nationalism developed in the 1930s and 1940s, responding to the earlier diasporic ethnie nationalism among both English and Chinese. Ibrahim Yaacob complained in 1941 that there were still too many who thought of themselves as Minangkabau or Boyanese, or as subjects of a particular raja instead of as members of the Malay *bangsa* pure and simple (Milner 1995: 269). One of the new Malay newspapers responded to the demands of Malayan-born Chinese for political rights in Malaya with the words: 'The Malays have rights not because they were born here but because they belong to the Malay *bangsa* and are the first *bangsa* that owns the land' (cited Omar 1993: 18). As with all such definitions, of course, the problem of how to measure racial identity became the greatest irritant. Like earlier British administrators, the Malay radicals wanted to find the 'real Malay—*Melayu jati*—excluding both Anglophile aristocrats and the part-Indian or part-Arab Muslims of Singapore and Penang (Roff 1967: 244–5; Nagata 1981; Omar 1993: 16–18).

During the Malayan Union controversy of 1945–6 what had been a minority view became politically dominant as the voice of UMNO, the Malay party formed around the ethno-nationalist idea. Malay loyalties should be given to the *bangsa Melayu* rather than to the separate Malay rulers or to the British. *Hidup Melayu* ('Long live the Malays') replaced the deferential *Daulat Tuanku* of salutation to royalty as the slogan of the *bangsa* (Omar 1993: 198–9).

The British were obliged to back down from their Malayan Union project and replace it with a Federation of Malaya in which the centrality of Malayness was explicitly expressed. In effect the 'Malayan' civic nationalism the British belatedly sought to encourage after 1945 was rejected in favour of an almost equally recent ethnic nationalism. The Malay press throughout the controversy denounced *bangsa Malayan* as foreigners. Federation of Malaya might be just acceptable in English, but only so long as it was understood as a translation from the real (Malay) name of the country, *Persekutuan Tanah Melayu*—Federation of the Malay Lands. The Anglo-Malay committee that recommended the name noted that 'the Malays took the strongest exception to being called

---

[1] In this it followed by a half-century the *Selompret Melajoe* of Semarang (1860), which sustained the third of my nineteenth-century meanings of Malayness, below (Adam 1995: 23–57).

or referred to as Malayans' (cited Omar 1993: 107). Citizenship, the British stipulated, was to be extended to those who regarded Malaya as their real home and had lived there for fifteen years, but this was distinguished sharply from nationality (*bangsa*). The constitutional report insisted that citizenship:

was not a nationality, nor could it be developed into a nationality ... It is an addition to, and not a subtraction from, nationality, and could be a qualification for electoral rights ... and for employment in government service ... [But] oaths of allegiance would be out of place. (cited Omar 1993: 109)

The Federation of Malaya was emphatically designed to be a state constructed around not simply a core culture, but a core ethnie. The defining identity, or nationality, was to be *bangsa Melayu*. On the eve of Malayan independence in 1957 the conflict between ethnic and civic nationalisms had to be skirted around again, in a formula which finally granted a single Malayan nationality, but only after hard bargaining for concessions which would acknowledge the definitive position of *bangsa Melayu* at the core—chiefly in symbolic forms and the 'Malay privileges' in education and government service.

One of the greatest benefits of the formation of Malaysia in 1963 was that it at last created a neutral and artificial name for the country distinct from that of any ethnie. It thereby could in principle, like Indonesia and the Philippines but unlike Thailand, Burma and Vietnam, emphasise the national identity without necessarily marginalising minorities. But there were still profound tensions between the concepts of core ethnie and of neutral citizenship. Lee Kuan Yew's Singapore was expelled from the new country after less than two years because his vigorous campaign for a civic or territorial nationalism—'Malaysian Malaysia'; the assertion that 'We are here as of right'—was considered by Alliance leaders as certain to lead to violent conflict with Malay ethno-nationalism (Mahathir 1970: 122).

The most forceful case for a core ethnie within Malaysia was that of Malaysia's longest-serving prime minister (1981–2003). Dr Mahathir's 1970 book, *The Malay Dilemma*, written in the aftermath of the traumatic 1969 riots, argued the ethno-nationalist case both in terms of the need for protection, and prior rights to the land. Leaning heavily on the example of Australia and the US, he argued that every country has a 'definitive people' who were the first to set up states in the territory in question. Since the aborigines did not do this, it was the Malays in Malaya, and the English-speaking Christians in Australia, who defined the core culture and set the conditions by which subsequent migrants were admitted (Mahathir 1970: 122–6).

Because Dr Mahathir had strong credentials with ethno-nationalists, he was well-placed as prime minister to move Malaysia towards some long-term resolution of the tensions between ethnic and civic nationalism. In opening UMNO to non-Malay *bumiputra* in 1994 (an important issue for the peoples of Borneo), and still more by declaring the future goal of a *bangsa Malaysia* as part of his Vision 2020, he raised the possibility of movement towards a civic state nationalism of Indonesian type (below). The remainder of his term, however, saw little progress in this direction, but rather a gradual shift towards religion as a sharper boundary between Malays and others, and an entrenching of the New Economic Policy as the cornerstone of 'Malay supremacy' (*ketuanan Melayu*), rather than its original purpose of economic equality.

As UMNO became more embattled in the twenty-first century, this issue of Malay supremacy became a major political one. Dr Mahathir's former deputy, Anwar Ibrahim, established a new multi-racial party after being bitterly attacked by Mahathir, expelled from UMNO and prosecuted for corruption and sodomy (the latter charge eventually overturned after Mahathir's retirement in favour of Abdullah Badawi as prime minister in 2003). In successfully steering this party to huge gains among all ethnic groups in the 2008 election, in partnership with predominately Chinese Democratic Action Party (DAP) on one side and exclusively Muslim Pan Malaysian Islam Party (PAS) on the other, Anwar and his new colleagues promised to end discrimination against non-Malay citizens in the states they controlled. Though not dissimilar to the PAP critique of 1963–5 in its attack on cronyism and corruption in the guise of Malay privilege, Anwar's campaign proved to have far greater credibility as articulated by a former leader of UMNO at a time when nepotism and corruption were seen to have reached new levels. In response to establishment cries of 'Malay supremacy under threat' (*Mingguan Malaysia* 13 April 2008), Anwar was understood to have scored a major propaganda victory through a new slogan of 'the people's supremacy' (*ketuanan rakyat*), articulated in a post-election rally of 14 April 2008.

Malay ethnie nationalism, of the 'protective' type analysed in chapter 2, had had an exceptionally long innings in Malaysia. In its UMNO form it had, however, been unable to expand its agenda to become an inclusive type of state nationalism of civic kind. By 2008 there were claims that this was a kind of 'failed nation' (Sani 2008). On the other hand, the sense of threat that had given rise to this brand of ethnie nationalism in the 1940s, when there were very few Malays in the modern economy, was unconvincing to a new generation who had seen the Malay population increase to some 60 per cent of the whole (*bumiputra* were 65.1 per cent at the 2000 census), and Malay domination of the patronage economy including state industries, the judiciary and the universities. The argument for marginalisation and impoverishment was being more credibly made by Indian workers, migrant workers and the indigenous peoples of Borneo. At the time of writing, it seemed conceivable that a new and more inclusive nationalism might emerge.

Malayness as revolutionary state nationalism—*bangsa* Indonesia

In the cities of the Netherlands Indies a Malay-speaking urban population of mixed origins took root in the nineteenth century, for whom Malay was predominately a *lingua franca* and a language for popular written expression. It had little to do with ethnicity, and was less used as a label for a particular commercial diaspora than in the previous century. In fact the majority of those who first turned modern Malay in romanised script into a vehicle of print journalism were of mixed Chinese-Indonesian descent and generally labelled 'Chinese'. The Dutch had never followed the English path of referring to all who spoke Malay as 'Malays'. Malay had been the *lingua franca* of the Dutch empire in the Archipelago since the mid-seventeenth century, and it was the principal language of the new Christianised minorities in Ambon and Minahasa. As a vague collective term for the inhabitants of the Archipelago, 'Malay' did not recommend itself to the Dutch. They used the term 'native' (*inlander*) in everyday disparagement of the people now known as Indonesians, an option not available to the English in the Straits, who used the loose and pejorative 'native' for all the Asians under their authority. When they sought to be neutral the Dutch called their non-Chinese subjects Indians (*Indiers*), and the Spanish did the same in the Philippines. When in the early years of this century the novel idea began to spread among the people of the Dutch-ruled Archipelago that they were a collective unity, they initially used the Malay version of this term—*orang Hindia*—to describe themselves.

The relationship between state and *ethnie* was profoundly different in Indonesia. The colonial cities of Netherlands India, as of Malaya, represented a sort of melting-pot where people from diverse origins came to see a common adherence to Islam as the most important thing that separated them from Europeans, Chinese and stateless unbelievers like the Balinese, Bataks and so on. Unless quickly assimilated into the Chinese or European communities through marriage (an option only available to women), the people brought to Batavia, Makassar,

Palembang or Medan by slavery (before 1800) or by the attraction of commerce, quickly became Muslim as an indication that they were civilised and urban. This new identity was generally called Islam, though in some of the cities and coastal areas of Sumatra, Borneo and the Peninsula it might also be called Malay, while in Semarang and other cities of Java, the loose ethnic marker associated with Islam was 'Javanese', even if Malay was the principal language spoken in the city. Thus a Chinese writer of the 1780s complained that Chinese who stayed too long in the cities of Java forgot 'the instruction of the sages' and 'do not scruple to become Javanese, when they call themselves Islam' (cited Raben 1996: 242–3). In the early twentieth century Javanese became a self-conscious label for those who spoke the Javanese language as their mother tongue, and the Malay-speaking people of Batavia, of very mixed Balinese, Chinese, Makassarese and other origins, adopted the name 'Betawi', and were so recorded in colonial censuses.

Though Islam remained the key marker of common identity, and served as such in the first modern mass movement, Sarekat Islam, this religious affiliation did not present itself as a nationalism in the sense of defining the boundary of the core ethnie. Among the first to feel the stirring of an Indies-wide anti-colonial secular nationalism expressed in the Malay language were Indonesia-born non-Muslims classified as *peranakan* Chinese and Indo-Europeans. As this nationalism became more popular in the 1920s these pioneering figures were marginalised, but educated Christian Ambonese, Minahasans and Bataks continued to play prominent roles in defining the nation. After 1914 Marxism made a heavy emphasis on race and religion seem old-fashioned.

The first newspapers serving the polyglot majority population of the colonial cities were Malay-language publications set up by Eurasians and Europeans in the mid-nineteenth century. The literary standard of printed Malay that began to form the basis of creating a new urbanised ethnie during this period was in Roman script and characterised by straightforward expression, somewhat influenced by Dutch and Chinese (Adam 1995). It became in the 1920s the only serious candidate for the language of anti-colonial nationalism, Dutch and Javanese both having fatal flaws for that role.

The name for this national language and cultural identity was more problematic. Neither *Melayu* nor *Jawa*, the two indigenous labels with claims to both antiquity and comprehensiveness, was ever seriously considered. Both had been clearly established in Dutch and later in educated Indonesian discourse as particular ethnie, separate 'races and tribes', according to the English rendering of the *landaarden* of the colonial census. Until the 1920s the only way to describe the new pan-colony identity was 'Indian' (Dutch *Indier*; Malay *orang Hindia*). The esoteric term 'Indonesia', used in some European linguistic and anthropological circles since the nineteenth century and popularised to some degree in the weighty *Encyclopaedia van Nederlandsch-Indië* (1918) as the term for the Malayo-Polynesian language family, was therefore readily embraced by students in Holland as a new all-encompassing identity. In 1924 they changed the name of their students' association to 'Perhimpunan Indonesia', and its journal to the rousing *Indonesia Merdeka*. Young Minangkabau intellectuals such as Muhammad Yamin and Dr Mohammad Amir, who had championed a unified Sumatran identity with the Malay language as its special glory, quickly became champions of a broader Indonesian identity. Yamin had published a patriotic poem extolling his Sumatran identity in 1920 (*Tanah airku*), but in 1928 he was keynote speaker at the Indonesian Youth Congress, making a strong case that Malay had already become the national language—*Bahasa Indonesia* (Noer 1979: 249–53; Reid 1979a: 286–7). Within four years of being launched in Holland, the concepts of an Indonesian nation and language spread through the political organisations in the colony.

The privileged students at colleges and senior high schools in the main colonial cities, very far removed from their birthplaces and mother tongues, had begun in the 1920s to form youth associations deriving from their ethnie or their islands—Jong Java, Jong Minahassa, Jong Sumatra (primarily Minangkabau, and therefore challenged by Jong Batak). In 1928, guided by the growing enthusiasm for broader solidarities, most of these groups came together for an Indonesian Youth Congress. They subscribed to a stirring oath of imagined unity—'one fatherland, Indonesia; one *bangsa*, *bangsa Indonesia*; one language, *Bahasa Indonesia*'. The larger language groups had already been in process of reimagining themselves as mobilised ethnie—*bangsa Jawa*; *bangsa Bugis*, and so on. But here, earlier than in Malaysia, the social Darwinian idea of competition between races, and the logic of being educated together in Dutch schools, had worked towards a broader definition. Its core was an agreed compromise, a *lingua franca* dissociated from any particular group. There was a core culture, in the sense that Minangkabaus and coastal Sumatrans spoke Malay as mother tongue, and for decades they would dominate the nascent literature in Modern Indonesian. But because Ambonese, Minahasan and Kupang Christians, *peranakan* Chinese, and various other urban minorities had spoken the same language for centuries, it was not perceived as belonging to any ethnie. The nationalists proposed, in effect, the radical and difficult path of building a bounded state without a core ethnie.

The Indonesian federalists of 1946–8, who sought with the poisoned chalice of Dutch help to build space in Indonesia for the autonomy of various ethnies and regions, fought a losing battle against the emotional pull of *bangsa Indonesia*. Several of the federal states, notably the one in East Sumatra that had contained the wealthiest Malay rajas, attempted to build an enthusiasm for *bangsa Melayu* or even for the hybrid *bangsa Sumatra Timur*. But when Sukarno passed through the capital of this doomed state in 1949 he proclaimed to cheering crowds at the airport: 'There is no *bangsa* Kalimantan, there is no *bangsa* Minangkabau, there is no *bangsa* Java, Bali, Lombok, Sulawesi or any such. We are all *bangsa* Indonesia. There is no *bangsa* Sumatera Timur. We are part of a single *bangsa* with a single fate' (cited Omar 1993: 209). The destiny of every ethnie within the former colony was to be no more than a *suku*, a 'tribe' with all its parochial associations.

Indonesia's anti-colonial nationalism, then, has been more territorial than ethnic. To this extent it may seem to have a stronger basis for developing in a civic direction, like some of those in Western Europe and the New World. At moments, in 1945–54 and again in 1998–2000, there did indeed appear to be strong forces trying to push it in that direction. On the positive side the core culture defined by nationalism seemed to be inherently plural in religion, culture and ethnicity, in a way analogous to that of India, if not Western Europe. As one lays out these broad comparative options, however, the need seems inescapable for a third type which we might call revolutionary or post-revolutionary nationalism, inviting comparisons with the Soviet Union, Yugoslavia and China rather than India. Like the revolutions in those systems, Indonesia's revolution of 1945–50 sought to consolidate its national project through a mixture of force, a heroic revolutionary myth which invalidated the distinct pre-revolutionary histories of ethnies and regions, and a heavy central direction of education.

During the Sukarno era when the only acceptable form of identity politics was the revolutionary assertion of a new Indonesian identity, the older idea of 'Malay' as a minor ethnic category within Indonesia (1.6 per cent in the 1930 Netherlands India census) was hard to defend. The hybrid coastal culture had a higher destiny as the new Indonesian identity. Insofar as Malayness was also something more specific, it suffered as the 'feudal' culture of the East Sumatran and West Kalimantan sultanates discredited during the revolution. But a new form of sanitised cultural competition between ethnie emerged in the depoliticised atmosphere favoured by Suharto (as described more fully in chapter 6). Particularly in ethnie-obsessed North Sumatra, everybody needed to find their own ethnie (*suku*) if only to balance the well-formed and assertive Batak ones. As a creole historically open to newcomers, Melayu was initially less hard-edged than its rivals in mobilising for political purposes (van Klinken 2007: 67–8).

Nevertheless, by the 1980s *Melayu* had taken its place as one of the recognised six North Sumatran cultures which had to be displayed on public buildings. The once-discredited Malay royal families were able to lead this return, making use of the importance of the Deli sultan's grandiose Maimun palace for tourism, and of their capacity to gain support for the ruling Golkar party on the basis of traditional hierarchies. An overarching Malay association was founded in 1971, and encouraged the building of a Karo house in the grounds of the Maimun palace in 1974 to ally with the Karo Bataks against the more dangerous and 'alien' Tapanuli Bataks. This was followed by the elaborate commemoration of the founding of Medan, which was somewhat fancifully attributed to a Karo chief who came to the coast in 1590 and converted to Islam, thus becoming the prototype of the polyglot Malay community.

In the ceaseless competition in North Sumatra for appointed office and the patronage that came with it, Mandailing (or Angkola) Batak were generally more successful both at the level of North Sumatra governor and Medan mayor (Pelly 1994: 122–39). In the late 1980s, however, the Malay lobby captured the mayor's position through Bachtiar Djafar, and in 1998 the governor's position through Major-General Tengku Rizal Nurdin (the 'Tengku' reflecting his aristocratic Malay status). With these victories Malay culture was re-established, for the first time since the Revolution, as the predominate ethnic marker of Medan, though self-defining 'Malays' are less than 10 per cent of its population. This was symbolised through an annual Malay Cultural Fair (*Pekan Kebudayaan Melayu*) on the Central Square, and in the 1990s by imposing on public buildings in the city a symbolic feature deemed to be Malay, in recognition that this was the original culture of the Medan area. This is represented by the yellow fascia found around the Maimun palace, in turn built by Dutch engineers in the 1890s to reflect what they saw as local and Moorish elements.

Melayu as ideology

Since Brunei's declaration of independence in 1984 as 'forever a Malay Islamic monarchy', Malayness has been a more prominent feature of that country than is true for either of its neighbours, despite appearing to have relatively shallow roots there. In the literature of the sixteenth century, Brunei people were described by their place of origin or as

Luzons, because of their reputed closeness to the people with whom they traded in Manila Bay. With Islam, Brunei undoubtedly became part of the high culture of Malay letters, though not playing as large a part in it as Aceh, Palembang, Johor, Patani or Makassar. Although the tradition of Brunei rulers includes early contact with Johor, sometimes involving marriage to a Johor princess, Brunei did not seek to play a role in the conflicts among rulers who claimed descent from Melaka. Brunei seemed distinctive enough, through its pluralistic Borneo populations, its unique and in some respects archaic form of spoken Malay, and its links with China and the Philippines as well as the Malay world, to be the centre of its own world.

It is not clear when the Islamic elite of Brunei began to see themselves as 'Melayu', but the nineteenth century European fashion of classifying peoples by race or nation rather than place seems likely to have had something to do with it. English writers such as Hugh Low, Henry Keppel and James Brooke use the phrase 'Brunei Malays', to distinguish the Muslim population of the capital and the court from other peoples of the interior. Once the British Residency was established in 1906, British habits of counting and classifying enjoyed greater influence. 'Malays' were counted as 54 per cent of the population at the 1921 census, 49 per cent in 1931, 41 per cent in 1947, 54 per cent in 1960 and 66 per cent in 1971 (Brunei Census 1971: 82). The reasons for this variation were in part the rapid rise in the Chinese population by immigration in the period 1921–60, and some immigration of Malay population thereafter. The biggest factor, however, seems to have been changes in classification.

While the early censuses under British control found ever more ethnic groups distinct from Malays in the strict sense, the 1959 Constitution that returned self-government to the sultan insisted that the major groups held to be indigenous (Malay, Kedayan, Bisayah, Dusun and so on) were all 'Malay' in a legal sense. Subsequent censuses took this declaration literally. The report of the 1971 census appears to have had different authors for its English and Malay sections, at least as regards ethnic divisions. In English the report states that the Malay group in the census 'consisted of the Malays, Kedayans, Bisayah, Dusuns and Muruts. Also included were those who called themselves orang Brunei, Belait, Tutong.' It goes on to explain that this was 'to standardise the term "Malay" as applied here with the term "of the Malay race" as applied in the Brunei nationality Enactment 1961'. The former ease of classifying people according to their place of origin, the English report noted, had tended to break down with urbanisation, population movement and intermarriage, so that 'there are now little differences between the various groups' (Brunei Census 1971: 34). The Malay text, while briefer on these matters, added that:

Melayu means the grouping of indigenous groups of the Melayu race. It contains Malays, Bruneis, Totong, Belait, Kedayan, Dusun, Bisayah and Murut. This division of communities is to avoid the mistakes found in the 1960 census, since many indigenous communities acknowledged themselves Malay because they follow the Islamic religion. (Brunei Census 1971: 5)

A *titah* (order) of the king in 1984 already referred to the concept of *Melayu Islam Beraja* (MIB: Malay, Muslim, Monarchy), and it has been particularly emphasised since 1990. In that year the Academy of Brunei Studies was established at the University, and undertook responsibility for teaching the obligatory undergraduate course in MIB. MIB has subsequently been repeatedly enunciated as part of the official philosophy of the state, around which a national identity in the fashion of Anderson's 'official nationalism' might be built.

Of the three elements in this trinity, 'Melayu' is the most interesting, since it emphasises not Brunei's national uniqueness or its Bornean heritage, but its membership in a supranational culture whose centre might appear to be elsewhere. In practice the limited formulations of Malayness suggest that it is seen as consolidating existing traditions rather than seeking some external standard. 'Melayu in MIB means the consolidation of inherited Malay values, customs and culture as the dominant cultural heritage in national culture' (Umar 1992: 10). It does, however, establish as normative a standard Malay language essentially the same as that in Malaysia, and some aspects of Malay high culture at the expense of local tradition. More notably it seeks either to marginalise or incorporate minorities. 'Clearly, this state is not a multi-racial or multi-religious state. This fact does not arise from any spirit of anti-non-Malay or anti-non-Muslim, but what has to be stressed is that this state is the property of Malay Muslims' (Hamid 1992: 27).

Brunei's experiment with Malayness as a core identity is the youngest of the three examples discussed, and it is much too early to assess what effects this move may have on popular consciousness and the sense of identity in the state in the long term. Despite some of the rhetoric of its apologists, MIB seems not intended as the basis of a future ethnic nationalism. It is not sufficiently distinctive from its neighbours for that purpose. As long as the monarchy remains the central political fact of Brunei, nationalism of any but a contrived 'official' sort will be viewed with suspicion.

In conclusion, it needs to be remembered that Melayu has been a wonderfully absorptive form of creole, welcoming maritime migrants and uplanders to enter together a commercial, coastal ecumene. As it became firmly identified as an Islamic identity, however, it also developed a sharper edge towards what it was not: not the highland pig-eaters, not the clannish Chinese, not the arrogant Europeans. When this pan-Archipelago Malay-speaking community acquired a secular name for itself as Indonesian, it was embraced enthusiastically by modern-minded urban-dwellers. In the 2000 census that measured ethnicity for the first time since 1930, 'Indonesian' was not allowed as an option though it would certainly have been popular among urbanites of mixed parentage. Instead, many such people declared themselves 'Malay', or the closely related 'Betawi', the two most inclusive creoles which thereby increased fastest since 1930 (Suryadinata et al, 2003: 12). In Sabah, where it also carried political advantages, the Malay percentage increased five-fold between 1920 and 2000.

The negatives of the Malay category became particularly important in the protective colonial environment of Malaya, however. There British influence ensured Melayu would be turned into race despite its quite contrary origins, and would become the base of a defensive type of ethnie nationalism.

5   Aceh: memories of monarchy

In chapter 1, I argued that most pre-colonial Southeast Asian societies were relatively state-averse. The identities which gave human societies a sense of belonging were shaped by forces other than those of the bureaucratic state. Kinship networks, market cycles, water-sharing for irrigation systems, sacred sites, religious rituals and popular performance helped to shape coherences which in most cases were more enduring and concrete than the states which competed over them. Before the nineteenth century, most of the Indonesian Archipelago's populations were in uplands away from the dangerous coast, and its states were not theirs; they were coast entrepots dependent on international commerce and ideas (Reid 1997: 67–77). Sriwijaya, Majapahit, Melaka and the Batavia-based Dutch Company (VOC) all developed some economic power and political charisma from their role as mediators of international commerce to populated interior regions. But they did not 'rule' those hinterlands in a sense which could create permanent identities in their subjects. Their legacies were a charisma to which various subsequent dynasties laid claim, not the shaping of a single self-conscious ethnie-state.

Within this pattern, however, Burma and to a lesser extent Siam went some way down a path of equating ethnic identity with the state. In Southeast Asia's 'age of commerce', a few Archipelago port-states also developed enough internal power as novel 'gunpowder empires' to give rise to new ethnies. Makassar, Banten and Aceh at their seventeenth century apogee were strong enough to develop some state nationalism based on military mobilisation, dynastic pride and Islam, though with necessarily shallow historical roots (Reid 1988–93, II: 212–13). The Makassar, Banten and Aceh identities and languages of today are descended from that heritage of the age of commerce. However the Dutch conquest of Makassar in 1669 and Banten in 1684 transformed these monarchies into unhappy client states, only one among several local dynasties and other sources of political community. The identity itself seemed often in danger of absorption by larger neighbours, Bugis, Javanese or Sundanese.

The Aceh sultanate remained, however, a focal point for pride and identity until 1874. In this sense it entered the category of 'stable maritime consolidation' which Lieberman (2003) devised to describe the Siamese state by the early nineteenth century. The only power to exceed it in this direction in the Archipelago was the Dutch East India Company in Batavia, which metamorphosed into the Netherlands Indian State after 1815. It was that maritime consolidation which introduced the concept of a modern sovereign state to most Indonesians. Aceh, however, resembled the Mainland monarchies in continuing into the modern era of competitive consolidation an intact sovereignty from the age of commerce. Despite the frequency of its succession disputes and the weakness of its bureaucratic capability, Aceh had, in fact, greater continuity of untrammelled sovereign rule from a single city than any Southeast Asian capital except Hanoi.

Aceh's monarchy as resistance

The most reliable of Acehnese chronicles begins abruptly: 'The first to rule the kingdom of Aceh Darus-Salam was Sultan Ali Mughayat Syah [d.1529].' (Raniri 1966: 31). The no-nonsense Islamic purist who penned these words obviously had little time for legends of descent from Alexander the Great, miraculous divine intervention, or links with the Chinese emperor, such as appear in other chronicles. In fact there are a few older apparently royal Islamic graves in the area of Banda Aceh, a long-standing trade centre of Lamri only 50 km to its east, and a Malay chronicle tradition tracing the origin of the Aceh dynasty to Champa, conquered by Dai Viet in 1471. But Raniri correctly identified the conquests of Ali Mughayat in the 1520s as the origin of a self-consciously Muslim sultanate uniting the whole of the north coast of Sumatra in opposition to Portuguese intervention.

When Marco Polo (1292), Ibn Battuta (1353) and the earliest Portuguese (from 1509) reported on this coast, it had been divided into a number of competitive port-states each speaking its own language, the most important in general being Pasai and Pidië. Ali Mughayat Syah profited from widespread outrage at Portuguese intrusion, naturally led by the Muslim merchants who had been its target, to establish Islam as a common bond which united rulers and merchants against both foreign Christians and interior animists. For the remainder of the sixteenth century the Portuguese were forced to look for pepper elsewhere as the Acehnese remained their most implacable opponents. The Portuguese were usually on the defensive, having to withstand ten Acehnese attempts to eject them from their major stronghold of Melaka between

1537 and 1629. The character of these assaults as *jihad* (holy war) was well attested by both Portuguese and Malay sources. It carried over into numerous battles with the interior peoples of Sumatra, who in defence saw their identity involved in resisting Islam and defending their forms of spirit worship touched by Hindu-Buddhist ideas.

Aceh became at this time the eastern pillar of the global Sunni Muslim struggle led by Ottoman Turkey. In the 1530s, and twice in the 1560s, the Ottomans sent military assistance to help Aceh against the infidel Portuguese. A 1568 decree of the Ottoman Sultan Selim II explained that he was sending help because: 'The Sultan of Aceh says that he is left alone to face the unbelievers. They have seized some islands, and taken Muslims captive. Merchant and pilgrim ships going from these islands towards Mecca were captured one night [by the Portuguese] and the ships that were not captured were fired upon and sunk, causing many Muslims to drown.' (cited Reid 1988–93, II: 147).

International connections

This Turkish connection ensured that Aceh would see itself differently placed from the sultanates positioned around the Java Sea. States like Palembang and Banjarmasin were always involved with coastal Javanese politics, and acknowledged the appeal of Javanese culture even when they were in conflict with specific Javanese states. For them, interactions with the Dutch successors to Javanese maritime power were inescapable. By contrast, Aceh never had significant contact with Java, but much with the Malay states of the Peninsula and Sumatra, where it loomed as the major power until the mid-seventeenth century, and with the Middle East, South India and the countries around the Bay of Bengal.[1] Because of its trade connections, it had more South Indian and Arab elements in its population, and in court roles including the royal dynasty itself, than did other Indonesian peoples.

In the sixteenth century this openness was demonstrated not only by the Turkish connection but by the number of Arab and Gujarati scholars making Aceh their home. In the first half of the seventeenth century when we have the first English and Dutch reports, Aceh emerges as a major port of the Bay of Bengal, with traders from the Red Sea and Pegu

---

[1] This contrasts with the older north Sumatran Sultanate of Pasai, conquered by a Majapahit fleet in the 1350s, the maximum demonstration of Java's maritime power. This is celebrated in the Pasai chronicle apparently written in Java (Hill 1961: 93–101), but not noticed in the Aceh chronicles, which pay little attention to Java or indeed to Pasai.

(lower Burma), and ambassadors from Siam as well as the European courts adding to its cosmopolitanism. From the mid-seventeenth to the mid-nineteenth centuries it was both an independent refuge for private traders of all kinds against the demands of the monopoly-inclined European companies, and a factor in Anglo–French rivalry in the Indian Ocean (Reid 2005, ch. 3).

From an Acehnese point of view, Turkey was the most important of these relationships. Although the diplomatic and commercial link was broken when the Dutch and English Companies reoriented the spice and pepper trade to the sea route around Africa, popular legends kept the idea alive that Aceh had a particular relationship with the caliphate in Istanbul. The embodiments of this memory were the Turkish flag, adopted for use on Acehnese vessels, and some enormous Turkish cannons, the largest of which was named 'a single measure of pepper' (*lada secupak*) to reflect a legend that this was all that was left of several shiploads of pepper sent to Istanbul to persuade the Caliph to extend military support to Aceh. In the period 1840–74, as the Dutch advanced menacingly along both coasts of Sumatra, this link was reinvented on both sides as a 'protectorate' by Turkey over Aceh which should exclude the claims of any other European power.

While the sixteenth century had presented Aceh with a bi-polar choice between the Muslim network and the Portuguese, the seventeenth opened with a plethora of choice. The Dutch, English and French all ensured that their first ships into the Indian Ocean, in the period 1598–1604, would call at Aceh as the major source of pepper and spices free of Portuguese influence. The first Dutch fleet, from Zeeland, quarrelled badly with the Acehnese sultan perhaps because local opponents successfully portrayed them as republicans. The second compensated by bringing an impressive letter from Prince William, and taking back to the Netherlands an Acehnese embassy to him (1602). For the English, James Lancaster carried a personal letter from Queen Elizabeth to the Sultan, although she had died before the ships arrived in 1602. This cordial exchange, and another in 1612, enabled later English supporters of Aceh's independence to claim that Aceh was Britain's oldest ally in Asia. The French, finally, arrived in 1604, and the best account of seventeenth century Aceh is that of the French admiral, Beaulieu, who was in the city trying to buy pepper for several months of 1621 (Beaulieu 1666).

Aceh was not ultimately very attractive to the European powers. They were troubled by the fixed antipathy of successive seventeenth century rulers towards allowing any wealthy merchants, domestic or foreign, to build defensible stone structures, 'lest they fortify themselves against him' (Martin 1604: 39). In addition, Sultan Iskandar Muda (r. 1607–36), the most powerful and absolutist of Aceh's kings, was a monopolist as effective as the European companies themselves, seeking to control as much as possible of Aceh's pepper and to enforce its sale at inflated prices. The Dutch and British Companies preferred to establish their bases in Batavia (1619) and Bengkulu (Bencoolen, 1688) respectively, where they could fortify themselves on a permanent basis.

Aceh paid a price in discouraging the major pepper-buyers, but in the long term this stern policy ensured that it retained its independence. Even when mercantile interests were better protected under the more consensual regime of four successive queens (1641–99), and well into the eighteenth century, there were periodic rebellions against monarchs who seemed too ready to allow concessions to foreigners. Sultan Mahmud Syah (r. 1760–81) was one such, who allowed the English East India Company to set up a factory in Aceh in 1772, only to have the territorial aristocracy (*ulèëbalang*) threaten to overthrow him if the permission were not withdrawn (Lee 1995: 52–6). In the eighteenth century both the French and English repeatedly considered the advantages of Aceh's untrammelled independence and extremely strategic location, but concluded that the military cost would be far too high. The English Company opted instead for Penang in 1786 because: 'To form a settlement there [Aceh] of safety and advantage, a force sufficient to subdue all the chiefs would be necessary' (Francis Light, cited Lee 1995: 80). This type of popular hostility to foreign influence over a weak but symbolically central state was an important factor in many Asian nationalisms—the outrage at state humiliation (OSH) nationalism explicated in chapter 1. Aceh was frequently affected by it in an Islamic idiom.

In the 1660s the Dutch Company had prized away Aceh's most lucrative dependencies, tin-rich Perak on the Peninsula and the pepper-growing centres of the Sumatran west coast. Aceh's remaining exports, betelnut, gold, benzoin and such tin and pepper as continued to reach Aceh to avoid Dutch control, were primarily of interest to Indian (notably Tamil Muslim *Chulia* merchants) and India-based European country traders. At the end of the eighteenth century, however, pepper cultivation boomed in the northerly part of the west coast still within Aceh's domain. This brought the long-distance traders back in greater numbers than ever, with the New England traders of Salem and Boston alone sending twenty vessels a year in the best seasons. Until the 1840s the pattern was a free-wheeling one, with American, French and British shippers dealing directly with the *ulèëbalang* who controlled the small pepper-exporting ports, and the sultan getting what small share he could from the profits through a tribute the *ulèëbalang* were expected to pay.

Periodically violence erupted between buyers and sellers of the pepper. Three times naval warships were called to 'punish' the alleged Acehnese offenders. The Americans burned a coastal village in 1826 and again in 1838, without any official contact with the sultanate. When a French gunboat followed suit in 1839, however, it led to a short-lived interest in Paris for establishing its needed Asian base in Sumatra. The energetic Sultan Ibrahim Mansur Shah (r. 1838–70) pursued such an alliance in the 1840s, as a potential buffer against the advancing Dutch. Louis-Philippe sent an impressive letter to him in 1843, and in response Ibrahim despatched an envoy in 1849 with letters for both Paris and Istanbul. The French had, however, already decided that they should not risk offending their Dutch allies, and shifted their attention to Indo-China. An Acehnese envoy was received by Louis Napoleon in October 1852, but both sides had by then decided that the relationship would not bear substantial fruit. The leader of the Acehnese delegation had, in fact, sent his deputy from Cairo to Paris, while himself taking up the more exciting option of Turkey (Reid 2005: 164–75).

This Ottoman connection had been kept alive by the pilgrimages of wealthy Acehnese to Mecca and by the largest settlement of Arab migrants in Southeast Asia, many of them influential sayyids from Hadhramaut. It was revived in the age of steam and telegraph in the chimerical hope that it might prove effective in holding off the Dutch challenge. The envoy of 1849–50 received a warm response which officially confirmed Turkey's suzerainty and protection over Aceh and Sultan Ibrahim as legitimate ruler. When the Crimean War broke out Ibrahim sent 10,000 Spanish dollars as a contribution to Turkish expenses, and received in return the highest Ottoman honour, the Mejidie. In 1868, and more desperately after the Dutch attack in 1873, there were further appeals for Turkish protection. However, no more than France was Turkey willing to disturb its crucial alliances on behalf of a far-off 'vassal'. The Turkish government offered its mediation between Aceh and the Netherlands in the light of its historic linkage, but only in a diplomatic form that could be brushed aside in The Hague (Reid 1969a: 119–29; Reid 2004: 236–8).

If Aceh was to be another Siam, it could only be by bringing Britain into play as the factor to balance Dutch aggression. But there were several reasons why Britain was not willing to stand up to Holland, as it did to France in Bangkok, in order to preserve Aceh's independence. Firstly, Holland was seen less as a competitor than a client of Britain, and therefore the safest candidate to occupy uncolonised territories of potential strategic value. Secondly, the sultans had been less able than the Thai kings to monopolise relations between their subjects and the outside world, as there were too many Acehnese river-ports accessible to foreign commerce, and too many foreign traders interested in maintaining that openness. British interests, including those of the Penang and Singapore merchants involved in the pepper and betelnut trade, were not generally identified with bolstering a strong sultanate against its subjects, in contrast with policy towards Siam. Finally, credit must be given to the strategic skill of kings Mongkut and Chulalongkorn in Bangkok, in consulting the British and other powers about which Europeans to take on as modernising advisors. Aceh's capital was as cosmopolitan as Siam's before 1850, with Asia-based Europeans, Arabs and Tamil Muslims taking the place of Chinese in Siam. But Acehnese rulers always had to deal with Islamic and anti-foreign sentiment among their subjects, the kind of nationalism I have categorised as anti-foreign outrage. In the crucial 1860s and 1870s, this factor forced the sultans to pursue the chimerical Turkish hope more actively than the conceivable but frequently abrasive British one. Combined with the difficulty of controlling its subjects, this gave Aceh an unruly and even 'piratic' image in the European capitals.

The most important dissenter from the dominant British policy line on Aceh was Stamford Raffles, who tended to envision the long-term role of Britain as a kind of protector of Malay monarchy against what he saw as the corrosive effects of Dutch monopoly. In 1810, he had already advocated a British treaty with Aceh to 'preserve the tranquillity of the country, prevent it from becoming a nest of pirates and cut off a vast source of illicit trade' (cited Lee 2006: 79). In 1819, he achieved this goal by signing an Anglo-Aceh Treaty with the contender he considered more legitimate in an Aceh civil war, in which most Penang merchants had supported the other candidate. This spelled out a defensive alliance and the terms for a British agent in Banda Aceh, but the agent was never appointed and the Penang government did not follow through. Only five years later, Britain signed the contradictory London Treaty of 1824, assigning Sumatra as a whole to a Dutch sphere. In a confidential exchange of notes with the treaty, the British promised to 'modify' their treaty with Aceh accordingly, and expressed the confidence that the Dutch would take 'no measures hostile to the King of Acheen'. The Dutch in turn undertook to ensure that Aceh, 'without losing anything of its independence', would accept 'moderate . . . European influence' in the interests of commerce (Reid 1969a: 12).

Since the British never fulfilled their part of this arrangement, and the Dutch were busy elsewhere until the 1860s, Aceh remained unaware of its changed status in European eyes. Its anxiety about Dutch ambitions began when the Dutch occupied the west coast border area of Singkil and Barus in 1839–40, and intensified when Dutch control on the east coast extended up to previously Acehnese-claimed Langkat and Tamiang in 1862. This was the period Aceh attempted to pressure Turkey to make good its 'protection', and to interest France, Britain, Italy or the United States in a treaty that would exchange some contested border area for protection. In 1862 Sultan Ibrahim evidently despatched the Italian adventurer Cesar Moreno, later prime minister of Hawai'i, with instructions to interest a European power in such a treaty, which he subsequently attempted in vain in Rome and Washington. In 1868 an influential Arab-led faction, but apparently not the failing sultan himself, sent an envoy to Istanbul to ask the Ottoman Sultan 'to inform all foreign peoples that we are under the protection of and subjects of the Sublime Porte, so that henceforth no other Government will be permitted to interfere in our affairs' (translated in Reid 1969b: 76).

When Sultan Ibrahim died in 1870, the sixteen-year-old nephew who succeeded him as Sultan Mahmud Shah (r. 1870–4) was less able to control the fissures that emerged in dealing with the Dutch threat. Different figures were associated with overtures to Turkey, with everyday trading relations with British and Chinese in the Straits Settlements, with the speculative international quest for allies, in particular the United States, and with holding off the Dutch through negotiation. These differences became crucial once Britain released Holland from any constraint in attacking Aceh through the 1871 Sumatra Treaty. The ambiguities between them were used by the more jingoistic Dutch party as a pretext for invasion in 1873 (Reid 1969a: 79–97). Despite them, however, the traditional sentiment of resisting foreign control held remarkably consistent through sultan, courtiers, ulama and *ulèëbalang*.

Unity behind this banner was facilitated by the unusual ineptitude of the ill-prepared Dutch attack in 1873, its defeat, Holland's subsequent need to 'avenge its honour' rather than compromise and its abolition of the sultanate when Mahmud died in 1874. In contrast to other Archipelago situations facing Dutch advance, however, there was already a widespread anti-foreign OSH sentiment. This type of nationalism was directly connected with the perceived status and independence of the Aceh monarchy, but it was also bolstered by the way Islam had been used over the centuries to buttress Aceh's wars, and by historical memories of resisting European threats in particular. It should be sharply distinguished from the sentiments surrounding Malay monarchy discussed in chapter 3, which valued the supernatural charisma of legitimate dynasties yet was historically adapted to sharing power with a variety of outsiders.

The resistance motif of 1873–1945

Aceh had only a few days' notice of the first Dutch attack in March 1873, yet was able to gather about 3,000 armed defenders of the royal complex and fortified mosque. After the unexpected Dutch defeat, the Acehnese had time to mobilise to confront the 8,500-strong second Dutch expedition in December 1873. Several influential *ulëëbalang* from the Pidië region brought up to 500 fighters each to the capital, while half the population of some pepper-growing regions on the west coast reportedly departed for the impending war. Dutch intelligence placed the expected number of defenders of the central symbolic points at anywhere between 10,000 and 100,000 (Reid 1969a: 97, 109).

The Dutch nevertheless took the mosque and citadel in a six-week campaign. They dug in defensively, in the hope that the Acehnese would submit without adding greatly to Dutch losses from war and disease, which nevertheless mounted to 1,470 by April, 2,373 by the end of 1874 and 5,374 by the end of 1876. But the fears of earlier potential imperialists proved correct, and Aceh had in effect to be conquered piece by piece. The death of the young Sultan Mahmud from cholera made a negotiated peace still more difficult. Resistance to the Dutch became the touchstone for leadership. Even such an effective unifier of the resistance as the talented Arab Habib Abdur-rahman az-Zahir lost credibility as soon as he tried to negotiate an honourable peace (1878). What the Dutch called a 'war party' was constituted around a provisional capital at Keumala in the hills behind Pidië. During the substantial periods when the Dutch adopted a defensive posture to limit casualties, they found themselves effectively under siege. When they went on attack Acehnese forces withdrew beyond their reach in one of the first demonstrations of successful guerrilla strategy (Reid 1969a: 180–217, 296).

Although a ten-year-old prince was proclaimed the new Sultan as Mohammad Daud (1874–1903), he could only add some charisma to the war party. Spiritual leadership of the resistance passed increasingly to the most intransigent *ulama*, for whom the idiom of Islamic martyrdom was the ingredient needed to inspire courage in the face of overwhelming odds. The most prominent of these *ulama*, Teungku Syech Saman di Tiro, wrote to his less heroic fellow-countrymen in 1885:

Do not let yourself be afraid of the strength of the unbelievers, their fine possessions, their equipment, and their good soldiers ... for no-one is strong, no-one is rich, and no-one has fine armies than the great God (be he exalted) ... and no-one gives victory or defeat but God (be he praised and exalted), the Lord of the Universe. (reproduced Zentgraaff 1938: 17)

Despite these heroics, the relentless Dutch policy of pursuit and destruction of Acehnese warriors throughout the country, adopted in 1898, convinced the majority of *ulèëbalang* over the next five years that there was no point in continuing the battle. By 1903, when the sultan submitted and abdicated his throne, there was a stable administration resting on cooperating *ulèëbalang*. Nevertheless many *ulama* continued to exhort resistance, and the highlands remained unpacified. Only after a further 14,000 Acehnese and Gayo were killed in their upland redoubts, including all seven sons of the resistance leader Teungku di Tiro, could the war be considered over in 1914.

Submission to superior force was not acceptance. The new generation born during the war saw themselves as a conquered people, their humiliation accentuated by the hated forced labour they were obliged to give to the conqueror for twenty-four days every year. Some thousands migrated to the British domain on the Peninsula. A few *muslimin*, as the guerrillas were called, continued to hold out in the hills to the end of the Dutch administration. Their numbers were fed by revolts every few years, the last in 1937. The west coast was particularly disturbed during the 1920s when communist agitation reignited the hopes of a general uprising. Hundreds were killed, and hundreds more arrested after taking part in sacred oaths to resist. In addition, several Acehnese every year sought release from their humiliation by launching themselves in frenzied individual attacks on a Dutchman.

The *ulèëbalang* were the bedrock the Dutch regime needed to build a more normal colonial society, and in consequence they were permitted more autonomy than rulers elsewhere. Yet even here the Dutch trod with immense care, liable to attack both from the older-style rulers jealous of their privileges (like one who publicly murdered the Dutch official who crossed him in 1913), and from the young Dutch-educated cohort from whom they hoped the most. The latter were the first to perceive Indonesia-wide political movements, notably Sarekat Islam in the period 1916–22 and the Muslim reformist Muhammadiah from 1928, as a means to restore Acehnese pride (Reid 1979a: 15–21). Such national organisations, however, were patronised in Aceh almost exclusively by non-Acehnese residents and a sprinkling of these westernised *ulèëbalang*. Most Acehnese grew more distant from their *ulèëbalang* precisely because of the latter's Dutch education and Java connections.

The education offered by the colonial government to Acehnese commoners provided basic literacy in romanised Malay. It was at first deeply resented as another imposition of the infidel conqueror, and parents preferred to send their children to the *ulama* to study the Quran and imbibe 'hatred and scorn for the kafir' as one Dutch governor put it

(Swart, cited Reid 1979a: 21). From the 1920s, however, the more popular Islamic stream began to borrow some of the modern methods of the government schools. It was the young products of these reformist Muslim schools who in the 1930s finally caught the enthusiasm for progress that had infected other young Indonesians two decades earlier.

The embodiment of this new surge of hope was a purely Acehnese organisation of the reformist schools and their *ulama*, established in 1939 with the acronym PUSA (Persatuan Ulama Seluruh Aceh). Its chairman was a charismatic younger *ulama*, Teungku Daud Beureu'eh (1899–1987), who had founded a modern-style school in Pidië despite having all his education in traditional Acehnese religious schools. This organisation offered young Acehnese for the first time the heady experience of an empowering modern organisation, strong enough to generate its own modern-style teacher's college and monthly *Penjoeloeh* ('Torch'). This journal was able to claim in 1941 that PUSA represented 'the voice of the Acehnese people'—a novel concept influenced by Indonesian nationalism but consciously distinct from it.[2]

Although such an instrument would have appalled their predecessors, Dutch officials in 1939 were indulgent towards PUSA precisely because it was not part of the national Indonesian movement that was then their primary concern. They were also prepared to allow it to be used as a counter to the often arbitrary powers of the *ulèëbalang*. Its journal and its rallies quickly did become avenues for criticism of the more authoritarian *ulèëbalang*, who responded vigorously by using Muhammadiah to attack it (Reid 1979a: 25–31).

The final Acehnese revolt against the Dutch, and the most successful, was largely the work of PUSA. The Japanese occupied Penang and northern Malaya in mid-December 1941, but it was another three months before they invaded northern Sumatra. A PUSA activist and *ulama*, Said Abu Bakar, surprised the Japanese fifth-column specialist, Col. Iwaichi Fujiwara, by seeking him out to offer active support with no particular *quid pro quo*. He told Fujiwara, 'the people of Aceh were extremely hostile to the Dutch Government, but also to the *ulèëbalang* because they also oppress the people, even more than the Dutch ... They are not afraid to die in the name of Islam' (Fujiwara 1966: 200–1).

Fujiwara sent him back with a number of other young Sumatrans he rounded up in Malaya, but no physical support at all. He had expected at best some sabotage in Japan's favour. But despite the changes of the 1930s, Aceh proved as ready as ever to revolt. After an initial uprising

---

[2] Tiro Tjoet, in *Penjoeloeh* 5/6 (March/April 1941). It is possible that this pseudonym, 'little Tiro', represents the then teenager who would later call himself Hasan Tiro (see below).

that killed Dutch officials in the Seulimeum area on 23 February 1942, a concerted movement of sabotage and disruption began on 7 March, five days before the Japanese arrival. Facing hostility even from those they had most trusted, the Dutch decided to withdraw three days later, leaving Acehnese to receive the Japanese on their own.

Since no demands for independence were made of the Japanese, it is difficult to classify the motives for this revolt as nationalism, either of an Acehnese or Indonesian sort. The strongest demands by Said Abu Bakar were for freedom from forced labour and tax, and punishment of the *ulèëbalang* to whom PUSA was most opposed. The anti-foreign and Islamic sentiments were still the most widespread, galvanised by modern mobilisation through PUSA, as well as anti-imperial nationalist ideas among the influential *ulèëbalang* who took part.

The new Japanese rulers of Indonesia quickly learned the same bitter lessons as the Dutch about the Acehnese resistance theme. A young but traditional *ulama* not linked to PUSA began denouncing that organisation for having 'driven out the dogs and brought in the pigs'. Despite numerous mediations to try to persuade him to resist, he prepared his students for death through meditation and recitation (*ratib*). In November 1942, he and over a hundred followers were massacred by Japanese troops, though not before killing eighteen Japanese with their knives and spears. Another generation of martyrs had arisen (Reid 1979a: 112–13).

Aceh within Indonesia

Aceh at the Japanese surrender in August 1945 was a very different place than it had been in 1942. Both Dutch and Japanese assumed that its notorious anti-foreign attitude would prevent the Dutch from regaining their colonial position there. Aceh for this reason was the only region Dutch and Allied troops never seriously attempted to control during the conflict of 1945–50. Some Dutch officials hoped it would fall out with Java quickly enough to enter Dutch federal plans voluntarily—though that was not to be. For their part recalcitrant Japanese soldiers saw Aceh as the safest bastion to continue the war against the Western Allies, since Acehnese had proved their willingness to pay a very high price for independence. Japanese defections to the Indonesian side were particularly numerous there, including 150 Japanese military personnel in Singapore who took two ships to Aceh three days after the surrender in an attempt to continue the war (Reid 1979a: 185–6).

Yet Acehnese themselves appeared stunned by the Japanese occupation and its sudden ending. Japanese mobilisation of both Islamic and *ulèëbalang* elites had been so intense, and the mutual fears of the two groups so profound, that their first thoughts were about how this new turnaround would affect that balance. In the event it was the youth trained or mobilised under Japanese auspices who took the initiative in continuing the Indonesia-wide independence preparations begun under the Japanese military at the end of the war. They brought the PUSA leadership and other influential *ulama* onto this side, convincing them that defending the new Indonesian Republic could be considered a continuation of the historic struggle of Aceh for its independence and dignity. These were precisely the terms of a declaration conceived by youth but endorsed by four of Aceh's leading *ulama*, two PUSA and two traditionalist, on 15 October 1945:

> Every segment of the population has united in obedience, to stand behind the great leader Ir Soekarno, to await whatever commands or obligations are put before them. It is our firm conviction that this struggle is a sacred struggle which is called a HOLY WAR (*Perang Sabil*). Believe therefore, fellow-countrymen, that this struggle is like a continuation of the former struggle in Aceh which was led by the late Teungku Cik di Tiro and other national heroes.[3]

The most prominent *ulèëbalang*, who had been promoted to the leading government positions successively by Dutch, Japanese and Republican regimes, were rightly wary of this alliance between mobilised youth and the more militant *ulama*. Stirred by a curious mixture of *jihad*, Marxism and nationalism, this alliance in December 1945 destroyed the forces of the most militant *ulèëbalang* in the polarised Pidië area, who had unwisely opposed the Indonesian Republic and made contact with the Dutch. Thereafter they killed or imprisoned all the established *ulèëbalang* throughout Aceh, including those who formally represented Indonesian Republic authority. PUSA thereby became the strongest political force in Aceh, able to ensure an effective and, by the standards of the revolution, unusually stable government in Aceh throughout the struggle which ended with Holland's transfer of sovereignty to Indonesia in December 1949 (Reid 1979a: 185–217).

The possible independence of Aceh was not publicly mentioned in 1945, any more than in the rebellion of 1942. Supporting the Indonesian Republic had appeared the heaven-sent channel to achieve the goals of the *ulama*-led populism of PUSA, to be rid of outside rule, both Dutch

---

[3] 'Makloemat Oelama Seloeroeh Atjeh', 15 October 1945, in *Semangat Merdeka*, 29 November 1945. Capitals in original. The controversial character of the statement for the Dutch-educated *ulèëbalang* officials is suggested by the six-week delay before publication. The newspaper publication noted that it was 'approved' by Tuanku Mahmud, a descendant of the sultans who had distanced himself from *ulèëbalang* interests, but only 'seen' by the most senior Republican official and *ulèëbalang* in Aceh, Teuku Njak Arif.

and Japanese, at the same time as destroying their *ulèëbalang* rivals. Since the Republican government was on the military defensive in its Java heartland, conceding all its cities to Dutch occupation by late 1948, it desperately needed Aceh's support. Far from determining policy for Aceh, it had to accept the 'social revolution' of which its agents were the victims. Hatta had also wisely chosen as Medan-based governor of Republican Sumatra a lawyer whose main qualification was that he was Acehnese. The most powerful figure in Aceh was in reality the popular Daud Beureu'eh, which was acknowledged by the Republic in giving him exceptional powers as military governor of Aceh in 1947. The role of the central Republican government for Aceh was to legitimate the Acehnese upheaval and to provide appealing words of defiance of the Dutch and support from the world, faithfully reported in Aceh.

The most persuasive articulation of this identification between Aceh's historic struggle and the new Indonesian Republic paradoxically came from Hasan Mohammad Tiro, later prophet of Aceh independence. Born in Lammeulo, Pidië, in 1925, Hasan was a great grandson through his mother of Teungku (Tgk) Syeh Saman di Tiro.[4] He was educated in one of Tgk Daud Beureu'eh's Islamic schools and in the PUSA-created teacher's college at Bireuen. He later claimed to have been very impressed as a schoolboy by an old man seeking him out to tell him 'never to forget your heritage, and to prepare yourself to lead our people and our country to greatness again, like your ancestors' (Tiro 1981: 1). He was certainly unusually conscious as a young man of the Tiro heritage of Acehnese resistance and the need to link it to current issues. The late Isa Sulaiman (pers.comm.) believed his hand was evident in the 15 October declaration above, and other statements connecting the Republican struggle with that of Tgk Chik di Tiro.

Hasan became chairman of the youth movement in Lammeulo at the moment it was preparing for a showdown with the militant *ulama* there. Later he wrote the Acehnese official account of that struggle to inform the Republican authorities as to its legitimacy (Sulaiman 2006: 143–53). He was one of the first young Acehnese to journey to the Republican capital at Yogyakarta to continue his studies at the newly-formed Islamic University. There he wrote his first historical work, dedicated to spelling out the notion that 'As it was in the past, Aceh is an indivisible part of the

---

[4] Hasan Tiro has created confusion about his age by sticking to a statement in his *The Price of Freedom*, p. 5, asserting that his declaration of Aceh independence on 4 December 1976 occurred on his fortieth birthday. His close comrades quietly acknowledged the 1925 date which I am using. Isa Sulaiman (2006: 126), however, put his birth date at 1923.

Negara Republic Indonesia, so also its history too is one undivided part of Indonesian history, and our slogan is one nation, one language and one fatherland'. It was the responsibility of historians such as himself to promote this Indonesian unity by rewriting the histories of each region so as 'to fashion one history for one Indonesian nation' (Tiro 1948: 1). He drew on the popular Dutch histories of the latter stages of the war by Zentgraaff (1938) and du Croo (1943), when the Dutch at last were able to acknowledge the heroism of Acehnese fighters such as the Tiros, while celebrating their own.

Hasan Tiro was well placed to convey to the Republican leadership his view of Aceh's past and present. When the Republican vice-premier, Sjafruddin Prawinegara, moved to the Aceh capital in August 1948 to ensure the Republic had a safe base should negotiations go badly, Hasan Tiro went with him as an assistant. The young man had a hand in persuading Sjafruddin to a view sympathetic to PUSA both on the position of the imprisoned *ulèëbalang* and on the need for Aceh autonomy. He issued a decree on 17 December 1949 constituting Aceh a separate Republican Province, contrary to the tidy three-way partition of Sumatra in earlier documents. Once this conflict was over Hasan Tiro went, with Sjafruddin's help, to New York to pursue his studies and help out at Indonesia's United Nations (UN) mission (Sulaiman 1997: 328).

His argument, however, that Aceh's history of anti-foreign struggle was a central part of the new Indonesian national history, was taken up enthusiastically by many others. Teuku Umar and Teungku Chik di Tiro had been known to every schoolboy using a Dutch textbook as the principal rebels whose defeat signalled the completion of the Dutch project of colonising the whole Archipelago. They were therefore given a prominent place in all the early Indonesian textbooks. When in 1959 Sukarno's 'Guided Democracy' regime began the practice of canonising official 'national heroes' (*pahlawan nasional*) as models for the country, such Acehnese warriors were prominent among them (Schreiner 1995). Similarly the success of Aceh in alone avoiding reconquest by the Dutch in 1946–9 made it the 'model' of how the revolutionary period was envisaged.

Sukarno's revolutionary and anti-colonial rhetoric made particular use of the Aceh case when he dominated the stage in 1958–65. The military-based regime of Suharto that replaced him in 1966 had no use for revolutionary rhetoric, but it did preserve the conviction that anti-Dutch struggle had to be the leitmotif of Indonesian history. Not only did it provide a conveniently unitary theme, it also confirmed the central role of the military, with the Indonesian National Army (TNI) as the legitimate heirs of those who fought the Dutch. Dr Nugroho

Notosusanto was the favoured professional historian of the military, charged since 1964 to develop a coherent history textbook, and a series of museums and monuments, to ensure armed struggle was the central theme of national history. As minister of education from 1983 he was able to ensure these views entered every school, with a new compulsory subject, 'History of National Struggle' added (McGregor 2007: 156–8). For the generation schooled in this way, Aceh was not simply a necessary part of Indonesia, it was the consummate model, the only part of the country whose history approached the ideal of military resistance.

As Hasan Tiro's career demonstrates, Aceh's military struggle could equally be seen as one dedicated to remaining out of the Dutch/ Indonesia project. In another, deeper sense, however, Aceh had genuine centrality in any construction of Indonesian identity and history. For the majority Muslims, it was the first bastion of Islam in the Archipelago, and the source of many of the classic texts of Malay-medium Islamic scholarship. The 'classic' era of Malay literature, in fact, belongs primarily to Aceh of the sixteenth and seventeenth centuries. In consequence Aceh is the only province to name its two leading universities after intellectuals (not militant heroes)—the state one after Syiah Kuala (the popular name of Abdurra'uf as-Singkili), and the Islamic one (IAIN) after Nuruddin ar-Raniri. Though less celebrated in either of the rival constructions of Aceh's past, these centralities remain important through the Indonesian language which Acehnese have always read and written more fluently than they do their own language.

It is critical, also, that Aceh entered Indonesia virtually without its traditional elite. The sultans in the port-capital, and a host of river-chiefs along the coastline who came to be known as *ulèëbalang*, had all had the historical role of mediating with the world outside. Many had become extremely cosmopolitan, better acquainted with diversity than most Indonesians of their time. Sultan Muhammad Shah (r. 1781–95) had spent some of his youth learning about gun-casting in a French shipyard in Ile de France (Mauritius), and spoke French and Portuguese as well as Arabic; his son Sultan Jauhar al-Alam employed Europeans by preference as his military commanders and political counsellors, and equally spoke good English. The pepper-trading rajas of eastern Aceh in the 1860s and 1870s owned extensive property in British Penang, which became the Acehnese window on the world. In the Dutch period the sultanate was no more, but the *ulèëbalang* were particularly cultivated by the Dutch, educated in modern ways, and to a considerable extent alienated from their people. Like the rajas before them, their compromises with foreign and *kafir* ways were often deeply unpopular with their subjects, among whom the OSH factor was profound. The elimination of this class from power during the revolution, and the unpopularity that ensued from the polarisation of the 1940s, meant that Aceh alone of Indonesia's provinces lacked the Dutch-trained elite accustomed to mediating with the Western world. The Islamic educated alternative elite were popular internally, but culturally very remote from the power-holders of post-independence Jakarta.

Aceh as distinct destiny: Daud Beureu'eh and Hasan Tiro

The end of the Indonesia-Dutch conflict, and the universal recognition of the Jakarta government from 1950, immediately transformed Aceh from Republican bastion to troublesome periphery. Alone of Indonesia's provinces, Aceh owed nothing to the diplomacy of the central government or the guerrilla struggle of its army. The success of the struggle meant the end of Aceh's short-lived effective independence. In January 1951 it was merged into the Republic's structure of larger provinces, becoming part of North Sumatra with its capital in Medan. Acehnese soldiers who had served in the province since 1945 were moved elsewhere and replaced by outsiders. The vigorous barter trade with the Peninsula, which had flourished during the revolutionary period, was now banned in favour of concentrating trade in Medan's port of Belawan. Daud Beureu'eh and most of the PUSA sympathisers he had appointed to office were replaced by Western-educated officials, many of them *ulèëbalang*-connected or non-Acehnese.

In September 1953, after several months of preparation, Daud Beureu'eh denounced the Jakarta government and declared Aceh part of the insurgent Indonesian Islamic State (NII), which Kartosuwirjo had proclaimed in West Java in 1949. Like Kartosuwirjo, but later and more emphatically, Daud Beureu'eh found his skills not needed and his thinking out of tune with the Western-educated elite now in charge of Indonesia. In accordance with his Quranic training, he could only justify his change of attitude to the Republic in Islamic terms, but outrage at the betrayal of Aceh's historical struggle was not far below the surface.

The Government of the Republic of Indonesia that now exists is not the Government we fought for in 1945 ... What it really is now is a *Hindu Government wearing a Nationalist shirt and very much resembling Communism*. It is patently anti-Islam, anti-God and largely run by the lackeys of the Dutch ... they also hold as their enemies those Indonesians who are Muslims, especially the Acehnese, because the Acehnese defended the Indonesian lands from being colonized by the Dutch Government. (translated in Aspinall 2006: 154)

Most telling of all was the statement of disillusion with the conclusion this same group had come to in 1945. 'In our hearts and souls we had viewed the Republic as a golden bridge [Sukarno's *jembatan mas*] to realising the true state for which we had longed from the beginning. It is now our view that this bridge is no longer a connection: it has become an obstacle' (Daud Beureu'eh, trans. Morris 1983: 202).

Jakarta responded forcefully, and its troops succeeded within two months in capturing the important towns and reducing the rebels to a guerrilla strategy in rural areas. The rebels had enough support to mobilise thousands of supporters to attack government military posts, but because they were lightly armed and unprofessional they suffered heavy casualties. The military responded in brutal ways that became well-known as a result of East Timor and post-Suharto exposés, but in fact date back to the revolutionary origins of Indonesia's military, its poor pay and discipline, and the frustrations of trying to deal with a generally hostile population unwilling to betray the rebels. After this initial unequal phase, the struggle turned to a guerrilla one familiar to both earlier and later periods.

Religion had been needed to justify the moral reversal with a national government so recently supported, but after this initial phase the rhetoric increasingly changed to a kind of ethnie nationalism. By 1955 Daud Beureu'eh had made clear that he wanted Aceh to be a federal state, regardless of how Islamic the central government might be. The rhetoric also became steadily more nationalist, appealing to Acehnese as 'descendants of the heroes and martyrs of Aceh, who were martyred defending the Islamic religion and their *bangsa* . . . Let us together defend the religion of Allah and the Land of Aceh' (Daud Beureu'eh 1954, as translated by Aspinall: 2006: 159). The 1955 declaration defined Daud Beureu'eh as the head of this state (*Wali Negara*) and Hasan Ali as its prime minister. Edward Aspinall (2006: 160) has correctly identified 'a genuinely nationalist sentiment' in the writings of the supporters of this first rebellion, already reading Indonesian troops as comparable to Dutch colonisers, as Aceh Independence Movement (GAM) spokesmen would routinely do later.

Jakarta sought to moderate Acehnese resentment by negotiating a series of concessions. The province of Aceh was re-established with prominent Sukarnoist *ulama* Ali Hasjmy as governor. A 1959 agreement effectively split the rebel group by promising that Aceh would become a 'special region' with authority in matters of religion, custom, tradition and education. Sabang, a fine deep-water port which had been developed by the Dutch on an island just off Banda Aceh, was declared a free port (1960). A state university was established in Banda Aceh,

Universitas Syiah Kuala, or Unsyiah. Daud Beureu'eh, supported by Hasan Tiro who returned briefly in 1959, continued to insist on the minimum concession of a federal state for Aceh, but many of his supporters accepted these lesser concessions from the government. With his movement badly divided, the veteran leader himself came down from the hills in 1962 and conceded that the struggle was over (Sulaiman 1997: 455–6; 2006: 133).

It quickly became clear, however, that the 'special region' would have no effect in limiting military control of Aceh. Once Sukarno's government was supplanted by Suharto's in 1965–6, amid traumatic massacres of the Left, the military constituted itself as the steel frame keeping Indonesia centrally unified. As a troublesome province with more justification for a military presence, Aceh had in practice less autonomy than other provinces, and a great deal more exploitation by military rackets of various kinds. Without shore-based infrastructure, the Sabang free port was a complete failure, and was closed in 1985 in favour of Batam. The University was a more effective step, providing a core of economists who would become after 1965 the technocratic partner of the military in bringing some development to Aceh (McGibbon 2006: 320–5).

Following the terror of 1965–6, in which young Muslim students enthusiastically partnered the military in destroying the left-wing parties which had previously been Jakarta's main supporters in Aceh, the province enjoyed its longest period of relative peace for a century. Infrastructure was repaired, and the exploration for mineral resources resulted in the discovery of vast reserves of natural gas at Arun, near Lhokseumawe. Mobil Oil signed the contract to exploit these reserves in 1973, and in consequence Aceh was in the 1980s one of Indonesia's largest earners of foreign exchange. The policy of the succession of pragmatic Acehnese economists in the governor's office from 1968 was not greater autonomy but a greater integration of the peripheral province into a booming Indonesian economy. Living standards increased along with Indonesia's as a whole, but by no means commensurate with the wealth flowing from the gas fields (Sulaiman 2006: 134; McGibbon 2006: 326).

Like the relative peace of the 1920s and 1930s, that of the 1970s and 1980s was based on both a negative factor, the defeat experienced by an older generation, and a positive one, the hope offered to a younger generation by education and development. In both cases the balance was tenuous, and dependent on outside factors. Those hoping for a renewal of the resistance motif gradually shifted their aspirations from the aging Daud Beureu'eh (already sixty-three when he conceded defeat) to his articulate young protégé Hasan Tiro. Tiro had remained in touch with his mentor through his elder brother Zainal Abidin, one of the leading figures of the 1953 revolt. From New York he publicly supported the rebellion and demanded that Jakarta stop its 'genocide' against the rebels. When Indonesia withdrew his passport, he was able to remain in the US, and indeed flourish modestly in international business, only with the support of some anti-communist friends there. During the Indonesia-wide Revolutionary government (PRRI) rebellion of 1958–9, led by his former Republican patron Sjafruddin Prawiranegara, he played a mediating role between Daud Beureu'eh's rebellion, the PRRI, and sympathisers in the US and South Vietnam willing to provide clandestine assistance to anti-communist causes. Having been such an enthusiastic supporter of the Indonesia idea in 1945, however, and aware of the international commitment to it, he was slow to abandon it altogether. In 1958 he published overseas but in Indonesian, possibly with CIA support, an argument for a federal and democratic Indonesia which would provide the necessary autonomy to Aceh (Tiro 1958). This was also the argument he made when he returned secretly from New York in 1959 to join the debates about making peace. Like Daud Beureu'eh he sought to hold out for a fully autonomous federal state, claiming to have various supporters for the idea in Indonesia and abroad (Sulaiman 2000: 328–9; 2006: 133–8; Nessen 2006: 181–3).

Having lost this battle Tiro kept his peace for the next decade, aware that Acehnese were weary of fighting losing battles. He was also undoubtedly aware of the deals being struck over the Arun gas field, and may have been hoping to play some part in them. But discussions continued among NII veterans about the right time and conditions to renew the struggle. The historical preoccupations which had in 1945 been used to support Indonesian anti-imperial nationalism, now drove him in the direction of Aceh ethnie nationalism. He claims to have given a lecture in New York in 1973, to celebrate the centenary of Aceh's defeat of the first Dutch expedition in March 1873. 'My speech ... was meant to be a clarion call for the Achehnese to rise again to honor their dead heroes and to take their place again among the free sovereign peoples of the world' (Tiro 1981: 62). When in 1974 Tiro was permitted to revisit Aceh as a potential businessman, in company with Singapore-based NII supporter Malik Mahmud, he found great interest in renewing the struggle on a more clear-cut basis of Acehnese independence. The hollowness of the gains made in 1959 now seemed apparent to this group (Nessen 2006: 184; interviews 2005).

Naturally the ailing Daud Beureu'eh was one of those the younger group of visitors met in the 1970s, and he reportedly passed his mandate for leadership of resistance to Hasan Tiro (interviews 2005; Nessen

2006: 185). Among those who sought to continue the resistance theme, independence was now the only option being discussed. In October 1976 Hasan Tiro felt ready to fulfil his 'destiny'. He returned clandestinely to launch the campaign for independence, seemingly more in a spirit of educating Acehnese about their past than beginning a serious guerrilla strategy. Battle-hardened NII veterans rallied to him, however, as planned, and in a small way, the guerrilla movement recommenced. On 4 December 1976 he declared Aceh independent in a jungle clearing, in a message heavy with historical claims.

Our fatherland, Acheh, Sumatra, had always been a free and sovereign state since the world begun . . . However, when, after World War II, the Dutch East Indies was supposed to have been liquidated . . . our fatherland, Acheh, was not returned to us. Instead, our fatherland was turned over by the Dutch to the Javanese—their ex-mercenaries—by hasty fiat of colonial powers. The Javanese are alien and foreign people to us Achehnese Sumatrans . . . 'Indonesia' was a fraud: a cloak to cover up Javanese colonialism. (Tiro 1981: 15–17)

In addition to emphasising the 'thousand year old flag' of Aceh, Tiro issued a new calendar marking ten annual holidays designed to remind Acehnese of their historical heroes (Tiro 1981: 53) To judge from his own account, he preached the message in the jungle that the important issue was not arms, but 'the crisis of national identity, the problem of the study of Achehnese history . . . Our true history has been subverted. When a people have forgotten their history, it is . . . like a man who has lost his memory' (Tiro 1981: 51). The military side of this beginning in Aceh was inauspicious. His deputy described him spending his time in the jungle writing a theatrical piece, in English and set to European music of the Baroque period, about Aceh's historical struggle from 1873 to the declaration of 1976 (Tiro 1979). Within a few months the military response to their modern guerrilla activity persuaded Tiro to leave Aceh with many of his principal lieutenants. Nevertheless the idea was spread that the resistance motif was again alive, this time on the basis of independence.

When Hasan Tiro struck a deal with Muammar Ghaddafi for the training of potential guerrillas, hundreds of young men proved ready to ship out from Aceh to Libya. Trained in the period 1986–9, this cadre of perhaps 250 men would become the hard core of the more substantial GAM forces that became a serious threat thereafter. The brutal military response to this more effective guerrilla operation began with declaring Aceh a Region of Military Operations (DOM) in 1989. Some 2000 Acehnese were thought to have been killed over the subsequent two years of repression, before the military again felt it had the upper hand. Nevertheless the military continued to exercise exceptional military powers until the fall of Suharto in 1998 (Kell 1995; Schulze 2006: 244–58; Robinson 1998).

The roots for Acehnese ethnie nationalism were deep, resting on a memory of state that was unique in Indonesia, as well as an exceptionally strong OSH factor based on personal memories of resistance to outsiders and suffering at their hands. For many these factors continued to nest within a genuine Indonesian nationalism as described in chapter 4. The centralised state education system had some success here as elsewhere in turning Acehnese into Indonesians, leading GAM activists to seek to burn schools as a major enemy of their cause (Reid 2006a: 231–3; 307–8). The developmentalism of Suharto's Indonesia brought positive results for some of the urban elite, though never on a scale that drove a high proportion of Acehnese (in contrast to Bataks in the following chapter) into lucrative positions in the bigger Indonesian cities. Aceh itself remained remarkably homogeneous in contrast with its pre-colonial history, with no large city attractive to outside migrants, and a climate relatively unwelcoming to non-Acehnese. Its older cosmopolitan elite was replaced to some extent with a technocratic one, but these too suffered a 'legitimacy deficit' as leaders of a restive province (McGibbon 2006: 325–9).

Democratisation and conflict

The strength of rival nationalisms had not been put to a serious test of democratic popularity until the fall of Suharto in 1998. The only free elections Indonesia had previously experienced were the national elections of 1955 (in a climate of instability in Aceh), followed by regional elections in Java only, the area least prone to ethnic separatism. These elections were contested at a time when expressions of particular ethnic or regional sentiment were still stigmatised as traitorous towards the victorious anti-imperial nationalism of the Indonesian Republic. Even in Aceh this mood, combined with physical repression of the NII rebellion, was sufficient to discourage any ethnie-specific or region-specific parties. The only parties of this kind that made significant gains were the Chinese-Indonesian Baperki and the United Dayak Party (PPD) in Kalimantan (Bertrand 2004: 51–3; 229n, and chapter 6 below).

The elections had nevertheless accentuated frustrations with the outcome of independence, epitomised by the 1958 PRRI rebellion affecting many regions outside Java. These discontents were physically suppressed in a series of military operations, but never dealt with. The mass killings of 1965–6 inaugurated the period of centralised Suharto government when questioning the military-inspired ideology was particularly dangerous.

Under the extremely constrained conditions of the New Order elections, only three parties were permitted, offering hardly distinguishable variations of the nationalist format. In an official atmosphere particularly hostile to political activity that was ethnic, religious or regional, even the gains made by Baperki and PPD were reversed. Ethnic sentiment was permitted only in certain essentialised cultural clichés, such as elaborate dress for weddings, cultural dance performances and quotations of architectural tradition, particularly in roof forms. Acehnese expression of this were the 'Aceh Cultural Festivals' held in 1972 and 1988, and the pattern of 'Acehnese' roof styles on government buildings in the 1980s, beginning with the provincial museum.

By contrast with this past, the experience of open-ended democracy at national level since Suharto's fall in May 1998 was a profound change. Under his immediate successor (and former vice-president) B. J. Habibie (1998–9) the press was freed, human rights institutions were strengthened, a free election for the national parliament was held in 1999, and East Timor was permitted a referendum which led to its separation from Indonesia. The president who emerged from the post-election horse-trading, Abdurrahman Wahid (1999–2001), had been Indonesia's most prominent champion of democracy and human rights. He sought, with mixed results, to remove the military from their central role in politics. He was unseated by parliament in favour of his vice-president, Megawati Sukarnoputri (2001–3), who oversaw remarkably peaceful elections in 2003 both for parliament and for a directly-elected president. By winning this last election handsomely and subsequently winning over a majority of parliamentary supporters to his side, President Susilo Bambang Yudhoyono could claim to have successfully completed a democratic transition in his first term in office (2003–9).

Such transitions usually destabilise the ethnic balance, and raise profound questions about the nature and boundaries of the political community. Just as in Europe in 1848 and 1917–18, democratisation in Asia could be expected to have consequences in redrawing boundaries and constituting new states. Of the forty-seven new states which joined the UN between 1974 and 1997, twenty-six seceded from countries within the first three years of a democratisation process. Since Indonesia had a unitary rather than a federal system like the Soviet Union and Yugoslavia, the predictable instabilities of the transition would not necessarily follow established internal boundaries. Ethnic, religious and regional tensions overlapped, and there could be no easy agreements where new demarcations would fall. The hundreds of thousands of victims of the South Asian transition to full democratic independence, as new boundaries were drawn between newly imagined religious communities, were a forewarning that Asia's transition would be no easier than Europe's. East Timor's separation from Indonesia, the only one to succeed in this initial phase of democratic euphoria, was bitter and bloody, and would have been much more so without UN intervention.

In Indonesia as a whole, the first three to four years of democratisation were frequently violent and murderous. The worst blood-letting was in the eastern islands of Maluku, where some 5,000 people died in fighting between Muslims and Christians, chiefly in the first years, 1999–2000. Muslim and Christian villages were so intermingled as to make separation impossible. But democratisation undoubtedly accentuated anxieties, fuelling both hopes and fears that existing compromises would be overturned by the new electoral system, and that elected local majorities would prove less tolerant than centrally appointed 'neutral' authorities (Bertrand 2004: 1, 114–34; van Klinken 2001). Such hopes and fears had begun to spark violence in Kalimantan even before Suharto's fall, as the military-bureaucratic consensus began to unravel. Sensing an opportunity to reverse through violence a marginalisation which had become increasingly acute through deforestation and in-migration, indigenous Dayaks began an orgy of blood-letting, chiefly against immigrant Muslim Madurese, in 1996–7 and again in 1999 (Davidson 2008). Another round of the anti-Chinese violence which had been a feature of Indonesia's twentieth century accompanied Suharto's fall in 1998 (see chapter 3 above). In total some 10,000 Indonesians were killed in ethnic and religious violence between 1997 and 2001.

In Aceh the initial period of apparently limitless democratic possibilities also raised the stakes. The press was freed from censorship in 1998, and political leaders right up to the president's office denounced military atrocities as part of the Suharto oppression. Led by a plethora of new non-governmental organisations (NGOs) dedicated to human rights and democracy, Acehnese became emboldened to attack soldiers verbally and in a few cases physically. In the lead-up to the East Timor referendum of August 1999, pressure mounted for a similar solution to the long-term problems of Aceh. A student movement, SIRA, was formed in February 1999 to campaign for a referendum on independence. In September it prevailed upon an important group of *ulama* (calling themselves HUDA) to condemn the murders and other human rights violations committed by the military, and to call for a referendum. With this support, and discreet backing from GAM, SIRA pulled off a mass rally of several hundred thousand people in Banda Aceh on 8 November 1999. Faced with such a throng, local religious and political leaders felt obliged to line up behind the referendum campaign.

From this point the Aceh Independence Movement began to look like a government in waiting. Its military commander, Teungku Abdullah Syafiie, hitherto hunted and invisible in the hills, appeared regularly on the front page of the local press. Although the guerrilla forces of GAM only operated in half of Aceh's districts (primarily along the northern coast), plantations, shops and offices in a much wider area paid contributions to its treasury, including even some government offices in the provincial capital. Many of the thousands of villages in Aceh paid GAM 20 per cent of the 10 million rupiah each annually received from the central government in development funds (interviews, 2000).

On the ground, however, the Indonesian military (TNI) continued to retaliate against those it defined as its enemies, including burning villages where its soldiers were attacked. Despite declarations on all sides that there would be no more violent repression, 534 people were killed in Aceh in the seventeen months following the end of the military emergency in August 1998, of whom eighty-seven were members of the army and police (*Kompas*, 24 December 1999).

In 2000 the killing roughly doubled in intensity, even as moves began to negotiate with GAM towards peace. The violence now frequently became anonymous, targetting high-profile figures formerly deemed immune. Members of parliament, party leaders, prominent NGO figures such as the New York-based activist Jafar Siddiq Hamzah, and the rectors of both the main state universities, were kidnapped or murdered in cold blood. In January 2001 the TNI raided the GAM headquarters and killed its guerrilla commander Syafiie, just three days after the Aceh governor had invited him for peace talks. On both sides there were multiple conflicting policies, and the military elements were more inclined to achieve their sectional aims through covert violence that could not lead to prosecution (Djalal 2000; *Los Angeles Times*, 5 October 2000).

This increasing tempo of violence was accompanied by multiple political moves, both to legislate measures to address Aceh's grievances, and to negotiate an end to the fighting. In both respects Abdurrahman Wahid's presidency was innovative, albeit disorganised. He responded to the peace-making initiatives of the Henry Dunant Centre in Geneva, leading on 12 May to the first agreement between the GAM leadership of Hasan Tiro and Malik Mahmud in Sweden and the Wahid government. They agreed to a 'Humanitarian Pause' in the fighting to take effect on 2 June 2000. This failed in practice to halt the killing, but established an important precedent, incompatible with the state nationalism of earlier Indonesian governments, for low-key foreign mediators to act as convenors of various joint GAM-RI monitoring committees.

Figure 5.1 Aceh government banner celebrates cessation of hostilities between the Indonesian Republic (RI) and GAM, 2002

Despite many setbacks, the two sides signed a substantial Cessation of Hostilities Agreement (CoHA) on 9 December 2002, which did finally curb the violence. Soldiers from two Association of Southeast Asian Nations (ASEAN) partners, the Philippines and Thailand, joined the GAM and TNI monitoring teams to investigate breaches of the peace by either side (Reid 2005: 352–3) (see figure 5.1).

Attempts to reach agreement on autonomy within the Indonesian framework began with the passing of an Aceh autonomy law by the Indonesian parliament in July 1999. This was widely rejected in Aceh as trying to give life to the discredited Aceh 'special region' deal of 1959. A more consensual drafting effort under the Wahid government led to the NAD Law of July 2001, so called because it renamed the province Nanggroe Aceh Darussalam (NAD), using the ambiguous Acehnese term *nanggroe* rather than either of the Indonesian terms *negeri* (town, principality or community) or *negara* (sovereign state). Because it included a generous concession to Aceh of 70 per cent of the oil and gas revenues for eight years, and 50 per cent thereafter, it did gain support among many Acehnese politicians. But almost none of it was effectively implemented before military rule was re-established in 2003 (Miller 2006: 301–10).

Megawati came to power in July 2001 with a state nationalist agenda inherited from her father, Sukarno, and much closer ties than her predecessor with the military. If she nevertheless continued the negoti- ation and autonomy initiatives of her predecessor, it was partly because she was too weak to do otherwise, and specifically because of the leading role on Aceh policy of her security minister, former General Susilo Bambang Yudhoyono. SBY, as he was known, was well aware of both the weaknesses of his army, and the international pressures to resolve this long-running sore. He appears to have tried to make the CoHA peace work, but eventually lost the battle with more hawkish elements in the military, many complicit in the business deals for which it was notorious (Kingsbury and McCullough 2006). After TNI-connected militias had stymied the peace by driving out the monitoring teams, Jakarta decided on a military solution. On 19 May 2003 martial law was declared and a self-styled 'invasion' influenced by Iraq war imagery was arranged for the media, with parachute-drops on an airport and city already controlled by the TNI. Between 40,000 and 60,000 army and police units were concentrated in Aceh during the ensuing two years, substantially the largest force in Aceh's 130 years of intermittent military occupation. All the GAM negotiators of the peace process were arrested along with many NGO activists and peacemakers, the local press was tightly controlled and the most aggressive military actions since 1990 were undertaken against GAM guerrillas (Schulze 2006: 247–55). The United States, which had encouraged the peace process at its outset, was not well positioned to urge moderation on a Muslim country after its own invasion of Iraq.

On 26 December 2004, Aceh was hit by the most destructive tsunami and one of the worst earthquakes of modern times (see figure 5.2). By this time the TNI had reduced GAM to the kind of guerrilla core it had been since 1990, but by dint of much greater pressure than before on an awakened civil society. Fortunately President Yudhoyono was by then better established with a popular mandate than any of his predecessors. He responded effectively to the devastation, allowing the military forces of the US, Australia, Singapore, Malaysia and other countries to move relief supplies in quickly. The president had already shown a cautious interest in renewing negotiations with the GAM leadership in Sweden. In the aftermath of the massive international relief effort, he authorised ministerial-level negotiations and substantial concessions. Both sides understood that such an unprecedented human tragedy, and equally

Figure 5.2 Debris of the tsunami surrounds the miraculously intact main mosque of the Aceh capital, December 2004

unprecedented international response, required a generous new start to reconstruct Aceh in peace. This time it was the Helsinki-based Crisis Management Initiative which brokered the peace deal, agreed in July and implemented immediately upon its signature on 15 August 2005.

In relation to the unitary bias of Indonesian state nationalism since 1945, the peace agreement was a remarkable reversal. It granted to Aceh 'authority within all sectors of public affairs' except those excluded—defence, foreign affairs, monetary and fiscal matters, justice and freedom of religion. Aceh would have its own flag, crest and hymn, and a cere-monial head of state called a *wali nanggroe*, the term which GAM had applied to Hasan Tiro. Aceh could raise its own external loans and international investments, administer its ports and airports, and enjoy 70 per cent of the revenues from oil and gas 'and other natural resources' in perpetuity. In return for GAM's acceptance of Aceh's place within Indonesia, its fighters would receive an allocation of land or a pension, and be permitted to play their part in the regional election of officials. An exception was made to the 1959 decree that only nationally organised political parties could contest elections in Indonesia, giving GAM members the opportunity to create or support an Aceh-specific party for the first time.

Some of these generous concessions were diluted by the Indonesian parliament which had to enact them into law. But an election for governor and deputy-governor was held in November 2006, only six months behind schedule. To the surprise of those reading media coverage of the campaign, the two teams closest to GAM emerged on top. The spirit of Aceh's ethnie nationalism among ordinary Acehnese was well captured in an Acehnese epic poem (*hikayat*) recited at one of the campaign rallies:

> This is a leadership, for better or worse, that always supports the nation [*bangsa*].
> Don't let the *bangsa* fall under oppression, even if it means living in the jungles.
> Please brothers and sisters, understand that our struggle has not ended.
> We haven't reached our destination; don't walk off while we are still midway.
>
> (*Hikayat of Imam Jun*, 2006,
> cited in Crisis Group International 2007)

Irwandi Yusuf, former GAM political negotiator and political prisoner, duly took office in February 2007 with an impressive majority of votes cast.

The ethnie nationalism of Aceh, sustained by a strong memory of state and of resistance to the intrusion of outsiders, had come to terms with the state nationalism of Indonesia, sustained by post-revolutionary centralism built on anti-imperial rhetoric. As Michael Keating (2001: viii, 102–33) has argued persuasively, when communities come together with different nationalist expectations and experiences, providing for differential claims on the state can be the strategy most compatible with justice and democracy. Aceh has had a very different memory of state and tradition of nationalism than have most Indonesians. Its relationship to Indonesian state nationalism is clear but distinctive.

Despite the absence of major cities or educational hubs in their province, and the painful conditions they have lived under, the number of Acehnese outside Aceh remains a very small proportion of those within. Aceh university administrators plan on the basis of 95 per cent of the hundreds of graduate students sent abroad after the tsunami coming home, as Acehnese students have in the past. Acehnese break into their own language, out of the formal Indonesian in which government and university proceedings are conducted, more frequently than do other Indonesians, and rejoice in this sign of both solidarity and jocular informality. Yet there is almost no writing in Acehnese, and even the GAM-schooled present governor has done little to introduce it into schools. What sustains Acehneseness seems primarily to be the tight identification with 'our' Islam (not necessarily that of outside pundits), pride in the historic sultanate and their immensely costly resistance to outside domination, and a resentment against the way they have been treated by Jakarta and by other Indonesians. Acehnese have long conceived themselves a *bangsa*, and responded warmly to the nationalists' evocation of solidarity with this *bangsa* rather than the *bangsa Indonesia* of the 1928 proclamation.

6 Sumatran Bataks: from statelessness to Indonesian diaspora

As explained in chapter 2, states had relatively little direct control over the inhabitants of the tropical rain-forests of Southeast Asia when compared with the great river systems of the temperate zone. For many peoples of the Southeast Asian uplands in particular, statelessness was not simply a negative absence or slowness to develop states, but a deliberate rejection of the manner in which trade-based coastal states had been experienced as a threat to their way of life. The highland populations of northern Sumatra, collectively known for several centuries as Bataks, will be our prime example of this category.

Like terms elsewhere in the region such as Toraja, Dayak, Dusun, Alfur or Karen, the term Batak was probably first used by coastal people as a generic descriptor of highlanders outside the boundaries of the civilisation defined by states and scriptural religions. These highlanders constituted the great majority of the population of Sumatra before 1870, and were themselves divided by a range of linguistic and cultural variations. They therefore defined themselves internally in terms of location, river-valley, dialect or descent. Yet when dealing with outsiders they appear to have accepted the broad label Batak, even including its 'savage' associations which served to intimidate potential intruders. The historical options for such peoples were either to be individually assimilated to the coastal states, or to forge new identities of sufficient breadth to demand a position of equality with the state-based identities of the coasts. This chapter takes the shifting identity-marker 'Batak' as a case study of how this transition was negotiated in the modern era.

For many centuries the Bataks perceived no collective identity, as each lineage and valley was separately organised. They spoke a wide spectrum of local dialects, comprehensible to those in adjacent valleys but not to those further away. The northern Batak dialects (today's Karo and Dairi) were part of a different and mutually incomprehensible language family from the southern (today's Toba, Mandailing and Angkola), with Simalungun another intermediate category. Those Bataks who identified most closely with the states of the coast, Aceh in the north or Deli,

Langkat and Asahan in the east, eventually became Muslim, and thereby rejected the Batak label as part of a pagan past. The Gayo people of highland Aceh, in particular, have a language closely related to Karo and Dairi, as well as some acknowledgement of common descent, and were probably at one time called 'Batak' by their neighbours in the cosmo-politan ports. In the seventeenth century, however, they accepted Islam and the primacy of the sultans of Aceh, and thus rejected any association with the category Batak. Toba, the largest group, have most confidently asserted their Batakness, and this in itself has in the nationalist era made other groups less inclined to do so.

During the past century all Batak groups migrated outwards, from the highlands which long protected them from malaria and hostile attack, to the more fertile and increasingly developed lowlands. They thereby came into intense contact with other groups, and found them-selves minority groups in large complex cities. For them, as for others, the modern definition of ethnicity is essentially urban—competitive, secularised and abstracted from the reality of life in the homeland, which now represents a set of symbols to be manipulated on the national, urban stage. This chapter traces that process.

Historiography

The highlands of Sumatra, despite being more densely settled and culturally sophisticated than the lowlands before the twentieth century, remain a striking case of Eric Wolf's (1982) 'People without History'. Ashis Nandy points out that it is the statelessness, rather than the inaccessibility, of such peoples that has denied them a history. In his view, modern secular history as practised in the academies is inextricably linked as a mode of analysis with the modern nation-state and its rise. History traces the lineage and legitimacy of modern states, and distorts our understanding of the past by doing so (Nandy 1995).

For academic authors 'Batak history' has seemed almost a contradic-tion in terms. There have been only a handful of academic theses, all focused on the period since the late nineteenth century incorporation into the modern (colonial) state. Even these have not been published in English, though a useful broad coverage by Daniel Perret (1995) was published in French.

Bataks of the nationalist age, on the other hand, have written popular histories in Indonesian, overwhelmingly focusing on the figure of Singamangaraja XII (1845–1907). After armed resistance to the Dutch effectively ended with his death in battle, some millenarian cults continued to celebrate his memory at a time when it was otherwise pushed to the margins of Batak consciousness by the influence of Christianity and modernity. The cult appears to have been revived and linked to anti-Western (pro-Japanese) nationalism by some of Singamangaraja's descendents of the Sinambela *marga*. They succeeded in convincing the Japanese military administrator of Sumatra to travel from Bukittinggi to Tarutung on 9 December 1944 to celebrate the third anniversary of the 'Great East Asia War' by laying flowers on the grave of Singamangaraja XII. The Japanese military administrator joined the son, Raja Tarita Sinambela, and the ninety-year-old widow of Singamangaraja XII to praise his fighting spirit as the essence of the Great East Asia War and of Indonesian nationalism (*Kita Sumatora Sinbun* 18 November and 11 December 2004 [1944]). The Guided Democracy period (1959–65), in which Sukarno sought to revive a revolutionary anti-Western spirit, gave further opportunities to the supporters of this cult to mobilise support to have Singamangaraja recognised as a 'national hero', Sukarno's method of reconstructing local histories into a nationalist mode. This was accomplished in November 1961, making him the first Sumatran accepted into the pantheon (Schreiner 1995) (figure 6.1).

This shadowy priest-king henceforth had a double role: as principal Batak link to the powerful national myth of the Sukarno and Suharto periods, but also as mediator with the cosmos and protector of at least some Toba Bataks against external threat. Although his predecessors in this role were scarcely known to history (in the academic sense), a creative use of Batak writings (*pustaha*), oral traditions and historical imagination have enabled some to push the history back through the eleven previous generations of Singamangarajas (Tobing 1957; Parlindungan 1965; Sangti 1977; Situmorang 1993). This lineage could represent the simulacrum of a state story, a key for later Batak intellectuals to claim equality with other Indonesian peoples who featured more prominently in Indonesian history through their states.[1] The first Indonesian book to call itself a 'Batak History' was hailed by its publisher with the words, 'until this time it can be said that there was no book of "Batak History" of a general and complete kind, which was on a level with the histories of the kingdoms that formerly existed in the northern Sumatra region and/or Indonesia' (Sangti 1977: 3).

'Batak' in the historical record

In terms of voices speaking directly from a vanished past—inscriptions and archaeological evidence from within and the information of

---

[1] This historiography is discussed more fully in Reid 2006c.

Figure 6.1   Statue of Singamangaraja XII erected in Medan to celebrate
his national hero status, 1961

travellers from without—we are at a serious disadvantage with highland
peoples such as those in Sumatra. Tomé Pires, our most reliable recorder
of all manner of states and societies in sixteenth century Southeast Asia,
also fails us here. 'There are many heathen kings in the island of Sumatra
and many lords in the hinterland, but, as they are not trading people and
known, no mention is made of them' (Pires 1515: 165).

As with all shadowy protohistories, the question arises with Batak
whether we are on safer ground tracing the history of a place, the domain
occupied by the six major Batak ethno-linguistic groups of today's North
Sumatra province, or of a people called Batak or identifiable in some

other way. And if the latter, what does this concept mean before the period of national self-definition in the twentieth century?

In terms of place, archaeological evidence has thus far yielded three major urban complexes in the North Sumatran area prior to the Islamisation of coastal ports. All must have been important gateways for the trade of the interior highlands, though on the borders of what is thought to be Batak territory today. Starting with the oldest, they are:

- the camphor and benzoin port of Barus on the west coast, flourishing from the eighth to thirteenth centuries, and recently excavated by a French team (Guillot 1998–2003);
- the east coast port of Kota Cina, near Medan, which flourished from the twelfth to fourteenth centuries, and must have had a role in the presumably Karo-Batak kingdom of Aru, a major maritime power from the thirteenth to sixteenth centuries (Milner et al. 1978);
- The Buddhist temple complexes of Padang Lawas, and particularly the fortified settlement of Si Pamutung, near the confluence of the Pane and Baruman Rivers. The ten inscriptions (two of which are in Batak script) on these sites, the Chinese ceramics associated with them and the architectural remains, all confirm occupation between the tenth and early fourteenth centuries but a peak probably in the eleventh to twelfth centuries. The sites may be associated with the kingdom of Pane mentioned in both a Cola inscription (1025) and the Nagarakrtagama of Java (1365), as well as later texts. Although in the extreme south of current Batak territory, its location 200 km up the Baruman river, near an important east–west corridor of trade, suggest an important medium through which Indian and Buddhist ideas reached the Bataks (Miksic 1996; Perret et al. 2007).

While archaeology may hold many future surprises in this area, these three sites must have been among those through which Indian (especially), Chinese, Javanese and other 'state' influences entered the Bataklands at this time, and acquainted their inhabitants with the idea of states, not necessarily in any hostile sense. Kota Cina has been linked to the influx of Hindu elements among the Karo, and Barus to a different range of influences among Toba Batak. Padang Lawas remains mysterious as to its links to southern Batak, and the new excavations being undertaken there may prove to be an important key to a state-forming 'path not taken'.

The only element of 'Batakness' dramatic enough to be noted in the earliest sources was cannibalism. Foreign sources note its presence in Sumatra long before the term 'Batak' or any other feature which could be identified with it. Ptolemy was the first, around 100 CE, to record the

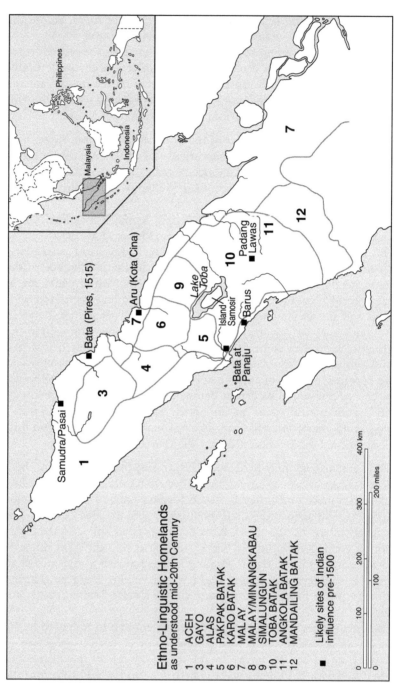

Ethno-Linguistic Homelands
as understood mid-20th Century

1   ACEH
3   GAYO
4   ALAS
5   PAKPAK BATAK
6   KARO BATAK
7   MALAY
8   MALAY/MINANGKABAU
9   SIMALUNGUN
10 TOBA BATAK
11 ANGKOLA BATAK
12 MANDAILING BATAK

■   Likely sites of Indian
    influence pre-1500

Samudra/Pasai

Bata (Pires, 1515)

Aru (Kota Cina)

Lake
Toba

Island
Samosir

Bata at
Panaju

Barus

Padang
Lawas

Philippines

Malaysia

Indonesia

0   100   200   300   400 km

0   100   200 miles

Map 2 Northern Sumatra

presence of cannibalism in what he identified as an island cluster of Barusae, presumably Sumatra. Following him a long series of Arab, Indian and European sources, including Marco Polo, attest to the existence of cannibalism in the island, including its more accessible north coast. Nicolo da Conti was the first European, in 1430, to use the term Batak (*Batech*) for this cannibal population in Sumatra (Yule and Burnell 1979: 74).

The term Batak appears even earlier in Chinese sources, but as a polity rather than a people. Chau Ju-kua (1970) has an obscure reference to Bo-ta as connected with Sriwijaya, while the Yuan (Mongol) dynastic chronicle mentions Ma-da next to Samudra (Pasai), both offering tribute to the imperial court in 1285–6. Ma-da would be pronounced Ba-ta in Hokkien, the likely language of trader informants.[2]

This thirteenth century Bata appears to have survived to the beginning of the sixteenth century, the first great watershed in Batak self-definition because of the confrontation with Islam. About 1515, before the rise of Aceh, Tomé Pires (1515: 145–6) described a loosely Muslim kingdom of 'Bata' in the same area, which in his case was given the added precision that it possessed the sources of petroleum in the Tamiang-Perlak area, later a precious resource for Aceh. The fact that the king was listed as Muslim and a son-in-law of the Aru (Karo?) king, also in some sense Muslim, indicates that the religious situation was still fluid, the inhabitants of the island recognised themselves by place rather than ethnicity or religion and that the natural centre for state-like formations for the interior peoples was at their points of connection with maritime trade. But Pires did not list this presumably hybrid Karo state as cannibalistic; that honour was reserved for the west coast area above Singkil (Pires 1515: 163).

This was the area of a Batak state for Mendes Pinto, writing of 1539. By then northern Sumatra had been transformed by the expansion of Aceh along the north coast, swallowing whatever kingdoms there were between itself and Aru including the 'Bata' of Pires. The Islamic expansionism of Aceh seemed already to have turned the term Batak definitively into a description of a people; a people defined by their resistance to this expansion. But it was still a people with a king, 'the King of the Bataks', whose capital was at Panaju, now on the west coast about eight leagues (50 km) up a river he calls Guateamgim, presumably one of the west coast rivers to the south of Singkil giving access to the camphor and benzoin land west of Lake Toba (Pinto 1989: 20–5).

---

[2] I owe this point to Geoff Wade.

Pinto makes his story of the Bataks a tragic one, with a king first refusing the offer of Islam and determining to fight the Acehnese sultan, then making a treaty and marriage alliance with him, which the sultan treacherously broke by attacking and killing his sons. The Batak king then assembled a major alliance of local chiefs to fight the Acehnese, whose Turkish reinforcements however proved too much for him. He retreated far up the river (Pinto 1989: 20–30).

This appears to mark the last of coastal 'kingdoms' associated with Bataks either by name or life-style. The ports were hereafter all Muslim and in varied degrees of tension with the people of the uplands, whom they labelled 'Batak' as those who had resisted the Acehnese *jihad*. Thus Barros, writing in mid-century, could report that Sumatra:

is inhabited by two kinds of people, Moros [Muslims] and *gentios* [heathens]; the latter are natives, while the former were foreigners who came for reasons of commerce and began to settle and populate the maritime region, multiplying so quickly that in less than 150 years they had established themselves as *senhores* [lords] and began calling themselves kings. The heathens, leaving the coast, took refuge in the interior of the island and live there today. Those who live in the part of the island facing Malaca are called *Batas*. They are the most savage and warlike people in the whole world; they eat human flesh. (Barros 1563: Dec III, Cap. 5:1)

This notion that Bataks were the ferocious cannibals of the interior was repeated by numerous European sources subsequently, and debated in the salons of the Enlightenment. For those of the upland people who did continue this practice after the Islamisation of the coast, it was a mark of their freedom, and a warning to the otherwise powerful outsiders not to trespass on it. The Malay sources of the coast were less concerned with this factor, but did share the definition of Bataks as those who resisted Islam and continued to eat pork. A seventeenth century Aceh text, the *Hikayat Aceh*, twice mentions Batak as an ethnic group. In an Aceh succession conflict of the 1590s it portrays the challenger stopping at Barus on the way to confronting his brother at the capital, and recruiting two upriver Batak *datu* (healers), 'skilled in the arts of sorcery (*sihir*) and magic (*hikmat*)', who successfully caused the king to become sick (*Hikajat Aceh* 1958: 92). A second incident is more surprising, portraying the young Iskandar Muda encountering 'an old Batak' on a hunt for a wild buffalo, who tricked the prince into giving him a sword and kris, and then scampered off into the forest (*Hikajat Aceh* 1958:186–7). This indicates that there were still villagers unincorporated into the Aceh state and religion very close to Banda Aceh, and that such people were called 'Batak'. This became in succeeding centuries a definition that many Bataks accepted. Nineteenth century witnesses assert that when Minahassan missionary teachers, and Chinese traders, penetrated into Batak areas for the first time they were also considered Batak, since they ate pork (Perret 1995: 60). External sources identified the different Batak groups through state-like rather than ethnic distinctions among the 'vast variety of tribes of Battas' (Anderson 1826: 209). John Anderson's mission to the east coast in 1823 also identified twenty-four distinct 'cannibal states' in the interior of East Sumatra, which today would be classified as Karo, Simalungun or Toba Batak. For the first time, however, Anderson did also make a rough ethno-linguistic distinction between the 'Karau-Karau [Karo]' and the 'Tubba [Toba]' as separate tribes with distinct languages, and also heard mention of fierce Pakpak in the far interior. The Karo were particularly distinguished from other Bataks by their industry and commercialisation, and avoidance of cannibalism (Anderson 1826: 222–6; 324–7).

In modern times the oral traditions of the Bataks do distinguish different though related origins of the different language groups, and also have their separate memories of hostile encounters with coastal Muslims. While there are some Hindu-Buddhist influences throughout the Batakland, these are understood to be stronger among Karos, who retained a practice of cremation and abhorred the cannibalism of their neighbours. One of the five Karo clans, the Sembiring (lit. 'the dark ones'), are remembered to have particular Hindu origins, including a sub-clan named Berahmana (Kipp 1993: 15; Rae 1994: 42–3). These and other oral traditions tend to confirm the connection between Karo identity and the quasi-Islamised Aru of sixteenth and seventeenth century sources.

Aceh attacked Aru on a number of occasions between 1539 and 1640, finally succeeding in dislodging the 'heretic' sultanate from the coast and replacing it with a Malayo-Muslim style of port-polity known as Deli. These events were remembered by Karos in the story of Putri Ijo (Malay: *Puteri Hijau*—'green princess'), who heroically led the last-ditch Karo resistance to the Acehnese at a fort the remains of which can still be found at Deli Tua, near Medan. While Aceh influence was never exercised directly over the Batak interior, the Karo also remember their four symbolic rulers, the Sibayak, as having been instituted by Aceh at its seventeenth century peak of influence (Singarimbun 1975: 6–8).

'Isolation' of the long eighteenth century

The aggressive expansion of Islamic Aceh in the period 1520–1630, at the expense of all the varied coastal states, ensured a separation not only between Bataks and Islam, but also between Bataks and the port-states of the coast. Batak 'statelessness' can be dated from this period, when states came to be associated by Batak with an aggressive 'other'. This statelessness was, however, qualified. The Karo and Simalungun on the east coast, and the Toba Batak on the west, each preserved from the earlier period a certain memory of state, often linked through tradition with Aceh. Thus the four *sibayak* (literally 'rich ones', perhaps a translation of the Acehnese and Malay *orang kaya*), who had a certain ritual primacy in the Karo area, and the four raja who held a somewhat stronger position in the Simalungun area, were popularly believed to have been inaugurated during the period of Aceh hegemony over the coast (Joustra 1910: 23; Kipp 1993: 215–17; Rae 1994: 63–4).

Many Toba Batak traditions also linked a principle of sacred descent with the coastal kingdoms they remembered—Aceh and Barus. The latter was a vital port for Toba Batak camphor exports in the long term, and therefore some ritual tribute was to be expected. Joustra (1910: 25–6) was struck at the surprisingly uniform set of traditions about the Barus link with Bakkara and the Singamangaraja line. The most accessible of these versions is now the Barus Hilir chronicle edited by Jane Drakard. This describes the journey of the founder of the Muslim dynasty of Barus Hilir, Sultan Ibrahim, through the Batak territories prior to establishing his kingdom on the coast. First in Silindung, and then at the Singamangaraja's sacred place of Bakkara, and finally in the Pasaribu territory, the local chiefs pleaded with him to stay and become their king. At Bakkara he urged the Bataks to become Muslim, because then they would be one people (*bangsa*) with him and he could stay as king. The Bataks responded apologetically, 'We do not want to enter Islam. Whatever else you order we will obey'. He therefore moved on, but not before fathering a child by a local woman, who became the first Singamangaraja. In each place agreements were sworn to by both sides, establishing the long-term relationship between upland Batak producers on one hand and coastal Malay traders on the other. These included establishing the 'four penghulu' of Silindung as a supra-village institution linked to the Barus trade (Drakard 1990: 75–80).

Since Barus and other ports on the west coast were themselves frequently under Aceh suzerainty, it is not surprising that Aceh also figured in Batak memory. Its ritual pre-eminence over the Singamangaraja line was acknowledged in various ways in the better-known nineteenth century, including the Singamangaraja's seal and flag, both of which appear modelled on the Aceh Sultan's. This link, mythologised in the mysterious Batak ancestor-figure Raja Uti, who produced no heirs but disappeared to Aceh, may go back to the troubled relationship of a Batak state with Aceh in the sixteenth century.

For the controversial Mandailing Batak author Parlindungan, however, and the Batak manuscripts of the 'Arsip Bakkara' he claims as a source, there was another powerful connection with Aceh in the late eighteenth century. He claims these documents reveal a treaty of friendship between the otherwise unknown Singamangaraja IX and Sultan Alauddin Muhammad Syah, known to have ruled Aceh uneasily from 1781 to 1795. The treaty purportedly agreed that Singkil was Acehnese, the Uti Kanan (Simpang Kanan?) area Batak, and Barus a neutral zone. But the Acehnese cannon which sealed the deal caused such havoc among some elephants at Bakkara that Singamangaraja IX was killed by one of them (Parlindungan 1965: 486–7).

As so often with Parlindungan's fanciful stories, there seems to be some factual basis disguised behind his cavalier style. In the 1780s the Singkil area was developed for pepper cultivation, and the limits of Acehnese control became an urgent concern. Acehnese raided the British outstation of Tapanuli (Sibolga) in 1786, and the British responded by attacking some Acehnese forts (Lee 1995: 67–75). This was indeed a time, in other words, when Acehnese would have sought to lock Batak suppliers and traders into their networks rather than the British ones.

Another intriguing vignette assumes some significance in countering the myth of Batak 'isolation' during the long eighteenth century. In 1858 a Frenchman or Eurasian called De Molac told a Pondichery newspaper that in the last quarter of the eighteenth century 'his family settled in the most savage part of Sumatra, established magnificent agricultural establishments there, acquired great influence among the natives and succeeded in reforming their customs'. The head of the family 'had recently been elected chief of the confederation of Bataks, a Malay people whose lands border Dutch possessions and the kingdom of Aceh' (*Le Moniteur Universel* 104, 4 avril 1858: 467). While the story was no doubt exaggerated, the supernatural expectations attached to later European visitors to the Batak highlands (Burton and Ward, Von der Tuuk, Modigliani) make it believable that there were predecessors in the eighteenth century.

Islam and Christianity in the nineteenth century

While Batak identity had been defined before 1800 by resistance to the Muslim states of the coast, the rapid Muslim advance in the first half of the nineteenth century complicated this equation thereafter. Some Sumatran students in Mecca came into contact with the militant Puritanism of the Wahabbi movement in the first years of the nineteenth century, and returned to overturn Sumatran Islam. The upland Minangkabau area to the south of Batakland had been Islamic since the sixteenth century, but the reformers insisted that compromises with local tradition, including cock-fighting, the worship of spirits and of Islamic saints and the sacred kingship of Pagarruyung, must all be forcibly eliminated. This movement, which the Dutch labelled Padri, swept through the Minangkabau highlands by force in the following twenty years, massacring the royal family of Pagarruyung and many other upholders of traditional custom (*adat*). Padri forces moved also into the southern Bataklands previously resistant to Islam, and one force penetrated as far north as Lake Toba, where it attacked Bakkara and killed the tenth of the Singamangaraja priest-kings. Their forces were forced to pull back, however, afflicted by disease, by the tough resistance of Toba Batak fortified villages, and after 1830 by the intervention of Dutch forces against them. Their venture into the Toba area served only to consolidate Toba Batak hostility to Islam, but the southern Batak who spoke a very similar Batak dialect became and remained Muslim, and thereby increasingly estranged from their non-Muslim Batak brethren. They tended to reject the term Batak thereafter as part of their pagan past, and as applying to their pig-eating northern neighbours.

The Padri incursion into the Bataklands is very poorly documented, except in the extraordinary book of Mangaraja Parlindungan, the sources for which remain suspect. Batak oral traditions in general agree that some of the most militant of the Islamic marauders who brought fire and sword to the Toba area were themselves newly converted Bataks. Singamangaraja X was killed by a militant Padri they called Si Pokki, around 1830 according to most authorities. Parlindungan, however, puts this event in 1819, and traces the source of the hostilities to cleavages within the Singamangaraja lineage itself. Tuanku Rao, the Padri zealot who ravaged the Bataklands, was in his reading an alienated Batak turned militant Muslim (Parlindungan 1965). In any case, these events marked a cleavage between the southern, Islamised Bataklands and the remainder of the Bataks, most of whom would come under Christian influence over the succeeding century. The Padris violently initiated a century of upheaval and threats to the Batak highlander way of life. Paradoxically, also, the death of Singamangaraja X at Padri hands enhanced the notion that this dynasty was a kind of magical protector of Batak integrity.

The next serious challenger to that integrity was Christianity. After some abortive forays by British and American Protestants in the early nineteenth century, a systematic mission to the Toba Batak was inaugurated by Ludwig Nommensen (1834–1918) and his colleagues of the German Rhenisch mission in 1862. He laboured particularly to have a Batak New Testament published as the first significant work in a romanised form of that language. The successful establishment of a Batak church as a result of these efforts is considered one of the greatest achievements of Protestant mission endeavour.

Mary Steedly (1996) has pointed out the importance of the link between the Protestant missionary revival of the nineteenth century and 'a framework of romantic primordialism' in language. The influence of German romanticism, particularly Herder's emphasis on the uniqueness and centrality of every language in the life of its speakers, led German and Dutch Protestant missionaries of the nineteenth century revival to seek to speak to each individual in their own language. The Protestant missions to the Batak all put great store on translating the scriptures into the vernacular and developing an indigenous literature. In the transition of these peoples to acceptance of a standardised form of their languages, this mission insistence on developing a printed form of the vernacular proved decisive. By contrast the highlanders who became Muslim tended to be led towards acceptance of the 'high culture' (Gellner's term) of Malay, or later Indonesian. Islam has historically tended to favour the big five inclusive 'high cultures'—Arabic, Persian, Turkish, Urdu and Malay—rather than encouraging writing and later printing in local vernaculars. Christian missions prior to the nineteenth century had also developed their teaching and sacred literature in the Malay *lingua franca*, which had thereby become the church language of Ambonese and Minahassans. For the purpose of Batak identity formation, therefore, it was important to have embraced scriptural religion **after** the German romantic revival.

The Rhenisch mission to the Toba Batak succeeded in part because as a German body it was conceptually separate from Dutch colonialism, and indeed preceded colonial control in the Toba Batak heartland. Between 1860 and 1900 the majority of Toba Bataks accepted Christianity, in a form which centred around the printed Batak versions of the Augsburg Confession and the Bible. Although there were areas of great tension between Batakness and Christianity, the second generation of Christians was able to conceive the uniform style of worship, belief and church governance developed by the Rhenisch mission as a part of the Batak identity, and the language used by the mission as a 'classic' form of Batak expression. In 1927 the mission was reconstituted as a Batak church, the HKBP.

The missionaries initially hoped that their printed Bible would unite the Bataks as Luther's had the Germans, despite the mutual unintelligibility of some Batak languages. This succeeded, however, only for those we now call Toba Batak, to the west and south of Lake Toba in North Tapanuli. Distinct Simalungun and Karo Batak identities were determined by a very different language (in the Karo case), and by the orientation of both groups to the east coast of Sumatra for outside contacts, with its much greater commerce and state-building tendencies on the shores of the busy Malacca Straits. Both Karo and Simalungun became more entwined with Malay coastal rulers, and from the 1860s with Dutch administrators and planters who preferred to work through the compliant rajas. Once Christian evangelism in the Toba Batak language had made enough progress that there were Simalungun pastors and educated laymen, these insisted on a separate liturgy in a separately standardised romanisation of their dialect (1928), and eventually a separate church (1952). In the longer term, ethnic churches each with their different literary standards came to define the boundaries of separate ethnies, the Batak sub-groups.

Those we now call Karo or Karo Batak were declared an objective of Dutch missionary work for political reasons, because of their proximity to the Muslim and anti-Dutch Acehnese (Kipp 1990). The expansion of the Rhenisch mission in that direction was therefore not encouraged by colonial authority, the work being entrusted to the Dutch Missionary Society (NZG). Karos appear to have accepted the broad exonym 'Batak' in the nineteenth century, but the Dutch mission favoured a distinctive term, to reflect the very different language in which they preached, to cater to Karo sensitivity to Toba domination, and to emphasise that the German mission should keep out of its sphere (Kipp 1993: 28–38; Steedly 1996).

The mission began printing Karo prayer books from about 1910, and in 1922 began a Karo-language mission journal, *Merga Si Lima*, which was influential by example and provocation even though it served only the tiny number (2–3 per cent) of Karos who were then Christian. In the 1930s other more ethno-nationalist publications began to appear among Karo. Although the Dutch Karo mission was a failure by comparison with the German Toba one, it had contributed greatly to the acceptance of a standard form of printed, romanised Karo, and hence of a self-conscious Karo ethnie by the time the colonial era ended. It was during the Japanese occupation, with Dutch missionaries interned, that Christianity began to seem an important part of this Karo identity. The mission churches declared themselves an independent Karo church (GBKP) and conversions multiplied.

Genealogy and identity

Today most Bataks are fascinated by their genealogical relationships, and believe themselves related to all other Bataks through a knowable descent line. This had once been esoteric knowledge, kept alive by Datus who rehearsed the oral traditions. Batak writing in the old bamboo-inscribed characters was not used for such matters.

In the 1920s, however, undoubtedly as a result of the interaction of curious Dutch and educated Batak officials working in the field of Batak customary law, a huge chart was compiled linking all Toba and most Angkola and Mandailing *margas* (patrilineages) with each other by tracing each back to branchings out from parent *margas* until reaching the ultimate source in Si Raja Batak. This chart appears to have originated in the labours of a Batak government prosecutor (*jaksa*), Waldemar Hoeta Galoeng, who printed it in Batak with an exposition of Batak genealogy linking all the Toba Batak *margas* to Si Raja Batak (Castles 1972: 184; Hutagalung 1991). W. K. H. Ypes, Resident of Tapanuli in 1921–5, wrote an endorsement for this book, but claimed in introducing his own weighty tome on the same subject in 1932 that he had compiled the information in 1926, after his retirement, by travelling around the Batak area recording information from elderly informants (Ypes 1932: 1–4). From the date of Hoeta Galoeng's publication, in any event, educated Bataks had access to a universal schema of their relationships. This has been enormously influential in establishing common origin and relationship as the key symbolic issue of Batak identity, particularly among the Toba for whom the system seems to work pretty well.

Dutch officials noted that the more dispersed *marga* had been tending to lose their sense of origin in the nineteenth century, and substituting legend. For example the Hasibuans of Padang Lawas, an area where Islam had made some gains, told Neumann in the 1880s that they were descended from 'one of the distinguished families of the retinue of Alexander the Great'. But in 1929, after the publication of Hoeta Galoeng's genealogy, this branch was convinced (rightly, in Vergouwen's understanding) that they were sprung from the extended *marga* of Huta Galung, and 'participated with zest' in the great festival where, 'for the first time in history, the entire Huta Galung marga assembled in ... the small territory of its origin in the middle of the Silindung valley; a gathering that made all the other Bataks envious' (Vergouwen 1964:18–19).

This effort on Toba genealogy appears to have provoked a rival construction by a Dutch missionary, J. H. Neumann, of the origins of Karo patrilineages. Mary Steedly (1996: 27) suggests that the missionaries may have half-consciously essentialised Karo origins to make it easier for Karos to let go of the old identities tied to particular spirit cults, and thus enter the modern world as Karo Christians. Certainly it has had that effect in modern times. Even though most evidence suggests diverse origins for the five Karo *margas* (Ypes 1932: 59–64; Kipp 1993: 15), a sense of common origin is a part of modern Karo self-perception.

The self-awareness of what became the three most coherent Batak ethnies—Toba, Karo and Mandailing—on the national stage can be dated to the 1920s, when the highlanders were becoming numerous enough in the cities to make their presence felt, and a mission-educated generation began to sustain ethnic publications in the romanised vernacular, Malay or Dutch. Up until about 1920 Bataks of any description who moved to the cities were quiet about their identity. Either they became Muslim and joined the broader urban Malayo-Muslim culture, or they passed themselves off as Minangkabau or Mandailing, who as Muslims had already established 'civilised' highland identities in the cities. But around 1920 the first Batak churches became established in both Batavia and Medan, and self-help clubs, newspapers and football clubs soon followed. Parada Harahap tells a story about the first Batak football club in Batavia in 1921, which at first was received with derision when it put up its sign at matches. But eventually 'they saw that people who had pretended to be *orang Padang*, whom they had regarded as clean and educated, turned out [to be Bataks], and spoke Dutch too' (cited Castles 1972: 181–2). The 1920s were marked by a great interest in Batakness, with unprecedented publications in Batak languages (never matched in the Indonesian era) as well as Malay dealing with *adat*, traditions and genealogy. The first Batak novels marked another stage in ethnie formation (Castles 1972: 183–4; Rodgers 1991a; 1997; 2005).

At the beginning of this flowering of Batak organisations, Muslims and Christians often cooperated, with the better-established Mandailing Batak Muslims willing to engage other Bataks whose dialect and *adat* was very similar even if their religion was different. But as Mandailing domination of Batak organisations was challenged by larger numbers of people they saw as still somewhat uncivilised, the Mandailings rethought their identity. A turning point came in 1922, when the first major inter-ethnic dispute broke out in Medan between two groups of South Tapanuli Batak Muslims who to outsiders seemed almost identical. A Muslim graveyard in Medan, owned by a Mandailing trust, had for forty years allowed all Muslims of South Tapanuli origin to be buried there, accepting that for practical purposes all could be considered Mandailing. But the curators suddenly stopped admitting people who still considered themselves to be Batak, generally those of Angkola, Sipirok and Padanglawas origin. Such peoples were required specifically to renounce their Batakness. A commission was formed to settle the dispute according to Muslim law, but it became only more bitter. The better-established Mandailings won this particular round, because of their better contacts and economic resources in Medan, but the issue had only arisen because other groups of Bataks were becoming educated and urban, and challenging the Mandailing domination by proposing 'Batak' as a more appropriate inclusive term. The leading Malay-language newspaper of Medan, the football club, a private school and a trading company which had been set up by Mandailing Bataks, all split into two rival organisations, one Mandailing and one 'Batak'—even though both at that stage were predominately Muslim. As an outcome of this furore urban Mandailings were even more convinced they were not Bataks, and formed a 'Mandailing National Committee' to demand that they not be listed as Bataks in the 1930 census (Castles 1972: 186–9). They won a partial victory (see below).

As a result of these disputes, the leading Sumatran city of Medan 'was changing from a 'melting-pot', in which immigrants were expected to conform to Malayo-Muslim culture, to a region of lasting ethnic diversity and competition' (Castles 1972: 189). But it was not clear at the end of the colonial period whether the political destinies of the different ethnies would also diverge.

The 1930 census, the last to count Indonesians by ethnicity until 2000, adopted the procedure of 'grouping as far as possible' the different ethnicities (*landaarden*)—'so as not to make the work of the tellers too complex and the processing and publication of the data too costly'. Groups would be sub-divided only in the main home base of the people in question. 'Batak' was taken as one group, who therefore appeared only as undifferentiated Batak when they were migrants outside the Tapanuli homeland. Within Tapanuli, where the overwhelming majority still lived, they were divided into seven *ondergroepen*. Of these Angkola, Karo, Padanglawas, Toba, Timur [Simalungun] and Pak-Pak [Dairi] were hyphenated as Bataks, while 'Mandailingers' were just listed as such. The census acknowledged that these sub-groups were far from fully established, however. On the one hand many declared themselves to be simply 'Bataks'; on the other many gave themselves more specific geographic appellations: Batak Samosir, Batak Sipirok, Batak Barus, etc, which were simply accumulated by the tellers into their designated sub-groups (*Volkstelling 1930*: IV: 15–17).

This method of state simplification was hugely important as a means of anchoring the seven groups in the mind of educated elites and influential outsiders as scientifically established ethnie. Dutch, Japanese and Indonesian higher authority tended subsequently to reinforce the categories as administrative ones, with some exceptions. Padang Lawas and to a lesser extent Angkola gradually merged into an overarching Mandailing identity because as predominately Muslim Bataks anxious to distance themselves from pagan or Christian Bataks they were administered together in a South Tapanuli district. When in 2000 ethnicity was again considered safe to reinsert in an Indonesian census, the Statistical Bureau tautologically clarified 'ethnicity is respondent's ethnicity' (*Suku bangsa adalah golongan etnis respondan*), seemingly allowing self-definition though only for large categories. In the outcome Dairi and Simalungun were too small to register in the top eight ethnicities, the details of which were given in the published census. Angkola survived as a major self-ascription in the highlands, though in diaspora Angkolas self-defined as a broader category—Mandailing, Mandailing/Angkola, Batak or Tapanuli. The surprise was that Toba Bataks split between those who declared as Toba (1.15m.), predominately in Samosir, in areas near the lake and wherever other Bataks predominated, and those who chose Batak or Tapanuli (3.2m., grouped together by the census), around Tarutung and overwhelmingly in the diaspora (BPS 2001: xx, xxxi, 74–6).

At the end of the colonial period, the government's proposal to devolve powers to a 'Batak Council' drove the division deeper than ever. As the Resident summarised the reaction, in North Tapanuli most opinion insisted that there should be one council for the whole proud Batak people, and that those of Mandailing too descended from Si Raja Batak, the mythical ancestor of all. Although Angkola and Sipirok chiefs also supported this idea despite their Islam, those of Mandailing fiercely maintained that they 'did not belong to the Batak group, that they could not and would not be called Bataks', that as Muslims they refused to join in a community of which the majority would be Christian and pagan, and that this was 'the unalterable opinion of the whole population of Mandailing' (cited Castles 1972: 268, 274; cf Rodgers 1981).

The growing ethnie nationalism of the Toba Batak, in other words, was emphatically not shared by the Mandailing of this period, who made 'religion the decisive criterion of identification', as Castles puts it, and unlike the Muslims of Angkola and Sipirok, 'let Islam rob them of their ancestors' (Castles 1972: 280). Besides religion, the emotive power of anti-imperial nationalism also played a role in defining Batak identity, less in competition with ethnie nationalism than in a layered merging with it.

This feature arose rapidly in the period 1917–20, a time when political innovation was at a peak throughout the Indies. A group of educated Toba Batak who had fallen out with the German missionaries for a variety of reasons formed the Batak Christian Association (*Hatopan Kristen Batak*, or HKB) in September 1917. Its leader was the charismatic Mangihut Hezekiel Manullang, who had expressed his disaffection from the stern paternalism of the missionaries by journeying to Singapore for training with the Seventh Day Adventists. His HKB was at times encouraged by Dutch officials who saw it as a counter to the leading Muslim organisation, Sarekat Islam, and at times by missionaries who shared its opposition to European plantations entering the Batak area, though for different reasons. But eventually it gained popularity by opposing both. In its journal, *Soara Batak*, and in mass meetings around the Batakland, it successfully fought the plantations which were being encouraged by some local officials, opposed forced labour on the colonial roads, demanded more schools and championed a stronger role in the church for the laity than conservative missionaries were prepared to give (Castles 1972: 123–70). All these issues brought the HKB more into alliance than confrontation with the growing anti-imperial nationalism of the time. The HKB faded as a unifying Batak voice in the 1920s, while Manullang and his key supporters became more involved with Sumatran and Indonesian nationalist organisations whose influence was limited to the towns. But a similar spirit of standing up to German missionaries and Dutch officials was evident in a breakaway church of 1927, the Huria Kristen Batak (becoming Huria Kristen Indonesia in 1946), which helped provoke the mainstream mission into reconstituting itself as a self-governing church under its own bishop (*ephorus*) three years later—the Huria Kristen Batak Protestan or HKBP.

Lance Castles' careful conclusion on the colonial period was that 'there was a growing consciousness among Tapanuli people that they were Indonesians, but ... the consciousness of *sukubangsa* (ethnie) membership was growing more rapidly' (Castles 1972: 173). In place of a sense of shame about their 'primitiveness' which had led earlier migrants to assimilate into Malayo-Muslim culture, there was an increasingly confident certainty of identity as Toba Batak, but layered within other identities both narrower and larger, including Indonesian. The intermediate idea of Sumatra, briefly prominent among students in the 1920s, never had much traction. Batak students left the Young Sumatrans' Union (JSB) in 1926 complaining of Minangkabau domination, but participated vigorously in the Indonesia-wide Youth Congress of 1928 that required them to declare that their only *bangsa* (nation) was *bangsa Indonesia* (Castles 1972: 177). Bataks had always defined themselves **against** their Muslim neighbours, whereas their minority position as Christians encouraged them to reach beyond Sumatra to fellow Christians in the east. Since the political and educational structures they operated in were Indies-wide, so were the horizons of educated youth. Bataks on the whole did not see themselves in opposition to Indonesia-wide anti-imperial nationalism, and were able to play their part within it in the turbulent 1940s.

The 1940s and the victory of 'Indonesia'

The response of once-stateless peoples to the political challenges and opportunities of the 1940s depended upon where they were located. The Japanese rulers of the 1942–5 period made sharp regional differences in the degree of nationalist mobilisation they allowed, which had knock-on effects when the Dutch attempted to return in 1945. Borneo and the islands of eastern Indonesia were regarded by Japanese planners as 'sparsely populated primitive areas, which shall be retained in future for the benefit of the Empire' (Benda *et al.* 1965: 7). They were allocated to the Japanese Navy for administrative purposes, enjoyed no concessions to nationalism until the last months of the war, and had a generally negative experience of the Japanese period. With some exceptions in Bali and South Sulawesi, the elites in these areas cooperated with Dutch plans to develop a federal structure. Formerly stateless upland peoples such as the Dayaks of West Kalimantan (Borneo), and the Minahassans and Toraja of Sulawesi (Celebes), threw up leaders who began to mobilise and politicise their respective ethnies for representation in the federal structures.

Among the most successful specifically ethnic political groups was the Dayak Association (Persatuan Daya, or PD) of West Kalimantan, led by the charismatic Oevaang Oeray. Despite the great linguistic diversity of the groups in question, they were united in opposition to the better-placed Muslim populations of the coastal areas and towns, symbolised by the sultans of Pontianak and Sambas who had claimed some primacy over them. In a populist style that would have appealed also to many Bataks, Oeray attacked the 'layered colonialism', whereby Malay and Dutch combined to oppress the Dayak, who in effect became 'the water buffalo that has to work and sacrifice for the raja and government' (cited Davidson 2008: 42).

The PD had seven representatives in the Dutch-created West Kalimantan Council of 1947–9, and won 31 per cent of the popular vote in West Kalimantan at the 1955 national election. The electoral process was clearly of great assistance to such an ethnic movement, enabled by popular support to recover from the otherwise fatal political handicap of having cooperated with the Dutch in the federal period. Even though Sukarno banned all such regional or ethnic parties in 1959 as part of his demolition of parliamentary democracy, Oeray himself was able to play his pro-Sukarno populist card to be appointed governor of West Kalimantan in 1960 (Davidson 2008: 45–51).

Sumatra, by contrast, was fully exposed to the revolutionary wave of 1945–6 in favour of a unitary and democratic republic. Parties formed through wholly local initiatives to support the Republic and oppose the

Dutch return declared themselves voluntarily and enthusiastically to be part of Java-based national parties. Some of this activity was the consequence of Sukarno's initial idea of having a single state party, a reincarnation of his pre-war nationalist party (PNI), which would embrace all the movements mobilised by the Japanese against the Allied return. Although this idea was stillborn in Java itself and revoked by Sukarno within two weeks, it lived on in Sumatra through the energy of Dr A. K. Gani, originally declared to be its leader for all Sumatra by Sukarno. The most militant movements mobilised by the Japanese among Bataks, especially Karo and Simalungun, to exploit their resentment of the dominant Dutch-supported rajas of East Sumatra, became officially members of PNI. Local Islamic organisations also declared themselves to be part of the umbrella organisation, Masjumi, set up by the Japanese in Java. A variety of Marxist organisations revived the pre-war communist party (PKI) as well as some competitors or united fronts, all on a national basis (van Langenberg 1976: 325–91; Reid 1979a: 172–7).

Rather than establishing an ethnic party like the Dayaks in Dutch-controlled Borneo, Muslim Bataks tended to support Java-centred Muslim parties, and Christian Bataks the Indonesian Christian Party (initially Parki, later Parkindo), set up by Protestant Christians in Java and extended to northern Sumatra in December 1945. The main Toba Batak church, the HKBP, threw its weight behind this party and indeed in many branches became indistinguishable from it, making this 'without doubt the most overtly ethno-centric of all the political parties' in Sumatra (van Langenberg 1976: 382, also 401). Parkindo still had a majority vote in many areas of the Toba heartland of North Tapanuli at the 1955 election. However Simalungun and Karo Christians, wary of Toba domination which they had managed to resist in their separate ethnic churches, were more likely to support parties such as the secular-nationalist PNI. Similarly Toba Bataks who had migrated during the revolution to occupy plantation land were much more likely to vote for the secular but more revolutionary parties, PKI and PNI, which supported their claims to retain the land they had seized as their 'gift of the revolution' (Liddle 1970: 92–7). The former sultanates of the east coast lost their power first through the violent 'social revolution' of March 1946 in which Bataks played a disproportionate role, and then by the legal rearrangements of the federal state the Dutch erected in East Sumatra, the Negara Sumatera Timur (NST). Nevertheless the NST did represent the interests of the former Malay establishment, and opposition to it in the period 1947–50 did consolidate support for the Republic among all the Batak groups (van Langenberg 1985: 113).

During the revolutionary period, both Toba and Karo Batak had been rather successful in using the republican army, the TNI, as a path to power. Unlike comparable groups in Borneo and eastern Indonesia, these Sumatrans had the opportunity to join the Japanese-trained 'volunteer' force, the *Giyugun*, for training up to first lieutenant rank, and Bataks responded strongly. Most of the Bataks trained in this way by the Japanese spent the revolutionary period as officers of the TNI which in the long run became the best weapon central government had in trying to bring the unruly warlords of the Batak area to heel. Many non-Batak, Muslim politicians and military leaders of East Sumatra had participated in the NST, and thus lost their legitimacy in the pro-Republican mood that followed its demise in 1950. Most Acehnese military figures were compromised by the Aceh rebellion of 1953. Curiously, it was precisely their military experience as agents of a modernising secular Indonesian government in combating various Islamist rebellions that led previously animist Karo Bataks to identify with Christianity. Nearly a thousand Karo officers and men stationed in Aceh did so at a series of mass baptisms at the beginning of 1953 (Rae 1994: 144–7).

As we noted in discussing Aceh above, the original Republican plan for a single Province of Sumatra gradually yielded to the older reality of ethnic blocks which had been labelled Residencies under the Dutch. First came the split into three provinces of North, Central and South, with the northern Province embracing three former Residencies—Aceh, East Sumatra and the Batak heartland of Tapanuli. Aceh regained its status as a province in 1959, and other former Residencies profited by being split off by Jakarta from their rebellious capitals during the PRRI in 1958. When Bengkulu was re-established as a province in 1967, Sumatra was again divided into eight provinces directly under Jakarta. Of pre-war ethnie-based Residencies only Tapanuli failed to make its case for provincial status, despite its size (it would have ranked fifth in population as a separate province) and relative coherence in terms of Batak *adat*. The ethnie formation of once-stateless highlanders clearly failed in realising even this level of political demands.

The reasons are two. Firstly, the historic difficulty Bataks had experienced in accepting higher political authority made Tapanuli hard to govern on its own. In particular the Muslim Mandailings were bitterly opposed to domination by North Tapanuli Christians. Secondly, most Bataks, and especially the Toba, had welcomed the destruction of the federal NST in East Sumatra, which had been erected partly to hold back Batak penetration of the fertile lowlands and their squatting on plantation land. Its demise opened the floodgates to land-hungry Toba Batak migrants (Cunningham 1958; Pelzer 1982). The merging of the two former residencies was therefore seen as an important victory of the revolution by many republicans, especially Bataks. Those who supported separating the two had been discredited by their association with the NST. Even the most determined Toba Batak ethnie nationalists, therefore, were inclined to see East Sumatra, and the rest of Indonesia beyond it, as an opportunity to escape the poverty of homeland rather than a threat to that homeland.

This acceptance of a North Sumatran and an Indonesian identity was made easier because a Christian Toba Batak, Colonel Maludin Simbolon, was military commander for North Sumatra from 1950, while most of the troops under his command (except for the restive Acehnese) were also Batak. As the most disciplined force in a very troubled region, Simbolon's army became increasingly opposed to the communist-led strikes and seizures of plantation land that were features of the 1950s, and also with the leftward drift of the Jakarta government. Like much of the new Sumatran elite, he resented Jakarta's attempts to stop the profitable direct trade with the British ports of Singapore and Penang.

In December 1956 Simbolon declared martial law and the rupture of relations with the Jakarta government. Like the Aceh rebellion of 1953, this act of rebellion rested on some fundamental ethnic, regional and religious considerations, but was overtly a rebellion aimed at reforming the Indonesian Republic as a whole. It was designed to obtain multiethnic support, but conspicuously failed to do so. The central military authorities quickly declared Simbolon dismissed, and replaced him as commander with a Karo Batak officer, Lt Col. Djamin Gintings. This immediately revealed that Simbolon's core support was Toba Batak. In a highly symbolic gesture, Simbolon's loyal mostly-Toba troops abandoned the multi-ethnic provincial capital, Medan, five days after the proclamation, in a retreat to the Toba heartland of North Tapanuli. There the rebellion sputtered on for several years, eventually forming part of the wider alternative government, the PRRI, declared by anticommunist and chiefly Muslim ex-ministers in February 1958. This PRRI was seen as such a threat to the Republic that it provoked a stern reaction from Sukarno and the TNI command (under a South Tapanuli Muslim Batak, General Nasution). They sent troops from Java which quickly ended the rebellion (Smail 1968). This episode certainly put Toba Bataks in confrontation with Jakarta, but there was no support from any quarter for a separate Batak state. Sumatran representation in the officer corps was markedly reduced by the dismissal of many as rebels, but the army remained the principal route by which Toba Batak could tap into power at the national level.

New Order prosperity and Batak diaspora

During Suharto's New Order of 1966–98 the political scene changed profoundly. After lurching from one crisis to another for twenty years, Indonesia had entered a condition of 'idealized absence in which nothing ... appears to happen' (Pemberton 1994: 7). First through repression, but ultimately with the apparent complicity of Indonesians anxious to be again *slamet* (secure against unforeseen events), national politics was rendered routine and uneventful. A phase of unprecedented economic expansion began, with its attendant urbanisation and mobility. As the boundaries and identity of the state ceased to be questioned, a strident form of anti-imperial nationalism was replaced by a surprisingly effective state nationalism which used a uniform education system, a mono-chrome nationalist narrative, monuments and public theatre of state to turn 'peasants into Indonesians'. Even as the roots of the new urban middle class in the many pasts and cultures of the Archipelago became increasingly tenuous, a non-political fascination with roots and tradition took the place of the political preoccupations of the 1950s and 1960s.

On the other hand the economic success of Suharto's long reign provided many opportunities for Bataks to fulfil their ambitions for status and inner strength (*sahala*). Their highland valleys had for centuries been much more densely settled than the fertile lowlands of East Sumatra, and their relatively high birth rate steadily increased the pressure on land. The Mandailings, as we have seen, did this first through Islam, accepting the low estimation of Batak-ness which most of their fellow Muslims had long held. Their diaspora began in the 1860s, to East Sumatra and Malaya. The phenomenon of Batak outmigration from the relatively crowded highlands around Lake Toba to the more abundant land and opportunity of the lowlands has been noted in the literature at least since 1936, when 42,000 Toba Batak were already settled as irrigated rice farmers in the adjacent Simalungun Batak area of East Sumatra (Tichelman 1936). Mandailing Bataks from South Tapanuli, quicker to profit from colonial education opportunities and as Muslims more readily fitting into the Malay establishment of the east coast, had been moving to clerical and commercial positions in the Medan area for twenty years before that. There were 45,000 of them in the east coast in 1930, more than half as many as the Mandailings remaining at home (Naim 1984: 49).

The large scale of Toba Batak migration to East Sumatra after the 'floodgates' of *kerajaan* and colonial control were broken in 1950 has been tracked by Clark Cunningham (1958), using particularly out-migration from sample home villages and statistics for the spread of the

Table 6.1 *Batak migrants in Medan*[3]

Ethnicity	1930 census	%	1981	%	2000 census	%
Toba	n.a.	<1	187,686	14.1	365,758	19.2
Karo	n.a.		51,651	4.0	78,129	4.1
Mandail/Angkola	n.a.	<5	154,172	11.9	178,304	9.4
Total	76,584		1,294,132		1,904,104	

Batak church. I applied similar methods to Cunningham's in 1995 to show that the scale and reach of outmigration continued to expand among the Toba, and since about 1970 has been equally spectacular among the Karo. The prosperity of the Suharto period improved transport facilities, and directed the flow of migrants increasingly to the fastest-growing cities and manufacturing zones of Indonesia. Since about 1980 both Toba and Karo prefer to leave their home province altogether to seek for work. They find the ethnic competition too tough at home, where they are always branded by their origins, while the opportunities for education, government employment and commerce are all greater in Java, the less-populated areas of the east and Borneo, and the new industrial zone of Batam, near Singapore.

Medan, Indonesia's third-largest city with two million inhabitants, was 31 per cent Batak by 1981 and 34 per cent in 2000 (table 6.1).

The number of North Sumatra-born migrants in other provinces increased from 188,326 in 1971 to 1,314,117 in 2005 (BPS 2006), the biggest numbers being in Riau, West Java and Jakarta. The 1990 census showed that nearly 300,000 people left the North Sumatra province in the five previous years, suggesting that in that relatively prosperous period Bataks became Indonesia's champion outmigrants (BPS 1994: 35).

The statistics of the main Toba Batak ethnic church, HKBP, systematically reported until the 1990s, show how the movement to Jakarta took off in the Suharto period. Reported HKBP membership in Jakarta increased twenty-fold in the period between 1959 and 1993 (table 6.2). These figures show at least 23 per cent of the HKBP membership was urban and outside the homeland by 1982 and 30 per cent by 1993 (table 6.3). The statistics substantially underestimate the urban

---

[3] The 1981 figures are from Pelly (1994: 308). Estimates for 1930 are based on proportions given for Deli-Serdang, the district of which Medan was the centre. The 2000 census figures may overestimate Toba Batak at the expense of Mandailing and Angkola, because I have classified the largest Batak category, those who described themselves as simply 'Batak' or 'Tapanuli' (grouped together), as Toba, whereas some Angkola Batak probably also identified in this way.

Table 6.2 *Growth of Batak church membership in Jakarta (Bruner 1972: 212 and Table 6.3 below)*

1939	725
1949	2,650
1959	8,750
1969	23,000
1982	91,645
1993	166,829

Table 6.3 *HKBP membership figures calculated from appendices in HKBP 1984 (1982 figures) and HKBP 1995 (1993 figures)*

	1982	1993
Jakarta (inc. Bogor, Depok)	91,645 [est]	166,829
Other Java	19,985 [est]	35,063
Borneo and East	5,000 [est]	14,946
Medan (incl. Belawan)	155,427	193,957
Sibolga	18,436 [est]	23,356
Siantar, Tg. Tinggi, Binjei	17,074 [est]	39,866
Total big city	307,567 [est]	474,017 [30%]
Total HKBP	1,326,260	1,596,025

proportion, however, since the church has a weaker hold on young Bataks who migrate to the cities before marriage and often marry non-Bataks there, while the churches which are explicitly Indonesian rather than Batak are more attractive to urbanites—the Methodists, Catholics, Pentecostalists, GPIB, as well as the two originally Batak churches which split from HKBP partly in the desire to be more national, HKI and GKPI. While these non-HKBP options may represent about a quarter of the Toba Batak population in the Tapanuli homeland, I believe that they would represent at least 40 per cent in the cities outside North Sumatra. A survey of Toba members of five churches in North Sumatra's second city of Pematang Siantar in 1992/3 showed the four others to total 57 per cent of the HKBP's membership, without adding the fast-growing Pentecostalists (Purba and Purba 1998: 34–5). The ethnic question in the 2000 census revealed 300,000 'Bataks' in Jakarta, a figure which included many Karo and Mandailing as well as the Toba of the HKBP statistics, but which on the other hand could be supplemented by the 275,000 Bataks listed for West Java, most of whom live in the sprawling area of greater Jakarta outside the city limits (Suryadinata et al. 2003: 19–20). Overall, it is a safe assumption that the number of Toba Bataks in diaspora exceeded the 700,000 still in the Tapanuli homeland well before the end of the century. A substantial majority of diasporic Tobas were urban.

The Karo Batak, by contrast, had little tradition of emigration until 1950 (Kipp 1993: 4), so that their transformation since then can be reckoned even more remarkable. Figures for 1992 in the headquarters of the Karo protestant church (GBKP), showed only 40 per cent of its members were then still in the Karo highlands (Tanah Karo), though 5 per cent if Sibolangit (outside the Karo *kabupaten* on the eastern side of the watershed, but long-standing Karo territory) were added. Given similar assumptions as with the Toba Batak church, that the church's hold is less tight in urban diasporas, the Karo population would already have been predominately diasporic at that time. A much larger proportion of Karos, however, lived within a few hours of their homeland villages, and therefore returned every year for village feasts.

My own research in Toba and Karo sample villages in 1995 confirmed the impression of Janet Rodenburg (1997: 1) that 'everyone leaves'. Young people who remain in highland villages are seen as losers, either lacking the initiative to leave or in the case of some women, tied by family obligations. My sample village surveys in 1995 showed spectacular rates of outmigration among young people. The above-average family sizes for which Toba Bataks are known were reflected in my sample, an average of seven children in the previous generation dropping only to five in the present one (BPS 1992: 78). One Toba village (Lumban Batu) surveyed in the densely populated island of Samosir in Lake Toba, had had over a hundred residents in the 1970s but only eight in 1995, though thousands returned for the occasional festive ritual. Another more typical village in Samosir had produced sixty-nine children since 1960, sixty-one of whom had reached an age (mid teens) when migration was possible. All but four (93 per cent) had done so, half of whom had left the island of Sumatra altogether.

These Toba samples were not particularly well educated, and became petty traders or urban workers. Karo Bataks, on the other hand, are today driven to migration pre-eminently by education (Kipp 1993: 56, 158–60). In my larger Karo highlands village case (Gunung, in Tiga Binanga), 90 per cent of those educated in approximately the last decade had left the village, and 45 per cent of this group had obtained university education—a figure hard to equal for a rural community anywhere in the world. Table 6.4 confirms the remarkable trend since about 1970 for almost all Karo children to be pushed through the highest possible education level as a means to betterment, and with consequent movement to a sizeable town.

Table 6.4 *Destination of children of Gunung, Tiga Binanga, Tanah Karo, 1995*

Parents' age	Present location of children			Education of children		
	In village	In province	Elsewhere	Primary or less	High school	Tertiary
75+	29	17	13	27	22	11
60–74	41	26	31	41	37	22
–60	4	14	24	2	20	18

Astonishing as this education rate is, in a district which first obtained a senior high school in 1966, it appears typical of the Karo Batak as a whole. One never meets a Karo who cannot point with pride to children or relatives graduated from this or that prestigious university. Karo parents feel ashamed if their children stay in the village. While Tobas are entrepreneurial emigrants, producing large families in the certainty that they will go off in migration rather than stay to be a burden to the family, Karos since 1970 have become hooked on education, and take justifiable pride in having travelled in the last forty years from being one of the least-educated ethnie in Indonesia to being the best-educated. While the first Karo graduated only in 1948, by 1974 a publication could proudly list 1,000 graduates, and estimates by 1995 were as high as 5,000 (Rae 1994, 139). Karo families are markedly smaller than Toba ones (average 3.5 children in the 1990s, and falling), largely because of the heavy burden of this education on parents. Whereas in the first phase of commercialisation of the Karo highlands through vegetable-growing, in 1930–60, the spur to saving was to buy a truck, and later a bus, this had changed by the 1970s to education.

The first generation of Karos who went through universities in the 1970s did well, and this confirmed the Karo conviction that education was the future. But their enthusiasm and that of other Bataks put huge pressure on the universities of the province. The three state institutions (one of which for the Islamic education stream) did little to meet the demand. Indeed North Sumatra had only half the state university student places that its population (5.7 per cent of Indonesia) would justify by Indonesian norms (1987/8). Since the province shares with Jakarta the bottom place in the national average of state university places to population, it is unclear whether this represents discrimination against Christians and Chinese, as they tend to allege, or rather simple state failure to keep up with middle class hunger for education. Instead there was a mushrooming of private institutions, some eighty in total by 1992 in the province.

While the state system admitted only 30 per cent more students between 1980 and 1990, those attending private institutions in North

Sumatra (usually Medan) increased seven-fold, so that by 1990 the 30,000 students of the state system represented only 20 per cent of the total student population, in contrast with other Sumatran provinces. While the best of these, those supported by strong religious organisations like HKBP and Muhammadiah, offered education comparable with the state system, the worst were ephemeral academies with minimal resources, often set up to justify some personal ambition. Increasingly disillusioned with these options in the 1990s, Toba and Karo young people sought entry to universities outside North Sumatra, convinced that they were discriminated against in their own state universities, and that competition to enter the public service after graduation was far easier in Kalimantan or Irian, or even in Java, than at home.

As latecomers to modernity, both Toba and Karo peoples had made remarkably successful transitions in three generations or less. Until the twentieth century they had been constrained within their highland valleys by antipathy to the states (and diseases) of the coast, despite developing complex agricultural systems which supported the highest population densities in Sumatra. The small island of Samosir in Lake Toba alone had 74,000 people at first count in 1907, and its population density of 110 per square kilometre was the highest in the Archipelago outside Java and Bali (Reid 2005: 55). The rapid acceptance of state authority, Christianity and progress by the 1940s enabled them to embrace modernity with a passion that propelled them out to the cities where all the wealth and opportunities were.

By the 1990s both communities were essentially urban diasporas scattered throughout Indonesia. If the diaspora already exceeded the homeland in population, it was totally dominant in wealth, education and dynamic. The political identity of each ethnie was overwhelmingly determined by this diaspora. One small example was a 'Karo Cultural Congress' held in 1995 in the homeland city of Brastagi. Of the 300 Karo eminences invited, 85 per cent were from the cities of the diaspora (Prinst 1996). This phenomenon is not unique to the Bataks, but they are Indonesia's most important examples of how community is maintained in diaspora.

Diaspora identity

Despite the transformation into a diasporic community forming a vigorous part of modern Indonesian identity, Bataks have remained extremely committed to their ethnies as re-imagined in the twentieth century. In the seventy years of nationalism and modernisation between the two censuses that recorded ethnic self-identification, 1930 and 1970, those self-identifying as 'Batak' or one of its sub-groups rose from 2 to 3 per cent of the Indonesian population (in numerical terms, from 1.2 million to 6.1 million (Suryadinata *et al.* 2003: 12–14). In the 2000 ethnic census that disallowed the categories 'Indonesian' or anything mixed, the tendency of urban respondents who had lost any link to ethnie origin was to identify with the dominant urban culture; hence the ethnicities to expand were Javanese (despite a birth rate much below the national average), Sundanese, and especially Betawi (the Jakarta hybrid category) and Malay (the closest surrogate for Indonesian). Bataks were the only true ethnie from outside Java to hold their own, by contrast with Minangkabau, Dayak and Toraja who all suffered high rates of assimilation in the cities. Bataks are regarded widely in Indonesia as the most clannish of ethnies and the most determined to maintain identity (Warnaen 1982). What holds these new Batak diasporas together?

A pronounced diasporic identity became clear only from the 1960s, in a New Order environment which made it not only acceptable but essential for each *suku* to proclaim a simplified short list of ethnic markers. Museums and theme parks have exhibited ethnic culture, the latter in particularly essentialised forms, while the push for tourist dollars has legitimated rituals, dress, music and house styles once denounced as 'primitive', un-Muslim, un-Christian and anti-national. Meanwhile the destruction of the Left removed the main pragmatic enemy of aristocratic and conservative culture, and the depoliticisation of national life shifted ethnic competition to cultural and economic domains (Kipp 1993: 109–14; Pemberton 1994: 152–81).

One might expect the obvious markers of Toba-ness and Karo-ness, as of other diasporic identities in Indonesia, to be language, religion (particularly for members of the ethnic churches) and birth in the homeland. All three are much less important than formerly and not at all important for many. Among the urban elite who set the tone of ethnic politics, the use of vernaculars is dropping markedly. Already in the 1990 census only 18 per cent of Medan people admitted to any local language as a mother tongue (BPS 1992: 39). Only about 9 per cent of Bataks (more than the 3 per cent of Minangkabaus) in Jakarta admitted in the 1990 census to speaking these languages at home (BPS 1990: 183–9). My surveys of university students in Medan, confirming the observation of Rita Kipp (1993: 198–9), showed more than 90 per cent speaking Indonesian even to their parents. The ethnic churches undoubtedly help Toba and Karo retain their language and identity in the cities more effectively than do Muslim Bataks, but in order to retain the attention of young people these churches themselves are now shifting to Indonesian in the cities. The fast-growing denominations—Pentecostalists and Catholics—use

Indonesian exclusively in the towns, while even the ethnie churches cannot hold the line on the use of Batak languages. They know they cannot hold young people unless they offer services in Indonesian, and the complete transfer to the national language in urban parishes seems only a matter of time.

The cultural activity of all the ethnie is itself now conducted in Indonesian. The conferences and seminars to promote each ethnic culture, the urban up-market weddings at which the *adat* of each group is displayed, are invariably in Indonesian. The periodic efforts to promote the teaching of the local languages in schools and to publish texts in them (typically reprints from the much more promising pre-war period) are mostly testimony that the battle for language is being lost.

The many schisms from the original Toba Batak church, the inroads of Catholics, Pentecostalists and Muslims, the much more complicated situation in the urban diaspora and the secular tendency of some educated leaders, have also made the ethnie churches less central in defining these identities. It is no longer certain that the leading officials (*bupati*) of the Toba and Karo homelands will be members of the dominant churches in each place, and official events require that Muslim, Catholic and Protestant figures all be represented when prayers are required.

Finally an increasing proportion, probably a majority in the twenty-first century, of Toba and Karo are born in the cities, not the homeland.

Yet the urban context brings its own competitive edge to ethnic mobilisation and boundary-fixing. North Sumatra and its capital Medan are justly famous as the most combatively plural places in Indonesia, with a kind of balance in both ethnicity and religion that generally prevents a descent into wholesale violence. Low-level ethnie violence on the other hand is endemic in Medan, where Karo, Acehnese and Toba are particularly noted for banding together to defend their clansmen against perceived bullying from other groups. The wealthier but vulnerable immigrant minorities, notably the Chinese, are seen as more inclined to rely on the police or protection racketeers rather than ethnie networks to defend them (Ryter 2002).

In the Suharto period when ethnic competition shifted to the cultural field, six ethnie blocks became sufficiently self-aware to demand a place in the Province's self-representation. These are Malay, Nias and four groups of 'Batak'—Toba, Mandailing (tending to absorb Angkola and Sipirok through the dominant Muslim factor), Karo and Simalungun. In reality, Javanese are by far the largest ethnic group in the Province, at 33 per cent, and the combination of Indonesia's first ethnic census in 2000 with the subsequent rebirth of provincial electoral politics have reminded its electors of this inconvenient fact. But as for the most part descendants of contract labourers brought in to work the massive tobacco and rubber estates of the colonial era, they could be disenfranchised as 'immigrants' to the Province, along with the more entrepreneurial Minangkabau and Chinese minorities. In the Provincial Museum, in the 'Medan Fair' theme park on the region's culture and in the architecture of key provincial government buildings of the 1980s and 1990s, these six indigenous (*asli*) cultures were the minimum that had to be acknowledged.

During the Sukarno period when communists and nationalists were seeking to build a revolutionary New Order, every aspect of local tradition, in *adat*, dress, architecture and speech, was demeaned as 'feudal', old-fashioned (*kolot*) and divisive. After the brutal crushing of the Left in 1965–6, localism made a cautious comeback. In the name of promoting tourism, building the pluralist culture celebrated in the national motto *Bhinneka Tunggal Ika* (many and yet one), and resisting Western individualism and anomie, it began to be acceptable and increasingly even desirable to flaunt one's ethnie culture. Former aristocrats were able to return from the dustbin of history as supporters of the new state party, Golkar, and as cultural exemplars of this lost tradition. Scions of the Malay sultanates demolished during the early revolution were particularly adept at positioning themselves to lead the Malay community's belated emergence as an ethnic competitor.

In the depoliticised atmosphere of Suharto's Indonesia, cultural competition occupied some of the space which the robust politics of the 1950s and 1960s had left vacant. For urban Bataks seeking their place in the Indonesian sun, this could not be represented by the village cultures from which they had escaped. New cultural simplifications had to be devised, sanitised and rendered attractive to serve their competition for a place in urban and national life. The tourist gaze sometimes helped clarify and justify the package of new identity-markers, but it was the Indonesian competition that defined them.

Six themes in particular stand out as markers of this new ethnie identity.

(1) **Genealogy** is crucial. Each Toba or Karo Batak must know their own patrilineal clan (*marga*) and that of their mother, which determines relationships with a host of other Bataks (see *adat*, below). In diaspora the complexity of mutual obligations and feasting cycles will be progressively attenuated, but because the clan name is used as a surname it cannot be evaded. Every Batak's surname announces the ethnicity of its bearer and to a considerable extent their relationships with other Bataks. Conversations with Bataks who meet will therefore begin by clarifying these relationships and establishing

what level of personal pronouns will be used in the conversation (among Karo this process, *ertutur*, is given much emphasis). Those who suppress the clan name, as many in the diaspora do, are to this extent announcing that they do not wish to be considered as Batak, and in particular do not wish to be bound by the *adat* requirements of marriage partner and relationships. This is more common among strict Muslims and Pentecostal Christians, whose faith readily reinforces the rejection of such *adat* requirements.

Diasporic Bataks have adopted a uniquely Indonesian institution (perhaps of Chinese origin), the monthly meeting of a credit cooperative (*arisan*), to help sustain their clan identity. Many urban Toba Batak *arisan* are restricted to members or marriage partners of particular clans, and use their meetings to collect money for members' purposes such as feasts, trips back to the homeland, or scholarships for their children. Many clans develop more elaborate urban associations, such as that described by Ed Bruner (1972: 220–8) for the Siahaan *marga* in Jakarta, which published a directory of its 532 family members (1970). The urban Karo, however, generally more recent migrants than Toba and closer to their village roots, tend to use village origin rather than clan as the basis for both small-scale *arisan* meetings and larger associations (Kipp 1993: 167–76).

(2) *Adat* (custom) was originally defined for Islamic purposes as the area of local custom which need not be swept away by religious norms, but has become Indonesian usage for the ritual and kinship requirements of particular ethnie. For both Toba and Karo Bataks, this means particularly the system of relationships between three categories of fellow-Batak—'birth-companions' or members of the same clan, whom it is considered incest to marry; the 'wife-giver' clan of one's mother and wife, to whom deference and even ritual service is due; and the 'wife-taker' clan one's own women marry, from whom it is natural to ask favours and assistance. This triad is described by Toba Bataks as the 'hearth of three' (*dalihan na tolu*) with reference to a three-legged cooking pot, and is considered the cornerstone of *adat*.

For the younger urban diaspora the problem is not so much avoiding 'incest', or marrying the *adat*-preferred mother's niece, as finding a fellow Karo or Toba marriage partner who can continue the *adat* relationships. Weddings, death-feasts and other rituals are partly still an occasion for young people to meet their kinsmen, dancing together and forming the right bonds. Karo students as small minorities in big city universities are particularly known for living together in the same hostels, and organising social activities where they can meet Karo students of the opposite sex and engage in the traditional style of courting dance (*guru-guru aron*) (Kipp 1993: 175–6).

Conferences are frequently held in the diaspora to discuss how *adat* can be preserved or modified in modern conditions. Handy guides are published in Indonesian to enable urban Bataks to fulfil the minimum requirements of their Batakness, and to prescribe in simplified form the correct *adat* procedures for weddings and funerals.

(3) **Links with the homeland** are changing, but no less important as smaller proportions of Toba and Karo Bataks live there. Increasingly marginal and backward in economic terms, the ethnic homeland becomes the scene where urban Bataks can act out their identity. For urban Karo, most of whom have fresh memories of homeland villages, the annual *kerja tahun* (harvest) feast in August or September, at which thousands of migrants will crowd into a village of only a couple of hundred inhabitants, is the major occasion for renewal of Karo-ness. In the rest of the year *arisan* and other groups meet regularly to prepare for the return and help save funds towards it. Peculiarly well designed to support migrants in a new urban identity, these associations will link 20–100 families from a particular village or descent group living in the same city.

For Toba Batak, New Year festivities have a similar though less important role to the *kerja tahun*. But the most important link to the homeland is now the industry of feasting and celebrating the dead, for whom increasingly elaborate monuments are erected. A succession of anthropologists from the 1920s through to the 1950s noted the collapse of Batak traditions in every sphere, including the habit of building stone (later cement) sarcophogi for the bones of important ancestors. But an extraordinary change began to take place in the 1960s, centred on the new practice of building not sarcophogi but collective tombs or *tugu* (monuments) for the reburied bones of a whole lineage. The change may have been influenced by the earlier success of supporters of Singamangaraja XII as national hero in erecting statues to him. The burst of *tugu*-building which transformed the North Tapanuli landscape from the 1960s suggests the growing importance of a 'homeland' as an ancestral place, where clans and lineages can celebrate their forebears while reburying them, and at the same time celebrate the bonds that continue to link them throughout Indonesia. Toba Bataks now revisit Tapanuli primarily for burial and reburial festivals. These serve to consolidate and strengthen the *marga* or lineage, to compete for status in a highly competitive Batak society, and to acknowledge

Figure 6.2 Modern Toba Batak monument (*tugu*), erected by the Manihuruk lineage, near Pangururang (Samosir), to rebury the ancestors

one of the great themes of the old Indonesian religion—the reciprocal helpfulness between living and dead (Pederson 1970: 85–6; Bruner 1983: 16–17; Reid 2002).

Whereas Minangkabau and other emigrants may be appreciated in their homelands for building mosques or schools, Toba Batak send money back primarily for ritual purposes. It is almost entirely the wealthy urban diaspora which finances the *tugu* and the huge feasts that utilise them (figure 6.2). It is also they who continue to build and maintain the traditional Batak houses that make the highlands so interesting for tourists. Nobody wants to live in such houses anymore, but many urban people like to keep faith with the ancestors from a village by maintaining a house, at which the periodic rituals of the village, clan and lineage can be held.

(4) **Dress** has evolved to become more simplified and sanitised for Toba and Karo as for every other ethnic (*suku*) of New Order Indonesia, to enable everybody to exhibit their 'tradition' at important ritual occasions, especially weddings. Most of this is simply the modernised Malay costume that spread throughout Indonesia under Dutch and mission impetus in the late nineteenth century, the *sarung*

kebaya for women, with perhaps some added item to show ethnicity; and for men a slightly different touch in headdress or jacket to a style of jacket and *sarung* which Dutch-influenced aristocrats throughout Sumatra had adopted in the late nineteenth century (before shifting completely into Western dress).

The key markers of distinctiveness which meet the ritual needs of today's urban Bataks are the handwoven cloth (*ulos*) worn as a scarf for Tobas, and the cloth worn as a high headdress (*tudung*) for Karo women. Weddings, as everywhere in Indonesia, became the pre-eminent site of competitive 'culture'. There people show off their *adat*, their dress, their music, to an inevitably mixed audience. They will call upon some recognised expert in *adat* to ensure that things are done in the appropriate manner.

(5) **Batak music and dance** in pre-Christian days were essentially sacral. The small Batak orchestra, comprising flute, string, gong and a characteristic narrow drum that gave the ensemble its name (*gondang*), was used to summon the spirits of the ancestors at every ritual occasion. The missionaries therefore banned this music, as well as the ritual dances, and replaced it with hymn singing in European melody but Batak language, at which the Toba in particular became adept. In the 1960s, however, the indigenous leadership of the Batak churches changed their position and began to celebrate the richness of local tradition even in Christian services. For the Karo church a key moment was its seventy-fifth anniversary in 1965, when laymen planning the celebrations included Karo music very successfully, without prior theological debate (Rae 1994: 30–1, 167–8; interviews). The post-independence generation felt that these animist associations had been broken, and were encouraged by the world-wide shift to cultural pluralism, with new theologies of enculturation influencing most churches with the notable exception of the Pentecostals. The Catholics, making rapid strides after Vatican II away from the universal prioritisation of Latin in the liturgy, became leaders of the trend after Pope John Paul II popularised enculturation in his encyclical *Redemptoris Missio* of 1990.

By the 1970s Batak music was also undergoing its own extension from older forms still played at death feasts and secondary burials, towards commercial, purely secular forms. Batak music and dance now grace every formal occasion where Bataks are in the majority. No wedding or important ritual event is complete without a dance, of one relatively simple form which all can learn and even awkward urban guests can readily participate in.

A tradition of private radio stations catering to local cultures had existed in Indonesia since the colonial 1930s. The Japanese period and the 'revolutionary' Sukarno period that followed suppressed most of them in favour of government-owned stations broadcasting only in Indonesian. In the Suharto period, however, advertising revenue made possible a spectacular comeback for private and ethnic radio. There were 217 registered private stations in Indonesia by 1974 and about 700 in 1997, and at least 40 of the latter operated in North Sumatra (Lindsay and Tan 2003, 17). At least 6 of these were Karo-owned and a larger number Toba-owned. Their popularity rose with that of the Batak music they played, which modernised and hybridised with the addition of an electronic keyboard and catchy vocals. The coming of ever cheaper forms of recording music, starting with the cassette tape in the 1980s, enabled local forms to recover some ground against the national, though at the controversial cost of losing some of its distinctiveness. The fact that both Karo (especially in Medan) and Toba are hugely overrepresented in owning and operating city mini-buses has made these another venue for celebrating ethnic music.

(6) **Architecture** too became important in the Suharto era as a particularly overt banner of identity. The handsome, sacrally designed stilt houses of the Toba Batak seemed doomed as they were destroyed in the troubled 1940s and 1950s and rebuilt as roomier, lighter modern houses on the ground. Wealthy urban families who would not dream of living in the dark old houses, however, began restoring or totally rebuilding those of their parents or grandparents for purposes of pride and ritual. In the larger and more communal villages of the Karo plateau, if my Gunung research site is typical, urban migrants have contributed to restoring or rebuilding the communal core of the village where vast feasts can be held at the annual regathering of migrant ex-villagers. These include the last remaining traditional eight-family communal house, the finest of the old rice barns (*jembur tengah*) beneath whose characteristic peaked roof the village elders used to sit and give judgement, as well as two modern buildings. One of these was a huge modern meeting hall, prosaically called by a Dutch word *los* (barn); the other was an intriguing replacement of the spiritual heart of the old religious order, the ornamented house (*geriten*) for the skulls and bones of revered ancestors, now turned into a symbolic link with the five founding ancestors through its five pillars.

Figure 6.3 Modern Church of GBKP with signature Karo roof, Medan 2008

In the 1970s touristic motifs from the highlands began to enter the cities. The first Toba Batak to become a major industrial magnate, T. D. Pardede, introduced the style to Medan with his upmarket Hotel Danau Toba, which lined its roof with a string of Toba-style upturned house roofs. Other smaller hotels owned by Minangkabau or Karo, each with their own roof-style to adapt, took up the challenge. Medan increasingly presented itself as a forum of architectural competition between the owners of different hotels, restaurants, ethnic associations, ethnic churches and occasionally even private houses (figure 6.3). Public buildings of the province, on the other hand, such as the Museum and the provincial assembly, faced demands to represent in its architecture each of the ethnie which made its case for inclusion as an indigenous *suku*. In the 1970s Karo, Mandailing and Melayu insisted on equal status with Toba, and by the 1980s the less assertive Nias, Dairi and Simalungun had also made their case. This apparent finality was disrupted by the robust democracy of the new century, and in 2006 the hybrid coastal identity of the Sibolga area on the west coast insisted on being a seventh category of representation—*suku pasisir* (coastal ethnie).

The accepted way of coping with this exuberance of identities was to include separate bands of decorative carving over the entrance to a provincial building, within the high pitch shared by most Batak houses (figure 6.4). At the level of Medan city, on the other hand, the relative success of Malay candidates in controlling city hall since the 1980s (see chapter 4), produced municipal buildings with a single motif.

Some of the inspiration for this battle of the kitsch was undoubtedly Taman Mini Indonesia, a giant theme park in Jakarta decreed in 1972 by President Suharto's wife, to represent the cultures of all Indonesia's provinces. It was quickly emulated at provincial level. Medan Fair was the theme park for North Sumatra. Each district (*kabupaten*) had to put in an entry, generally in the form of a traditional house which, along with certain markers of dress, thereby became the most recognisable cliché of ethnie culture. Many Bataks and others who had no personal knowledge of such architecture came to see and be photographed with 'their' ethnic culture, and the venues were even favoured for weddings as a means to stress ethnie connectedness without leaving the city.

Democratic politics and layered identity

After the fall of Suharto in 1998, Indonesia rapidly transformed itself into an effective democracy, with direct elections not only for president and national parliament, but eventually also for governors and district heads of each region. Accompanied by the devolution of very large portions of budgetary allocations to province and district level, this meant that the stakes in local politics became much higher than they had even been in Indonesia's history as a post-revolutionary centralised state. In the Ambonese area of Maluku, in western Borneo (Kalimantan) and in parts of southern Sulawesi, horrendous violence between Muslims and Christians or rival ethnic groups killed thousands of people. In East Timor, Aceh and Papua thousands more died in

Figure 6.4 The North Sumatra provincial museum deals with ethnic claims with a Toba–Batak designed roof style, Malay entrance and horizontal bands of decoration to represent seven different ethnicities

struggles to secede from Indonesia altogether (Bertrand 2004; van Klinken 2007; Davidson 2008). North Sumatra by contrast witnessed no talk of secession and few signs of more overt violence than usual, despite being notoriously the most ethnically and religiously divided of Indonesia's provinces. The reasons deserve consideration.

The changes described in this chapter transformed Bataks into dynamic, predominately urban and diasporic communities, for whom regional or ethnic separateness is no longer imaginable. They still feel many areas of competition with the larger Indonesian ethnies who dominate the state, but this competition is carried out on an Indonesian stage, in the Indonesian language, and with the aim of advancing Batak stakes in the symbolic and material resources of Indonesia. The generation educated in the 1970s and 1980s is redefining its ethnie identity in ways that suit an urban, competitive life-style. Having been aliens in the city up until the 1940s, Bataks are now one of its most recognisable and characteristic groups, noisily manning the buses and taxis that form its life-blood. The Bataks are an excellent example of layered identity, for whom both the ethnie and Indonesian identities are strongly internalised and expressed, but on different levels of social interaction.

The steady decline in the use of Batak languages is part of a process proceeding rapidly throughout Indonesia. Even though the 1990 census showed only 15 per cent of Indonesians using Indonesian in the home, the proportion was 37 per cent among urban Indonesians and higher still among younger and better-educated cohorts. Few of Indonesia's languages made the transition to printing successfully, and the absolute domination of Indonesian in the rapidly expanding school system after 1950 reduced most to 'dialects' used only for oral communication. As migrants to the cities, Bataks suffered more than most from this language loss. About a quarter of urban Bataks were recorded as using Batak in the home in 1990 (Lindsay and Tan 2003: 13–16, 196–9), more than other urban populations but far below that of rural populations. The decline of Toba Batak was undoubtedly slowed by the commitment to it of the ethnie church, HKBP, and the continuing resonance of the Batak Bible. In reprinting the 1926 genealogical work of Hutagalung, the modern editor insisted in his best Indonesian that because of such works, 'If the cultures of many ethnie in Indonesia have faded and seem to be disappearing, the Toba Batak culture shows some resistance' (Hutagalung 1991: iii). Yet in the bookshops today the only Batak works are the Bible and such nostalgic reprints as these. If Batak identity were dependent on the written language, it would indeed be terminally endangered.

The advent of a robust democracy to both the nation and the province has given more opportunities for Bataks to accumulate *sahala* (soul power) and status in their remarkably individualist ways, but not to advocate greater autonomy for their ethnie. The much less democratic 1950s, when Toba Batak aspirations to be masters of their own space rode on the military leadership of Colonel Simbolon, was in fact the last time when even the Toba Batak appeared united behind a political cause. Their HKBP church split in 1964 with the formation of the splinter GKPI, and in the 1990s was again racked with terrible conflict over its leadership which led to violence in several parishes. The open politics of the post-1998 era were embraced energetically, but pitted Batak against

Batak far more than it united them to claim the electoral prize. When the first open election for North Sumatra governor and vice-governor was held in April 2008, five pairings split the vote remarkably evenly. All but the winner, veteran Malay politician Syamsul Ariffin ('friend of every *suku*' as his slogan said), had a Batak in the team, three of them Toba. A narrow last place was taken by the team led by the Toba Batak mayor of Pematang Siantar, paired with a Javanese who failed to deliver the expected large numbers of Javanese voters.

The decentralisation of budgetary and other powers that marked the post-Suharto reform period might have been expected to help the Toba and Karo to manage their own affairs at least in the Tapanuli heartland. This too had the opposite effect. North Tapanuli, whose district government had long been the administrative support for efforts to unite Toba Batak and boost their culture and *adat*, split into four separate districts (*kabupaten*) under pressure of the competition for the new decentralised resources. First the area around the Lake split off as Toba Samosir, and then each of the two districts divided again. Toba Batak unity had long seemed more apparent and necessary to the diaspora than to the inherently diverse highland homeland.

And yet a Toba Batak and a Karo Batak ethnie have both clearly formed and will remain, nested within the Indonesian in a form we may call layered identity. More confidently than with other ethnie one sees this asserted even in diaspora, with high rates of marriage within the ethnie (some informants claimed over 90 per cent). The 'flaccid formulation' of folklorist dancing, clothing and children's games favoured by Suharto's cultural establishment was opposed, as Susan Rodgers (1991a: 85) pointed out, by a 'politically robust' Batak version of identity resting sturdily on their marriage alliance and genealogical systems. These Batak identities are now as in the remote past defined against the local Muslim identity of the Sumatran coast, an opposition enhanced by the sense of being a small and somewhat embattled minority as Christians in Indonesia. Yet Indonesian identity itself is in no way opposed, but embraced energetically as a complementary layer alongside the Toba (or Karo), the Christian, the Batak and the regional (usually expressed as a city—Medan). The Medan newspaper most active in boosting the unique heritage of Batak *adat* was also 'a tireless proponent of Indonesian nationalism' (Rodgers 1991a: 84).

Indonesia and its imperial predecessor are the only form of state the Batak have known. It is now also the only true nation-state they can readily imagine.

7 Lateforming ethnie in Malaysia: Kadazan or Dusun

At the end of 1995 the Malaysian government agreed that a fifth language could be taught in its schools, after Malay, Chinese and Tamil (long conceded to the three major communities in West Malaysia), and Iban (the largest of the Dayak languages of Sarawak, conceded shortly before). This language was called Kadazandusun, the latest mouthful to try to gain consensus among the indigenous peoples of Sabah (the northern corner of Borneo). At the last (2000) census the half a million people whose language this was or aspired to be were also listed as Kadazandusun. Going back through previous censuses, however, these were registered as two peoples, 'Kadazan' (104,924) and 'Dusun' (216,910) in 1991, merged into the larger Pribumi (indigenous people) category in 1980, all listed as Kadazans in 1970, and all as Dusuns in 1960 and previous censuses (see table 7.1). I will refer to them as KD in this chapter.

Given the importance we have attached to censuses in the toolkit of identity creation, these differences suggest a troubled path to ethnie formation. By contrast with the Batak counterpart in the previous chapter, Sabah represents a case of even later politicisation and ethnie formation, well after the nation-state it was asked to join in 1963 had taken shape. Whereas Bataks had an equal share with other ethnie in building anti-imperial nationalism and its state nationalist successor, the Kadazandusun remain outside and in tension with the Malay ethno-nationalism which has the central place in Malaysia's state nationalist project. On the other hand, Malaysia's federal structure, stitched together in multiple com-promises in marked contrast to Indonesia's revolutionary centralism, provides many advantages for regionally focussed minorities. The late formation and political program of a KD ethnie were closely tied to the lively state politics of Sabah, and the struggle to position themselves as its 'definitive people'. While they have lost that battle, they have achieved against considerable odds a stable niche within Malaysia's federal and plural system. The ups and downs of their passage towards a modern political identity provide useful tests of our basic propositions about Asian nationalism.

Table 7.1 *Ethnic percentages in Sabah censuses (Reid 1997: 124; Malaysia Census 2000)*

Census	1911	1921	1931	1951	1960	1970	1980[1]	1991	2000
Kadazandusun[2]	42.0	39.8	39.8	35.2	32.0	29.9		19.6	18.4
Murut	12.7	11.5	8.8	5.6	4.9	4.8		2.9	3.3
Bajau	11.3	12.7	12.3	13.4	13.1	11.8		11.7	13.2
Malay	2.9	2.3	2.1	0.6	0.4	2.8		6.2	11.7
Other indig[3]	14.4	13.2	13.0	16.5	15.8	13.5		13.6	14.3
Chinese	12.9	14.9	18.0	22.3	23.0	21.4	16.3	11.5	9.6
Indonesian	2.6	4.3	3.6	2.4	5.5	6.1			
Filipino	0.1	0.2	1.3	0.6	1.6	3.1		23.9[4]	23.6
Total population (000s)	215	263	277	334	454	653	956	1,735	2,603

Sabah's peoples

In the early twentieth century, the only Sabah languages which had been written down were still the 'exotic' ones—English, Malay and Chinese—and the only education available was in these languages. The dilemma of the KD throughout the twentieth century was whether they would join the modern urban educated world of competing nationalisms as a single people with a single written language, as two such peoples, as many,

[1] The 1980 Malaysian census listed all who were not Chinese or Indian as simply '*pribumi*' (native), including Indonesian and Filipino migrants.

[2] Listed as Dusun until the 1960 census, and as Kadazan in 1970. I added the 10,881 Rungus and the 20 Lotud of the detailed 1970 census to the Kadazandusun category, since this is where they were in previous enumerations. In the 1991 census I have aggregated the 216,910 reporting as Dusun and the 106,740 reporting as Kadazan, together with 19,000 estimated for Rungus Dusun. That estimate is based on a growth since the 1970 census of the same order (74.4 per cent) as for other Kadazandusun. The Rungus are clearly a 'Dusun' group by language, culture and mythology, but in the valleys of the Kudat peninsula they have resisted modern acculturation pressures more than others, and retain a longhouse residence pattern and chiefly swidden agriculture.

[3] In the censuses prior to 1970 specific ethnic terms are listed—Sulu, Orang Sungei, Brunei, Kadayan, Bisaya and Tidong—Brunei being the largest of these at each enumeration. In the 1991 and 2000 censuses all are listed as 'Other Bumiputra'. I have reduced this by 1 per cent (and expanded Kadazandusun accordingly) in both years to allow for the Rungus Dusun of Kudat. The 2000 census showed the 'other Bumiputra' category to comprise 10.5 per cent Muslim and 3.8 per cent Christian.

[4] The figures for Indonesian and Filipino represent nationalities (of recent migrants) not ethnicities. In the 1991 and 2000 census this migrant category is lumped together as non-Malaysians. It is the most controversial, and is reported differently in different releases of the census. Since the percentages do not add up to 100 per cent, this category including many illegals may be the residual one, which would expand it to 29.5 per cent in 2000. A Statistics Department release relating to 2005 showed Sabah's then total population as 3,015,000, of which 748,000 or 24.8 per cent were non-citizens (*Daily Express* 3 August 2008).

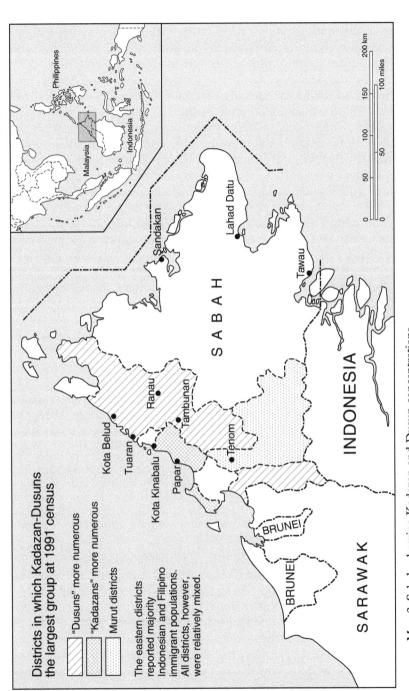

Districts in which Kadazan-Dusuns
the largest group at 1991 census

"Dusuns" more numerous

"Kadazans" more numerous

Murut districts

The eastern districts
reported majority
Indonesian and Filipino
immigrant populations.
All districts, however,
were relatively mixed.

Map 3 Sabah, showing Kadazan and Dusun concentrations

or as an assimilated part of the broader 'Malay' identity which often (though with plenty of ambivalence) presents itself as the proper label for 'indigenous' peoples within Malaysia (and perhaps even beyond it).

The British colonisers of North Borneo adopted the Malay term 'Dusun' to describe the majority agricultural population of Borneo's interior. In the usage of Brunei Malays it meant agriculturalists or uplanders, definitely contrasted with traders, townspeople and Muslims, and having the patronising or pejorative connotation in their eyes of rustics, unbelievers and primitives. Although 'Dusun' was often used as a residual category for all who were not Muslim or Chinese, the colonial government in its censuses and administration distinguished from them the 'Muruts' of the isolated valleys of the southern part of the state around Keningau and Tenom. As Owen Rutter (1929: 32) saw it, the Dusun was simply a more evolved Murut, having adopted agriculture where the Muruts remained relatively isolated hunter-gatherers. 'The Dusuns, located in a kinder terrain and influenced by more civilized peoples, have passed from a savage into a higher stage of development ... What the Murut is today, the Dusun was yesterday.'

These 'Dusuns' of colonial definition also appear to have thought of themselves as a single people, with a common myth of origin associated with Nunuk Ragang, a giant banyan tree thought to have been located at the junction of the Liwagu and Gelibang rivers to the east of Ranau. From here, perhaps after some cultural contact with Chinese, they believe they dispersed around the west coast of Sabah, developing their different dialects (Evans 1953: 187–8; Topin undated; Shim 2007; *Our Cultural Heritage* undated: 73–7). Already before the birth of Kadazan nationalism, an ethnographer reported:

> The Dusuns themselves, while they have no common name in their own language, do recognise all other groups of Dusun who came from the legendary village of Nunukaragan as their own people. Those who do not come from Nunukaragan are not Dusun. As far as I am able to ascertain, this criterion does effectively distinguish the group to whom the term Dusun is now commonly applied. (Glyn-Jones 1953: 117)

While upland groups in other areas, like the Bataks of North Sumatra or the Toraja of Sulawesi, eventually accepted with pride the pejorative label given them by coast-dwellers, this was to be a problematic process in Sabah. In the 1920s Rutter noted that many of the groups he called 'Dusun' did or could identify themselves collectively as 'landsmen' (*tulun tindal*), but those 'on the West Coast, particularly at Papar' called themselves Kadazan. The 'Muruts', each group relatively isolated in its valley, tended to deny kinship with other groups of 'Murut' let alone 'Dusun'.

Contemporary KD spokespeople believe themselves the 'definitive' original people of Sabah, using a term favoured by Dr Mahathir for the Malays. They identify the major Muslim groups (Bajau, Suluk, Brunei, Illanun and various Indonesians, as well as the currently popular 'Malay') as recent immigrants, and all the non-Muslim Borneo peoples as potentially or properly the 'indigenous' KD.

When British officials first counted the population in racial categories in the 1911 North Borneo census, however, the 'Dusuns' were listed as only 42 per cent of the population and Muruts as a further 13 per cent (against 15 per cent Chinese, 13 per cent Bajau, 13 per cent 'other indigenous'). Because of accelerating immigration and conversion to Islam, and the relatively much lower natural increase of the KD population than that of the immigrants, KDs were reduced progressively to less than 20 per cent in 1990. Since Muruts experienced a demographic crisis in the twentieth century, with populations falling even in absolute numbers, the combined KD–Murut share of the population dropped still more radically, from 55 per cent in 1911 to 22 per cent in 2000.

The invention of Kadazans

KDs had no indigenous writing system (unlike the Philippine groups to which they had some relation), and therefore no standard written form of the language. In 1921 the KD population was still only 2 per cent literate, almost wholly animist in belief and without benefit of education. The Catholic Mill Hill Mission, however, had begun in 1882 to open schools for the KD population on the west coast south of modern Kota Kinabalu. After a very slow and difficult beginning there was much faster development after the Second World War. By 1953 there were forty Catholic schools in Sabah with almost 6,000 students, the majority 'indigenous'. In the whole school system (including government and Chinese schools) there were then 3,385 students classified as 'Dusun' (*NBAR* 1954: 69). Most of these were KDs of the west coast studying in one of the forty Catholic schools, including the famous St Michael's Secondary School in the Penampang valley behind Kota Kinabalu. While less than 4 per cent of the native population was Christian in 1931, a quarter had become so by 1960 (Jones 1966: 60, 144). The government schools taught in Malay and the Chinese in Chinese, but the Catholic schools opted to teach literacy to rural folk initially through their local KD dialect, shifting gradually by the third or fourth year into English. From these schools, therefore, there emerged in the 1950s and 1960s a small elite of educated, Catholic KDs, fluent in English but also confident in speaking and writing their own language in romanised script. Although there were many pressures to adopt the use of Malay and English during everyday exchanges in the towns, familiarity with this standardised form of Kadazan language was reinforced through the many editions of the Kadazan Catholic catechism and prayerbook (*Vazaan doid Surga*; Rooney 1981: 144).

The majority of this educated group appears to have believed that they and their language were Kadazan. The British colonial government, however, still called the language 'Dusun' and doubted whether it was a single language or a range of dialects. The 1950s and 1960s could be read as a struggle between these two views, with the former emerging victorious. Although the process of standardising language through the use of an agreed form in education, the church, the state and the media was much later in coming to KD than to most other languages which have 'made it' into the modern world, that process was undoubtedly taking place among the first large cohort of educated KDs.

In January 1953 the *Sabah Times* was launched as the colony's first English-language daily, with about 1,000 subscribers by the end of the year. Most of these subscribers were no doubt Chinese and European, but the newspaper's Sabah-born editor, Donald Stephens (Australian father, KD mother), imaginatively included one page of news 'in romanised Malay and Dusun', as the government report put it (*NBAR* 1953: 131–2; *NBAR* 1954: 124–5). In fact, however, the KD section of the newspaper was called by Stephens 'Kadazan Corner', and it spelt the language according to the only system widely known—that developed for the dialect of Penampang and Papar by the Mill Hill missionaries, and dispersed by them to a wider spectrum of Catholic schools. Stephens justified this policy later:

It was done in answer to a natural rising pride among the Kadazan peoples and a knowledge of their desire to be known by their own name and not by a name which they feel had been nothing but a label hanged on them, put there by others without their consent ... I feel that if the Kadazans are ever to feel **one** that common link [of language] should be strengthened, and there was no better way of strengthening it than by trying to **standardise** the language. The obvious answer was to start with the Kadazan as spoken in the Penampang/Papar area because it is in this area that the people have gone a long way in having their language written down ... One could have picked the Kadazan spoken in Tuaran or Kota Belud or Ranau for use but because the Kadazan spoken in Penampang and Papar were the most commonly understood and had already been used as a written language (Romanised) it was obvious that the best choice was the Kadazan as used in Penampang/Papar. (*Sabah Times* June 1960)

The same group of educated Penampang KDs who began to write for this Kadazan Corner spawned in 1953 a 'Society of Kadazans', dedicated to uplifting the backward KDs of the area, and protecting and preserving their culture. Their cause was helped when the first modern dictionary appeared, a *Kadazan Dictionary and Grammar* written in Japanese internment by a Mill Hill missionary and published with Australian Colombo Plan help (Antonissen 1958). It shared their view both of the name and the spelling of the standardised language struggling to birth.

As an oral medium radio was not obliged to develop a common written standard, but it had a much wider appeal and is still remembered as having pioneered the Kadazan idea in the interior. 'Radio Sabah' began transmitting a few hours a day in 1953, in English, Malay and Chinese, to what were then 2,700 holders of radio licences. The first broadcast in what the government again called 'Dusun' was in 1954. At the beginning of 1957 this became institutionalised as a daily program of fifteen minutes, and 'the Kadazan people' responded so enthusiastically that this was raised progressively to thirty and then forty-five minutes a day by the end of 1957, and fourteen hours a week by 1960. In fact the inspiration for much of this success, Fred Sinidol, was an enthusiastic 'Kadazan' from Penampang, who took his 'Kampong Program' around the villages broadcasting the music of local artists, talks on old customs and news. While the majority of programs in the other languages were relayed from outside sources, the Kadazan program was wholly indigenous—over 60 per cent in the form of local music groups, some of whom walked up to sixty miles for the opportunity to record. This immensely popular program broadcast voices in a variety of local dialects, but did much to popularise the idea that they were all part of a single language group called Kadazan (*NBAR* 1953: 131; 1954: 125; 1957: 140–1; 1960: 159–61; 1961: 196; interviews).

The origin of the term Kadazan is still debated. Many believe it is derived from the word for 'towns'—*kakadazan*—and therefore designates the semi-urbanised coastal people as opposed to the Liwan—upcountry people of the area between Ranau and Tambunan (*Daily Express* 20 March 1987; Topin undated). Others think *kadazan*, or its interior equivalent *kadayan*, is simply a regional name long used for the people of the Penampang and Papar areas of the west coast, or that it means people of the land as opposed to sea-farers (Glyn-Jones 1953: 118; Harrison 1971: 58). Stephens and his supporters, however, preferred to interpret it as a term meaning 'our people', once accepted by all KDs but since 'forgotten' because of pressure from British officials not wanting to see the KDs proud and united (Donald Stephens in *Sabah Times* 30 June 1960; see also Luping 1994: 4–5). At the opposite extreme the anti-Kadazan activists of the United Sabah Dusun Association (USDA) later argued that it was not an indigenous word at all but derived from Malay *kedai* meaning shop or town, whence *kedaian* (people of the town) or in coastal dialect, Kadazan (Raymond Boid Tombung, cited *Daily Express* September 1994). There was enough ambivalence in the term itself and the motives for which it was adopted to lay the basis for much future difficulty. Peter Mojuntin was undoubtedly correct for his 1950s-educated generation in writing that 'nearly all educated or striving to be educated Kadazans have come to regard the word "Dusun" as derogatory when referred to them during the colonial days'. Their use of Kadazan, he thought, was part of their demand to be treated with as much respect as all the other races in Sabah (Mojuntin in *Sabah Times* 23 November 1967). Although these early nationalists were undoubtedly sincere in wanting to apply the label to all the indigenous people of Sabah, they could never dispel completely the associations of the term with urban sophistication. Already in the 1960s a field worker in Ranau noted that while the Dusuns of this area readily accepted that they were one people with the Penampang *evolués*, 'the idea that they, the people of Ranau, should be called ... Kadazan never was very popular' (Harrison 1971: 58).

Kadazan ethnie nationalism

The first KD cultural and social organisations formed in the early 1950s had, of course, used the term Kadazan in their names. These associations began to assume political importance when Donald Stephens, editor of the *Sabah Times* and the first KD to take major roles in government, became president of the Society of Kadazans in 1958. In 1961, with the sleepy condition of Sabah suddenly politicised by the proposal of the Malayan prime minister, Tunku Abdul Rahman, to incorporate the Borneo territories and Singapore into Malaysia, this society became a political party—United National Kadazan Organisation (UNKO). The KD delegates assembled from various parts of Sabah to form this association also voted to accept Kadazan as the name for all the indigenous non-Muslim groups—albeit with some significant dissenters.

Why did this Kadazan ethnic identity, fragile and innovative as it was, become the basis for the colony's infant politicisation, despite the preference of its British mentors for multi-racial political parties? The reasons are very similar to those which underlay the formation of the racially exclusive Malay party, UMNO, in Malaya in 1946, in somewhat similar conditions. The Malays of Malaya then, and the Kadazans of Sabah in 1961, believed that they were the underdogs in educational and economic terms, certain to be manipulated or absorbed in any

Figure 7.1 Donald Stephens proclaims Sabah's entry to Malaysia, 1963, with Tun Mustapha seated centre

multi-racial arrangement by the dominant Chinese and Muslims respectively. On the other hand the Kadazans also believed, like the Malays in Malaya, that they were entitled to political primacy by their greater numbers and greater claim to indigeneity, and would achieve it if they could act in a united fashion. The first years of political activity in Sabah appeared to support these hopes.

Firstly, Donald Stephens became the first chief minister, and led the colony's entry into Malaysia in 1963, with Muslim and Chinese leaders playing supporting roles (see figure 7.1). Secondly, some of the key symbols of Kadazan national identity began to gain acceptance among the various communities. A harvest festival (*Kaamatan*) centring around rituals honouring the rice spirit had been accepted by the colonial government as a three-day holiday for KDs in 1956, at the instance of the Annual Native Chiefs' Conference. Stephens championed this as a fair equivalent of Chinese New Year and Muslim Idulfitri, and it was accepted into the calendar of state-wide holidays in 1960. The *Kaamatan* quickly became a popular institutionalisation of Kadazan cultural pride, with dance, song, speech and sporting competition always climaxed by a beauty contest dedicated to the beautiful maiden Huminodun of the KD origin myth, the sacrifice of whose life gave birth to rice and the other essentials of KD agriculture. The term Kadazan was widely accepted by the educated elite, and there was little challenge even to the written form established in Fr Antonissen's dictionary. A Kadazan Cultural Association was formed in 1963, devoted to recording, maintaining and standardising Kadazan language, songs, dances and traditions. It also took over from an older youth association the organisation of the annual harvest festival (Roff 1969; Ongkili 1972: 50–3; Lupin 1994: 97–112).

The *bumiputra* challenge

Sabah joined Malaysia in 1963 with an alliance government superficially similar to that of West Malaysia, comprised of three parties each based in a particular ethno-religious tradition. Donald Stephens' predominately KD party changed its name in January 1964 to the United Pasok-momogun Kadazan Organization (UPKO) after reabsorbing the Murut followers of Datuk Sundang who had in 1961–3 opposed joining Malaysia before elections, and who preferred the term Pasok Momogun (people of the country) to Kadazan. The United Sabah National Organisation (USNO) was created by Sabah's most prominent Muslim, the Suluk Datuk (later Tun) Mustapha, who became the state's first indigenous governor, a supposedly ceremonial post analogous to the monarchs of West Malaysia's states. USNO was thereby left without a strong political leader, but it had the great advantage of support and sympathy from Malaysia's dominant party, UMNO. This party for Malay Muslims encouraged USNO's ambitions to become the Muslim-led party of all Sabah's '*bumiputra*' (sons of the soil), the term invented with Malaysia to replace Malay as the 'indigenous' category entitled to special privileges. These two parties were joined in the Sabah Alliance by the theoretically multi-racial but predominately Chinese and urban Sabah National Party (SANAP).

The Sabah Alliance had none of the stability of its West Malaysian equivalent. It was torn by the then debate between Lee Kuan Yew's 'Malaysian Malaysia' and Kuala Lumpur's model of racially defined parties accepting Malay primacy in return for guaranteed participation in government. Each of the Sabah parties had ambitions to become multi-racial, but on different presumptions. UPKO and UNKO competed over their different understandings of what indigenousness meant, while UPKO also competed with the Sabah Chinese Association (SCA), as SANAP had renamed itself under pressure from the Malayan Chinese Association, for the support of Chinese, many of whom had long and harmonious associations with KDs.

UPKO's vulnerability to Kuala Lumpur pressure was accentuated by the expulsion of Singapore from Malaysia in August 1965, and charges of disloyalty to Malaysia that were made against those who questioned the remaining balance of power. UPKO abandoned one position after another in an attempt to retain a place within the ruling Alliance: Stephens was forced out as chief minister in late 1964 by a combination of the other two parties; Stephens and the most effective of the younger Kadazan politicians, Peter Mojuntin, were forced to resign as president and secretary of UPKO in 1965; Mustapha moved from the governorship into politics about the same time, becoming chairman of the Sabah Alliance and refusing to relinquish the post as previously agreed to let UPKO have a turn. The 1967 state election confirmed UPKO as the party of KDs, as it won twelve of the fourteen seats with KD majorities. Nevertheless Mustapha, whose USNO had won fourteen seats, formed a government with SCA support and refused to have anything to do with UPKO. Far from being the 'definitive' people, it appeared that even a minority KD voice in government had disappeared (Ongkili 1972: 62–9; Clark Roff 1974: 52–62, 86–106; Luping 1994: 115–97).

In the depth of this crisis Donald Stephens startled most of his younger Kadazan lieutenants by seemingly accepting the argument of Mustapha that the *bumiputras* of Malaysia should unite behind Malay and Muslim leadership. In an emotional speech to the UPKO national council in December 1967 he moved that UPKO be dissolved and that all its members seek admission to Mustapha's USNO. 'The Kadazans, in order to be saved, must lose our sense of racialism or rather tribalism and not only accept all bumiputras as one but we must also learn to feel one' (cited Luping 1994: 240–1). Having persuaded his supporters to accept this act of political self-abnegation he himself retired from politics and later took up a position as Malaysian high commissioner to Canberra. Given the view of Mustapha and many of his Kuala Lumpur supporters that *bumiputra* unity could only truly be achieved on the basis of Islam, this same logic eventually led Stephens to embrace Islam in 1971. The KD's own leader had declared the whole adventure of Kadazan nationalism to be a mistake.

The decade which followed these decisions was a very dark one for any who believed in a separate identity for KDs or for Christians in Sabah. Sustained by control of the timber concessions which had always dominated Sabah's money politics, and backed by Kuala Lumpur, Mustapha moved to suppress the key markers of KD identity. His policy for national unity was 'one language, one culture and one religion'. Kadazan language was removed from all schools as they became part of the national system in the late 1960s, and the use of all languages other than

Malay and English in radio broadcasts was forbidden from 1974. Islam was declared the state religion in 1973, in defiance of one of the major points of the original Malaysia agreement, and state authority was used in a variety of ways to encourage Sabahans to become Muslim. In 1970–2 the majority of foreign priests and missionary workers were expelled (forty-one in 1970 alone), and the first Malaysian Catholic Bishop of Kota Kinabalu, a Sarawak Chinese, was refused a residence permit (Rooney 1981: 213–19; Loh 1992: 228–31; Luping 1994: 199–274).

Kadazan revival

This dark period proved the political crucible for a more substantial sense of identity to emerge among a younger generation of Sabahans. For many of the subsequent generation of leaders the formative experience of their youth was the confrontation of December 1972. Eight of the remaining Mill Hill missionary priests under notice of expulsion had decided that they could in conscience passively resist the expulsion orders unless reason was given for them. As the time decreed for departure approached, the youth of the Catholic schools took turns sleeping in the priest's house to guard against a sudden raid by the police. At 3 am on 2 December, the police field force struck at three Catholic Kadazan strongholds. In Papar and Tambunan they managed to cut the ropes of the church bells before the sleeping youths could ring them to summon the faithful, and the priests were spirited off to jail. In Kuala Penyu the police were less successful and 600 parishioners gathered in the night to block their approach. Only by calling up hundreds of reinforcements did the field force and riot squad manage to force their way through the crowd to take the priest away (Rooney 1981: 215–17).

This dramatic confrontation appears in the long run to have galvanised the KD forces, and sharpened the sense that KD identity lay outside Islam. All the churches now assert that the Mustapha persecution was a blessing in disguise, in forcing Christians to become more dynamic, more Malaysian and more lay-led. At the height of their difficulties the Catholics formed lay pastoral councils at parish and all-Sabah levels. The first chairman of the Sabah Pastoral Council in 1971 was Peter Mojuntin, the most charismatic of the younger KD political leaders. He had become secretary of UPKO at its 1964 formation at the age of twenty-five, and reluctantly accepted Stephens' call to join USNO in 1969, becoming one of the few Kadazans given a role as state minister in the Mustapha cabinets of 1970–5. Far from following Stephens into Islam, however, he accepted the role as principal Christian spokesman, frequently invoking the '20 points' governing Sabah's entry to Malaysia in an attempt to defend religious freedom.

Mustapha's fall in 1975, however, was brought about not by KD assertiveness but by the dissatisfaction of Mustapha's former supporters at his extravagant and authoritarian style and increasingly long absences. The last straw for the Kuala Lumpur government was his open threat to withdraw Sabah from Malaysia if Kuala Lumpur did not indulge his policies. At this the Malaysian prime minister, Tun Razak, encouraged the formation of an alternative party led by Mustapha's deputy, Harris Salleh. Harris appears to have believed he could only win a Sabah election against Mustapha by bringing the KDs on side, so proposed bringing Donald Stephens (now known as Tun Fuad) and Peter Mojuntin into the party. Berjaya was formed under the leadership of Stephens and Harris in 1975, and went on to defeat Mustapha's USNO in 1976. The support of KDs, and particularly of Christians, was critical in this victory, and they were rewarded with the ending of the cruder aspects of Mustapha's Islamisation campaign.

Although Stephens was the initial Berjaya chief minister, his death and that of Peter Mojuntin in a plane crash two months later was a further blow to KD hopes to return to the central place in Sabah politics. A Muslim (of mixed ancestry), Harris Salleh, took over as chief minister, and cultivated ever closer relations with Kuala Lumpur. The Harris state governments of 1976–84 presided over much federally driven modernisation of the state, and the emergence of a much larger group of educated KDs who could be considered middle-class. But the participation in government of prominent KDs (led by an academic, Dr James Ongkili, as deputy chief minister) did not satisfy the desire of this rising group for a sense of their own worth as a distinct people.

Educated KDs complained that their job prospects were curbed by the continuing bias towards Muslims in higher public service positions, and that Muslim dominance in the state was being promoted by the tolerance or even encouragement of Muslim immigrants from the southern Philippines and Indonesia. More fundamental a blow to KD identity was the acceptance by the Berjaya governments of UMNO's view that all *bumiputra* should see themselves as one people with one (inevitably Malay and Muslim) culture, in implied confrontation with Chinese and foreigners. Realising that the term *bumiputra* had become repugnant to many KDs, the state government adopted in 1980 the Indonesian term *pribumi* to designate all Sabah peoples of 'Malay stock and related groups'. The 1980 census thereby obliterated KD as a category, and classified those previously seeing themselves as the 'definitive' Sabah people in a common category with migrants who had very recently arrived from the Philippines and Indonesia (Loh 1992: 231–40; Luping 1994: 275–330).

With explicitly ethnic political conflict ruled out since Stephens' decision of 1967, the conflict between KD identity and the Harris government focussed on cultural issues. The Kadazan Cultural Association (KCA), which had clung to a tenuous existence during the Mustapha years, began a new lease of life with the election of Joseph Pairin Kitingan to its presidency in December 1976. Pairin was an Australian-trained lawyer new to politics, having been recruited as part of the Berjaya landslide in 1975, and elevated to minister and deputy president of the party after the death of Stephens and Mojuntin. He developed the KCA into a popular organisation with branches in each locality, and a particular role in running the annual harvest festival. The chief minister tried to head off this potential source of opposition by asking Pairin to merge the KCA into a multi-ethnic Sabah Cultural Association, but Pairin declined and the broader body had little life.

In 1981 the state government declared that the annual harvest festival, which had become the chief expression of KD ethnic identity, should become a 'people's festival' for all Sabahans. The government took over the running of the festival in May 1982, shortening it to one day, removing the harvest rituals conducted by animist priestesses (*bobohizan*) and restricting access on the pretext that Malaysia's king would come to preside over the event. The KCA determined to organise its own national harvest festival on the traditional lines in Pairin's stronghold of Tambunan. Despite a total boycott of this event by the state government, and a denial of all government facilities to it, the autonomous Tambunan festival became a triumphant event attended by those who called themselves Kadazans, Dusuns or Muruts from all over the state.[5]

This event established Pairin as the new hero of long leaderless KD identity. The KCA organised his anointing in March 1984 as *Huguan Siou* (literally 'brave leader'). Pre-colonial KD society had been truly stateless with no supra-local leadership, but war leaders had emerged periodically to resist impositions from Brunei or the British. This particular title was popular in Penampang and Papar by the nineteenth century, and had been rediscovered by Kadazan nationalists in 1964 to bestow on Donald Stephens, with the novel meaning of 'great leader' or even 'paramount chief' (a title invented by the Brooke government in Sarawak for Dayak officials; Luping 1989). Ceremonies in various places to have the *bobohizan* pray over him to strengthen him had some effect in

---

[5] The festival is lovingly commemorated in *Our Cultural Heritage*, undated.

uniting KDs in more remote areas behind the urban leadership. These developments, however, made his continued place in the Harris government extremely problematic, and a series of rows culminated in his resignation from Berjaya in 1984, and triumphant return to the state assembly in a by-election for his Tambunan seat in December of that year. Five months later Pairin was chief minister, his newly-formed PBS succeeding at the state election in overturning a Harris government grown corrupt and authoritarian. At the subsequent state elections of 1986 and 1990 Pairin's PBS gained even more handsome victories at the polls despite increasing opposition from Kuala Lumpur (Bala Chandran 1986; Tan 1986; Luping 1994: 331–464).

The Dusun challenge

The victory of the new KD hero appeared to remove the anxieties about the viability of a separate KD identity. A two-day state holiday was declared for the harvest festival, control of which was returned to the KCA; a magnificent KCA cultural centre was built in Penampang which became the site for subsequent Sabah-level festivals; the ethnic label Kadazan was again legitimated and the 'pribumi' one buried, and the first moves were made to have Kadazan taught in schools. Yet these victories brought with them the seeds of further division.

The adoption of the term Kadazan by the early nationalists of the 1960s had swept most, but not all, educated leaders along with it. At the 1961 meeting where Stephens secured the adoption of the term, six older leaders had voted to retain the term Dusun, and they included traditional chiefs of the interior Tuaran and Keningau areas. This dissent had given rise to the Dusun Lotud Association (of Tuaran) in 1960 and USDA in 1967. The leaders of these organisations were never more than a minority of educated KDs in the 1960s, and seemed an increasingly marginal one as independence and education brought new pride to the people who became officially known as Kadazan. Although Muslim leaders occasionally encouraged USDA when they saw reason to fear Kadazan nationalism, this was seldom the case in the 1970s. In 1979, however, as the Kadazan Cultural Association became more energetic, its Dusun equivalent returned to life with a successful request for equal time on Radio Sabah for 'Dusun' language broadcasts.

Linguists explain that the Penampang-Papar dialect which the Catholic missionaries developed as a written language was in fact at one extreme of the dialectic range that makes up KD. The consonants represented by the English sounds h, v, z in Penampang-Papar become l, w, y respectively in the majority of dialects to the east and north. In the early days of printed language the people of Tuaran and Tambunan learned to read the printed z as a y in the newspapers and Catholic prayerbooks that came to them from Kota Kinabalu. However, by the 1980s, they were no longer as tolerant about doing so, and began to call for their own 'Dusun' language. After little more than a year of the PBS government, it was reported that 'A few years ago if one asked a Dusun what race he is, the likely answer is that he is "Kadazan". Today, most of them, particularly those outside the Penampang and Papar districts, will perhaps proudly say that they are Dusuns' (*Sabah Times* 21 December 1986).

One reason for the change was the geographical expansion of education after entry to Malaysia, so that the coastal Kadazan no longer dominated the debate. Another was the spread of Protestant churches in the areas away from the coast which the Catholics had not reached. With the Protestants came the Summer Institute of Linguistics and the first professional studies of the variety of dialects in the interior. A New Testament appeared in the Dusun of Ranau in 1975, and a whole Bible in the Bundu Dusun of the Kota Belud area in 1990. With this greater currency of written variants other than coastal Kadazan, even Catholics of the interior began to expect their Kadazan prayers to be rewritten in Dusun.

The USDA had cooperated with the far more influential KCA in supporting the decisive Tambunan harvest festival of 1982. But the accession of the Pairin government in 1985 seemed to stimulate fears in the interior that the urban literati of the coast had hijacked 'Kadazan' identity for their own purposes. In late 1986 the press began to publicise allegations of resentment by 'Dusuns' that they were still the butt of jokes by urban Kadazans. 'In pubs in Penampang, drinkers laugh themselves silly with jokes of a barefoot Dusun not knowing there is a bell to get the bus to stop' (*Sabah Times* 21 December 1986). At the same time the USDA became more active with the return to its leadership of the ambitious Mark Koding, deputy chief minister in Pairin's government. By 1987, he was demanding that he and USDA be given equal responsibility with KCA in organising the *Kaamatan* festival, or else they would continue to organise their rival celebration in Ranau—known as *Kokotuan*, as if determined to be different (*Sabah Times* 19 March 1988).

In November 1988 the federal education minister, Anwar Ibrahim, during a speech in the Sabah capital, held out hope of introducing the teaching of Iban and 'Kadazan' in Malaysian schools (*Sabah Times* 21 December 1986). Pressure quickly mounted for a standard form of the language to be taught, and the KCA organised a large conference in January 1989 to promote agreement on it. In opening the conference

Pairin sought to lay the issue of a label to rest by declaring that Kadazan had already been selected in 1961, while urging delegates to concentrate on the substantive issue of the most widely acceptable forms of the language. This generated the most determined of offensives, coordinated by the USDA, for the term Dusun to be retained. 'The Dusuns', declared their spokesman, 'recognise and accept all ethnic names, including the Kadazan, hence we demand the full measure of respect and recognition due to us, and we will not accept any form of pressure to change our ethnic name' (Kalakau Untol in *Daily Express* 14 March 1989).

This assertion that the KDs were two people rather than one threatened all that Kadazan nationalism had stood for. It seemed confirmed by USDA sponsoring its own harvest festival in May, and a Dusun song festival the following month. Pairin devoted many of his speeches in the following months to calls for unity, which should not be lost for the sake of a label: 'What name we use for ourselves is a matter of our own choice ... My name is Pairin. I come from Tambunan. My birth certificate says that I am a Dusun. I am also known as a Kadazan and as a Bumiputra, a Sabahan and a Malaysian. All are acceptable to me' (*Daily Express* 19 May 1989). He frequently reminded listeners of their common mythological origin from the great tree Nunuk Ragang. In negotiations which followed the language standardisation conference, his KCA executives were prepared to grant the wider acceptability of the central Dusun consonants l, w and y. The name of the language proved much more emotive.

There is little doubt that Mark Koding and some other USDA leaders were using this issue to advance their own political ambitions, probably encouraged by non-KD leaders out to weaken the PBS government. Koding resigned from PBS to fight the 1990 state election with his own AKAR party. When it lost all seats contested even in the most 'Dusun' areas, it appeared that the political unity of the KD had survived this controversy. Nevertheless the KCA had clearly lost its battle to have Kadazan accepted as a unifying name for the KD people. In the census held within a few months of that election, twice as many people identified themselves as Dusun as called themselves Kadazan.

In August 1989 the KCA executive announced that the Association's name would be changed to the Kadazan Dusun Cultural Association (KDCA) 'to remove the impression that the KCA belongs to the Kadazan people only'. As Pairin emphasised as KCA president, 'We want to drive home the point that the Kadazans and Dusuns are one and the same people, no matter which ethnic name they prefer' (*Daily Express* 18 August 1989).

Coping without state power

Since the 1989 crisis the compromise appears to have been accepted that unity can best be achieved under the awkward banner Kadazandusun, one word for the language, though two words in the census category. The KDCA launched an ambitious programme in 1987 to develop a dictionary, eventually published in 1995 as *Kadazan Dusun Malay English Dictionary*. This provided two forms of each KD word, first the Kadazan dialect of Penampang and then the Central Dusun of Tambunan-Ranau. A shorter version apparently not authorised by the KDCA was brought out a little earlier by Jeffrey Kitingan as *Dusunkadazan Dictionary* (Kitingan 1994), which takes Interior Dusun as the key referent for each word, followed by Coastal Kadazan, Malay and English equivalents. The language introduced into schools in 1997 was named in this hybrid way, Kadazandusun.

The political unity which enabled KDs to dominate successive multi-racial Sabah Unity Party (PBS) governments stood the party in good stead in four successive election victories—1985, 1986, 1990 and 1994. In each case the party won almost all predominately KD seats as well as a share of the Chinese, Muslim and mixed seats. However the personal ambitions of the educated leaders undid these victories after the 1994 election. The twenty-five seats won by PBS in 1994 against the twenty-three of a Barisan Nasional coalition heavily backed by Kuala Lumpur, proved too narrow to stop the buying of assemblymen after the election—a common phenomenon in Sabah elections. The KD elected members, evidently convinced that the PBS could not retain government, began a race to be the first to defect and bring as many colleagues as possible with them, in the hope of being rewarded with top jobs in the new state government. Only three of the twenty-five elected PBS members were still with Pairin when this race was over (Chua 1995). The others joined a variety of parties within the Barisan Nasional (BN) coalition, each hoping he would be the KD to be allotted a two-year term as leader of the BN and the government in Sabah, in a three-way rotation of the top post with Muslim and Chinese that had been promised by the BN before the election. Bernard Dompok, member for the Kadazan heartland seat of Moyog, won this contest in the name of the largest of the defecting KD parties, eventually renamed after the historic UPKO of Donald Stephens.

Dompok's term as chief minister came to an end at the 1999 state election, when he lost his seat along with all the other KD candidates who had defected to the BN in 1994. The 1999 election was the first fought under electoral boundaries redrawn in 1995, which had ensured that twenty-four of the forty-two seats had Muslim majorities. Backed strongly by Kuala Lumpur, with Prime Minister Mahathir declaring that funds would be cut off if the opposition prevailed, UMNO succeeded in winning all the Muslim-majority seats. PBS, again representing the opposition, won seventeen seats including all those dominated by KDs. Having lost its earlier quest to redraw Sabah politics along the ethnic lines of the Peninsula, Kuala Lumpur had in effect succeeded in polarising the vote along religious lines (Chin 2004). As seen in the 2000 census, growing numbers of Sabahans (11.5 per cent in 2000 against 6.2 per cent in 1990 and 0.4 per cent in 1960) were willing to declare themselves Malays to join the winning team, but this base was still far from adequate to win elections. UMNO in Sabah had embraced all Muslims, and even accepted some KD Christians as members. PBS was faced with a similar dilemma to that of UPKO in 1967, of seeing itself condemned to permanent opposition and the non-Muslim indigenous people to increasing relative impoverishment as they missed out on development projects and the patronage that comes with office. In 2002, therefore, Pairin Kitingan led his PBS back to a subordinate place in a BN government, where it again had to jostle for influence with KDs who had a longer history of supporting Kuala Lumpur, notably Bernard Dompok.

This move has transformed Sabah from having the most interesting elections in Malaysia to the dullest. At the 2004 and 2008 state elections, held at the same time as federal ones, the governing party won all but one of the sixty state seats, the opposition destroyed itself with a plethora of squabbling candidates and independents did better than the national opposition parties. Pairin Kitingin's prestige as *Huguan Siou* maintained a certain unity among his followers despite the seemingly permanent loss of the struggle to be Sabah's definitive people. After the ease of its 2004 win of all thirty-two seats allotted to it in the BN intra-party deal, UMNO declared that it would abandon the rotation of the chief minister's position, and retain it always for the leading party. Pairin became deputy chief minister, as leader of the second party in the coalition with twelve seats. Bernard Dompok was arguably a stronger voice in government, however, having chosen the ruling party earlier than Pairin, and he used his position as a federal minister to become the principal East Malaysian voice opposing the drift towards Islamisation and 'Malay supremacy' in the Malaysian government. He had sufficiently reclaimed his position as a KD spokesman to be able to return to his heartland Kadazan seat of Panampang at the 2004 election.

Remarkably, despite the insignificant number of Malays in the state's population when it joined Malaysia, the Peninsula model of UMNO

Table 7.2 Sabah population by ethnicity and religion, 2000 (Sabah Yearbook 2007: 15)

	KD	Murut	Bajau	Malay	Other bumip	Chinese	Foreign	Total %
Muslim	100,968	11,698	342,421	303,497	273,092	8,589	510,238	63.7
Christian	359,210	70,054	383	–	100,776	81,475	98,634	27.8
Buddhism + Chinese religion	3,511	295	42	–	7,207	163,528	1,888	6.8
Tribal + 'no religion'	14,561	2,582	249	–	7,990	7,433	1,251	1.3
Total (incl. unknown)	479,944	84,679	343,178	303,497	390,058	262,115	614,824	100

dominance had by 2004 been successfully transplanted to Sabah. This was achieved through greater government patronage for those declaring themselves to be Malays or at least Muslims, but also by expanding the membership of UMNO in Sabah to include Christians and even Chinese, a useful precedent for non-racial politics in Malaysia more broadly. The rapid gains for Islam, both through internal conversion and mass migration from Indonesia and the southern Philippines, had ensured a Muslim majority by the 2000 census of 58 per cent of the population of citizens (including 101,000 KD Muslims, 21 per cent of the listed KD total), and 83 per cent of the foreign immigrants (see table 7.2). These demographic changes made the return of a KD chief minister rather unlikely, so that most of the KD political leadership concluded they should focus rather on seeking to work within the Malay-dominated system (Lim 2004). By comparison with the dangers of permanent opposition, having a stake in power was far more attractive.

The period since the loss of state leadership in Sabah has seen important gains towards ethnie consolidation on the cultural front. During the 1994 election campaign the federal government had again affirmed, as part of its strategy to break the PBS hold on KD votes, that Kadazandusun would be accepted as a community language in Sabah schools. Despite the renewed political divisions of the period 1994–2002, Pairin Kitingan and Bernard Dompok, as well as Kadazan and Dusun partisans, worked together to have Kadazandusun teaching begun at the first primary level in February 1997, using a standard based on the interior dialect of the Ranau and Tambunan area, but with some concessions to coastal dialects. KDCA favoured calling this the Bunduliwan standard, Bundu being one of the names of the coastal dialect, and Liwan of the interior. Starting with grade four in primary school, a further level of instruction was added in subsequent years until it was taught in grades four through six. A hundred primary schools were in the scheme by 1998, and 276, plus 31 middle schools, by 2004, when Kadazandusun was being taught by 775 KD teachers to 22,000 children in Sabah (Zawawi 2001: 134; Lasimbang 2004: 10; KLF 2007).

Although Bernard Dompok (chief minister 1997–9) was instrumental in the establishment of the Kadazandusun Language Foundation and the advancement of Kadazandusun through the primary school system, it may have been the very lack of effective political power since 1995 that helped the KD intellectuals, as in the 1970s, to cooperate better to have their language taught, Christianity defended and some symbols of their culture preserved. Just as the Bataks standardised and sanitised their tradition in the process of ethnie formation, a few attractive modernised

Table 7.3 *Mean income of ethnic groups in Malaysian Ringgit, 2004 (EPU 2006a: 59)*

Sabah ethnic groups		Other Malaysia ethnic groups	
Kadazandusun	2,037	Malaysia 'bumiputra'	2,711
Murut	1,638	Iban (Sarawak non-Muslim)	1,725
Malay	2,779	Malay (Sarawak)	2,717
Bajau (Muslim)	1,824	Melanau (Sarawak Muslim)	2,341
Chinese	4,248	Chinese (Malaysia)	4,254

elements of 'traditional' KD culture were made iconic—a standard black dress for both sexes, mythological common origins and the *Kaamatan* festival cleansed of the drunkenness which tends to embarrass urban leaders (*Borneo Post* 24 February 1995). The definition of non-Muslim indigenous unity was extended to include the Muruts, so that later politically correct formulations used the formula KDM—Kadazan Dusun Murut.

In economic terms the indigenous groups in Sabah have been relative losers in Malaysia's competitive rush to middle class status. Despite its oil and other resources, Sabah remains the poorest Malaysian state, with the lowest per capita income, 23 per cent below the poverty line compared with 3.6 per cent in the Peninsula, and more than twice the number of people per doctor and nurse (2,719 in 2004) than the national average (1,387; EPU 2006a: 58; EPU 2006b: 421). Within this relatively impoverished state, its wage levels kept low by the flood of immigrants, the 'Malay' populations have benefited from government patronage to move ahead of indigenous groups. Yet as table 7.3 illustrates, KDs have fared least badly among the non-Muslim indigenous groups of East Malaysia, despite their state overall having been punished by Kuala Lumpur for its long period in opposition hands. Although many factors may be at work here, the relative skill of KD leadership and growing coherence of KD political identity deserve some credit for the better outcome than the analogous group in generally richer Sarawak—the Iban.

Federalism and democratic elections undoubtedly helped the Kadazandusun to institutionalise their identity and their language within the decentralised Malaysian system. Despite being far less numerous and less fully in control of their own territory than were the Bataks in Sumatra's highlands, they allied effectively with Chinese and with other indigenous groups to win several electoral contests. By comparison with many other once-stateless groups, including the Bataks in Indonesia and the Dayak of Sarawak, they have been able to achieve a degree of unity behind charismatic leadership—Donald Stephens, Peter Mojuntin, Pairin Kitingan (particularly) and Bernard Dompok. Like Indonesian counterparts, on the other hand, they face inevitable language loss as people move away from the homelands to the polyglot cities. Many educated KDs themselves prefer to speak to their children in Malay or English, which are firmly associated with education and modernity (Zawawi 2001: 93, 99–101). A recent study of an interior area near Keningau where greater language maintenance might have been expected showed virtually all communication of school-age children with each other and with their parents was in Malay, with a very rapid progress of language loss from an older generation fluent in KD (Mahadhir and Tumin 2008). The Catholic Church, the chief impetus for the first attempt at language standardisation, consecrated its first KD bishop in 1993 (for Keningau) and its second in 2007 (for Sandakan). But even this bastion of KD identity now has most of its liturgy and all its administration in Malay and English. The agricultural rituals which formed the emotional centrepiece of the earlier harvest festivals are increasingly little understood by young KDs, and the 'pagan' priestesses who conduct them will all have died within a decade or two.

The time within Malaysia since 1963 has certainly not favoured the relative position of KD within Sabah, as Muslim conversion and massive immigration reduced their proportion of the state's population to around a fifth. Nevertheless they have established an increasingly stable ethnie with its own clear political program, and done so peaceably and creatively. This ethnie is now likely to endure.

8   Imperial alchemy–revolutionary dreams

The long history of states has played a large role, larger than is acknowledged in the literature, in the making of political identities. Those identities were fluid and multiple in equatorial Southeast Asia precisely because states had always held such limited leverage in that forest-and-water world. Modernity, however, cannot do without states. State-like formations and ideologies were brought to this region by successive waves of outsider traders. Prior to the years around 1900 these trade-based polities gradually became more like states, though the nineteenth century acknowledged only those ruled by Europeans (and eventually the Siamese with European advisors) as 'civilised' members of the globalising world order. In the twentieth century there was no further toleration of ambiguity or statelessness. World order required that all boundaries were demarcated, 'slavery', 'piracy' and an arms-bearing populace eliminated, and the status of all within those boundaries rendered unambiguous as subjects (Klein 1993; Tagliacozzo 2005).

Only the Siamese monarchy in Southeast Asia had been able to satisfy the demands of world powers sufficiently to survive this trauma. Kingdoms such as Aceh, Lombok and Sulu were incorporated into imperial states through wars short or long, while stateless peoples like the Batak and Kadazandusun for the first time confronted the standard package of state monopoly of force and law, finding the experience liberating as well as threatening. Malay sultans on the Peninsula and in Sumatra and Borneo continued their age-old roles of mediating between external powers and indigenous peoples, though their true powerlessness grew increasingly obvious to the dynamic worlds of identity formation in the cities.

Both the Dutch and British colonial constructs remained extraordinarily plural, in language, religion and political formation. Few in the 1930s (except the Indonesian nationalists) believed that they could or should ever become single nation-states. Yet the pluralism was so pervasive at every level that lesser ethnie nationalisms had even more difficulty making a successful bid for cultural and political coherence than the broadest anti-imperial nationalism. The idea of Indonesia was particularly seductive. It managed the alchemy of making the resented imperial infrastructure of state into a sacred symbol of identity. Its rootless artificiality ensured that it could generate anti-imperial and later state nationalism on the same level of abstract charisma as had the symbolic rulers of the Hindu-Buddhist past.

The above chapters showed some examples of ethnie formation, both around different concepts of pre-colonial state in the Malay and Aceh cases, and by building new identities for stateless peoples among Batak and Kadazandusun. There were other attempts to build ethnie nationalisms at the outset of the competitive twentieth century. Arab and Indian overseas ethnie nationalisms joined those of the Europeans and Chinese in directing attention elsewhere. Muslim reformers formed a range of different organisations, which assumed religion to be the appropriate basis for brotherhood. Minahassans and Ambonese formed into self-conscious ethnies on the basis of exceptionally high education levels and Protestant Christianity (Henley 1996). Javanese and Balinese aristocrats formed organisations designed to uplift and modernise their impressive cultures. Yet in colony-wide assemblies their voices sounded parochial and backward-looking. To make a case for one group, the idealists ultimately had to make the case for all.

The unitary ideal triumphed in Indonesia through the travails of 1945–50. In the following fifty years it was spread through highly uniform education and broadcasting systems, to the point that Indonesian identity has become a genuine, taken-for-granted part of the mindset of Indonesians who grew up within it. In the longest term this outcome may serve the country well, even including those groups that have been marginalised or suppressed by it in the medium term. In contrast with what appeared at the outset the lesser challenges of Burma or Malaysia to create a viable nation-state, Indonesia achieved that alchemy brilliantly. The essential ingredient in its successful mix was to have detached its sacred symbols of identity from any particular history or culture.

The costs of pursuing this unitary goal as ruthlessly and single-mindedly as the Indonesian army did under its first two presidents was very high. No goal of social engineering can justify the loss of so many lives, without speaking of the heedless erasure of cultures. Bob Elson weighs just this balance and concludes that much of the effort to protect the unitary idea 'was unnecessary, and a great deal of it counterproductive' (Elson 2008: 318). The counterproductive quality is plain to see in Indonesia's treatment of Aceh, which might well have remained in a unitary Indonesia without force if treated more imaginatively in the 1950s. But when comparing with the case of federal Malaysia, we must conclude that choosing more peaceful and democratic means at critical junctures would have produced different outcomes, not the same uniformity of layered identities. The reasons the Indonesian government behaved inflexibly at various junctures and its military resorted to violence were rooted in the same mind-set of 'eternal, unassailable, incontestable and inherited unity' that built Indonesian unity at any costs.

Post-revolutionary Indonesia and federal Malaysia

The boundaries drawn between British and Dutch spheres in what the British called 'the Malay World' were arbitrary. The peoples and histories in the space that came to be Malaysia were not fundamentally different from those that came to be Indonesia save for their more recent, immigrant quality. Indonesia had by far the more intractable assemblage of ethnies rooted in distinctive histories, languages and literatures. Yet it is Malaysia that has the complex federal system, while Indonesia remains, with China, the world's largest experiment in organising exceptional cultural diversity through a unitary state.

The reasons for these different paths lie in part with colonial history, but to a far greater extent in revolution. It is true that British colonisers accepted asymmetric and even eccentric arrangements in the interests of pragmatic empire-building. The monarchies that eventually comprised Malaysia had greater juridical sovereignty than any monarchs in Netherlands India (Emerson 1937: 53–4; Reid 2007: 146–8). It was the achievement of the state through revolution, however, that determined that Indonesia, like China, would be unitary. Had the sudden Japanese surrender in August 1945 not created a revolutionary opportunity, Indonesian statehood would have proceeded through a series of constitutional compromises between different regions and the Dutch, with some federal solutions the likeliest outcome. Does Malaysia's federal experience offer some insight into the kind of Indonesia that might then have emerged?

Fundamentally, what Elson calls 'the idea of Indonesia' would have been profoundly different. The romantic, sacrificial abstraction served by countless emotive rituals and even cabalistic repetitions of the 17–8–45 formula (the date of the independence proclamation) has been powerful in post-revolutionary Indonesia. State rituals and museums were designed to remind that this idea was conceived in blood, and further blood was permitted in its name. The revolutionary unitary ideal demanded the overthrow of the colonial rule of law, but it was force rather than constitutionality that filled the gap. By contrast Malaysia's legislative and judicial apparatus retained much institutional strength, and its military remained in the barracks. Its judiciary was eventually tarnished by Mahathir, but by contrast with Indonesia, Malaysia maintained a rule of law.

The toll of violence has been extremely heavy in Indonesia, mostly unpunished and much unrecorded. While some has served to confirm elite perceptions of dangerous primordial sentiments among the less educated, a great deal of the violence has been perpetrated or at least encouraged by the state. The thousands of casualties in the Malayan Emergency (1948–56) are comparable (given the different populations) to those in Indonesia's revolutionary and parliamentary periods, but there is nothing on the Malaysian side to put in the balance against the appalling bloodshed of 1965–6 in Indonesia, the 'mysterious killings' of 1982–5, the Aceh conflict in 1998–2005 and the ethno-religious vendettas of 1996–2002 (van Klinken 2007; Reid 2007: 158–61).

The manner in which the Kadazandusun and other Borneo peoples joined Malaysia was hardly an ideal of democratic consultation, but by contrast with the other side of the border, it was consensual, constitutional and peaceful. Each of the ethnie is acknowledged in the census (with the exception of 1980), in the school syllabus, and in the political system through ethnic parties and state assemblies. From the perspective of a minority ethnie struggling to maintain and develop its unique identity, the federalism of Malaysia has proved a far more congenial space. Democracy has also been better served through federalism. Not only does it give the regions what they appear to want; it provides essential experience for opposition parties at state level without the zero-sum game threatened by electoral change in centralised systems.

From the viewpoint of the nation-state, federalism and the ethnic party system can be perceived as dangers. Parties that mobilise on a state, ethnic or religious base have an interest in maintaining those categories and emphasising them at the expense of the centre (Brown 2007). They can more realistically secede because they have some of the infrastructure and leadership to do so. The departure of Singapore from Malaysia in 1965 demonstrates how that can happen, but also that it is not the end of the world. When Kuala Lumpur firmly opposed such secession, allegedly in the mind of Tun Mustapha in the 1970s and some Kadazan leaders in the late 1980s, it had abundant means to prevent such an outcome. India's survival in even more difficult circumstances has proved the same point (He et al. 2007).

The cost of Indonesia's revolutionary centralism can also be measured in economic terms. Maddison's comparative figures show Indonesian gross domestic product (GDP) per capita a little ahead of Malaysian in 1913 and still comparable in 1940. Indonesia suffered terribly from its revolutionary experience, which included a drastic rupture with the European firms that had dominated the high points of the economy, and a climate unfriendly to foreign investment until 1967. It failed to keep pace with Malaysia post-war reconstruction and post-1970 boom, falling to little more than half of Malaysia's gross national product (GNP) per capita in 1950 and close to a quarter today (Maddison 2001: 215, 304–5; Anderson 2008: 36–7; Reid 2007).

Though Indonesians for much of their history looked down on Malaysia as a backward-looking, neo-colonial construct, there is since 1998 a more wistful debate about where Indonesia may have gone wrong. Robert Elson (2008: 322) has made for the first time in the scholarly literature a persuasive case that 'there is no point in enforcing a false territorial integrity at the cost of the very values that must underpin the whole project'. The top-down ruthlessness and brutalisation was too high a price to have paid. The end did not justify the means. Nevertheless Jakarta has succeeded in turning its subjects into Indonesians, as Kuala Lumpur has not managed to turn its subjects into Malaysians. That Indonesianness involves a shared language, idiom, education and set of assumptions about the nation. It includes a layering process in which more local and particular identities are complementary to the Indonesian one, not in conflict.

Imperial boundaries

It is time to return to the question asked at the beginning of this book: whether nationalism is at a different stage in Asia than in Europe, or of a different type. If the former, should we consider the real challenge of ethnie nationalism to imperial borders to lie still in the future, when democratisation and mass education are further advanced? If the latter, do we need new models?

It is now hard to recall how heroic and improbable the Indonesian idea seemed in its early stage. A perceptive anthropologist who worked among Bataks in the 1950s then thought that in contrast with migrants in America, 'Batak individuals cannot join a distinctively Indonesian society, nor can they modify their culture in the direction of an individual model, for neither the society nor the model exists' (Bruner 1961: 513). There seems no question any longer that such a model does exist, for all those educated within the remarkably centralised post-1950 system. Anti-imperial nationalism was used rhetorically by Sukarno and bureaucratically by Suharto, and became the state nationalist project. The anti-imperial content had run its course by the 1990s, but it had done its work through the education system. The evidence of this book is that Bataks have become Indonesians, without ceasing in most cases to be Bataks. In varying degrees the same may be said for other ethnies within Indonesia. Aceh was and remains an exception, with its own ethnie nationalism based on a memory of state and of sacrifice. Yet there too the education system has worked its alchemy and provided much of the cultural frame within which Acehnese identity is expressed.

The process of democratisation after 1998 was the supreme test of whether this alchemy had succeeded. A half-century of experience with successful secession movements suggests that it is only the first flush of democratisation that is helpful to potential secessions. Those who did not break away from the Soviet Union in that moment of permissive euphoria did not get another chance. In Indonesia, too, it was the immediate successor to Suharto, President Habibie, who could offer a referendum to East Timor as a way of healing Indonesia's long-festering sore. Aceh also had its best chance at that moment, when the activists who had helped bring Suharto down were still influential, and democratisation appeared to include the right to the kind of government one wanted. Once parliamentary institutions were securely established, the politicians found that supporting state nationalism was more popular with their electorates than democratic principles. Secession very seldom occurs, indeed, in mature democracies (Dion 1996).

Indonesia's independent history, though no model of democratic constitutionality, does demonstrate that even very diverse empires can become nation-states. The alchemy by which this process occurred needs more attention, for it does have much wider application. Indonesia has made a remarkable transition to a democracy which appears increasingly stable. Indonesian identity has become a given component in the layered identities that Indonesians deploy. The Malaysian nation-state is in this sense less secure but has also made remarkable progress towards the goal. So successfully has the nationalist era been weathered that the principal challenge to both Indonesian and Malaysian political identity comes today not from ethnie nationalism but from religion in its new globalised forms.

Broader unities

The globalising economy and trans-national legal regimes raised in chapter 1 are also part of the answer to the future of ethnie nationalism. The more Southeast Asian countries become locked into transnational modes of production and exchange, and subscribe to international conventions governing such exchanges, the less significant its particular boundaries become. To some extent civic or territorial nationalism becomes an essential pragmatic underpinning of global integration, rather than the focus of passionate identity. As advanced economies become more multi-cultural, they curiously converge from the opposite direction with plural polities such as those in Southeast Asia. Is the pluralism of Southeast Asia pre-modern or post-modern?

The boundaries of Southeast Asia were fought over in the period 1940–80, as different nationalisms contended in the rapidly changing international situation. Thailand's irredentist claims against Cambodia (the most passionately felt because of Angkor Wat), Malaysia and Burma were briefly rewarded by the Japanese. French Indo-China was contested by various parties until the communist victories in 1975, and thereafter Cambodian and Vietnamese communists fought over their common boundary. Indonesia fought the formation of Malaysia in 1963–6 and harboured its domestic opponents, while the Philippines laid a claim to Sabah in 1962 and also refused to recognise Malaysia. At several points the Burmese government did not control some of its borderlands with China and Thailand. If new or reconfigured nationalisms were to make their claim for sovereign status, their chances were greater during this stage of post-colonial uncertainty.

Distrust remains along many of these borders, but since 1980 military confrontation appears a thing of the past. Recent territorial disputes between Malaysia and Indonesia, and Malaysia and Singapore were peacefully resolved by the International Court of Justice in The Hague (2002 and 2008 respectively). Stability breeds acceptance, and state nationalism does its work in turning even borderland peoples into citizens. But the international situation has also been helpful, of which the regional ASEAN was a key part.

The antecedents of the regional idea were all caught up with, and limited by, the Cold War. The first activists for the Southeast Asian idea had been on the left. A Southeast Asian League was established in Bangkok by the revolutionary groups in Indo-China and the left-leaning Pridi government in Thailand in September 1947, just before the latter was ousted in a right-wing coup (Goscha, 1999: 140–4). Subsequent efforts arose from the anti-communist side of the Cold War. The Southeast Asian Treaty Organisation (SEATO, 1954–77) was blatantly US-sponsored and contained only two Southeast Asian states; ASA (1961–7) contained only three. Only when an anti-communist, though theoretically still non-aligned, government took over in Indonesia could ASEAN be formed in 1967 with all the free-market states of the region—Indonesia, Malaysia, the Philippines, Singapore and Thailand, with Brunei joining at its independence in 1984.

ASEAN was far from a European Community, but was successful in developing an 'ASEAN way' rhetoric of consensus, and inserting itself as a necessary package in broader regional groupings. Some members had bi-lateral relations with the US, but in multi-lateral formations such as Asia-Pacific Economic Co-operation (APEC) all the ASEAN members had to be brought along. With its powerful and quarrelling neighbours to the north it played a very useful role of extending the regional idea through the ASEAN Regional Forum (1994), eventually grouping most Asian and Pacific countries, and ASEAN+3 including China, Japan and Korea (from 1999) annual meetings. In a globalising economic context, it helped redefine the way Southeast Asian elites thought about their neighbours, and thereby softened the tyranny of boundaries. Within that context, a series of 'growth triangles' sought with varying success to moderate the absolutism of borders and allow natural trade and investment flows across them. The first of them, SIJORI (Singapore–Johor–Riau, 1989), allowed Singapore capital to move to the neighbouring Indonesian islands as a low-cost manufacturing centre. Without the Singapore factor, regional groupings around the Malaysia-Thai border (plus northern Sumatra, 1993), the intersection of East Malaysia, the southern Philippines and Indonesia, and the Mekong basin had less success in overcoming regional distrusts.

Like the European Union, ASEAN sought to expand into former communist states as a way of wooing them towards more open markets and polities, and overcoming regional distrust. The bar however, was set very low, particularly under Dr Mahathir's aggressive chairmanship of ASEAN in 1997. Vietnam had been admitted in 1995 while still communist, and Mahathir was hoping to bring the remaining three, Cambodia, Burma and Laos, into membership for the thirtieth anniversary. The Cambodian strong man Hun Sen made that impossible by attacking the constitutional process that ASEAN leaders had been at pains to build there, but it was nevertheless admitted two years later. The problem of Burma has dogged ASEAN ever since, making both consensus internally and normal relations with the Western world externally a great deal more difficult.

Despite these difficulties, Southeast Asian states have been busy members of the international community, both within the ASEAN context and in the myriad other international organisations that now regulate the trans-national order. In Southeast Asia as elsewhere the international context is vastly different from that in which older nationalisms made their violent way in the Western world. On the one hand the world order has more means at its disposal to prevent nationalist disruptions to that order. On the other a consensual parting of the ways within a supra-national order, such as that between the Czech Republic and Slovakia within Europe, is hardly consequential enough to be worth dying for.

The imperial alchemy is working.

Glossary

A = Arabic; Ac = Acehnese; B = Batak; Ch = Chinese; D = Dutch;
I = Indonesian; KD = Kadazandusun; M = Malay

adat (A/I)	custom, tradition
arisan (M/I)	credit cooperative, usually meeting monthly in the houses of members
asli (M/I)	original, indigenous
baba (M)	local-born, Straits Chinese
bahasa (M/I)	language
bangsa (M/I)	race, nation
bobohizan (KD)	female shamans or priests
bumiputra (M)	'sons of the soil'
daulat (M)	sovereignty
hikayat (M/Ac)	historical epic (Malay); epic poem (Acehnese)
Huguan Siou (KD)	lit. 'brave leader'. Informal Kadazan cultural leader
hui (Ch)	(secret) society
jawi (A/M)	Southeast Asian (Malay-speaking) Muslim; Arabic script for Malay
jihad (A/M/I)	sacred struggle for Islam; holy war
kaamatan (KD)	harvest festival
kerja tahun (I)	annual village festival, notably Karo Batak
ketuanan (M)	supremacy
marga (B)	patrilineal clan, using same surname
merdeka (M/I)	freedom
negara (M/I)	state
orang (M)	person
peranakan (I)	local-born, creole
perang sabil (M)	holy war
pribumi (I)	native, indigenous

rixdaalder (D)	VOC silver coinage intended to replicate Spanish dollar, equivalent to 2.5 guilders
sahala (B)	soul power
suku (M/I)	sub-division, particularly a quarter, adopted into modern Indonesian for an ethnie
syahbandar (M)	harbour-master, port official
tanah (M)	land
tataba (KD)	a magical wand
totok (I)	outsider (Chinese-speaking)
tugu (I)	monument
ulama (A/M)	Islamic scholar (pl. or Arabic '*alim*')
ulèëbalang (Ac)	hereditary local chief or port-ruler in Aceh
wali negara (M)	head of (federal) state

References

Adam, Ahmat 1995. *The Vernacular Press and the Emergence of Modern Indonesian Consciousness (1855–1913)*. Ithaca: Cornell University Southeast Asia Program.

Ali Haji ibn Ahmad, Raja 1979. *The Precious Gift (Tuhfat al-Nafis)*, trans. Virginia Matheson and Barbara Andaya. Kuala Lumpur: Oxford University Press.

Andaya, Barbara Watson and Leonard Andaya 1992. *A History of Malaysia*. London: Macmillan.

Andaya, Leonard 1993. *The World of Maluku: Eastern Indonesia in the Early Modern Period*. Honolulu: University of Hawaii Press.

2001. 'The Search for the "Origins" of Melayu', *Journal of Southeast Asian Studies* **32**, iii, 315–30.

Anderson, Benedict 1983 [1991]. *Imagined Communities: Reflections on the Origin and Spread of Nationalism*. London: Verso.

2008. 'Exit Suharto: Obituary for a Mediocre Tyrant', *New Left Review* **50**, 27–59.

Anderson, John 1826 [1971]. *Mission to the East Coast of Sumatra in 1823*. Kuala Lumpur: Oxford University Press.

Anon. 1930. 'Islam dan Nationalisme', in *Soeara Atjeh* 1 April.

Antonissen, A. 1958. *Kadazan Dictionary and Grammar*. Canberra, Government Printer.

Arendt, Hannah 1968. *Antisemitism*. San Diego: Harcourt Brace Jovanovich.

Armstrong, John A. 1982. *Nations Before Nationalism*. Chapel Hill: University of North Carolina Press.

Ascher, William 1998. 'From Oil to Timber: the Political Economy of Off-budget Development Financing in Indonesia', *Indonesia* **65**.

Aspinall, Edward 2006. 'Violence and Identity Formation in Aceh under Indonesian rule', in Anthony Reid (ed.) *Verandah of Violence: the Background to the Aceh Problem*. Singapore: Singapore University Press, 149–76.

Baker, Chris 2003. 'Ayutthaya Rising: From Land or Sea?' *Journal of Southeast Asian Studies* **34**: 1.

Bala Chandran 1986. *The Third Mandate*. Kuala Lumpur: Bala Chandran.

Barmé, Scot 1993. *Luang Wichit Wathakan*. Singapore: Institute of Southeast Asian Studies.

Barros, João de 1563 [1973 [1777]]. *Da Asia*. Lisbon: Regia Officina.

Battuta, Ibn 1929 [1353]. *Travels in Asia and Africa, 1325–1354*, trans. H. A. R. Gibb. London: George Routledge.

Beaulieu, Augustin de 1666. 'Mémoires du voyage aux Indes orientales du Général du Beaulieu, dressés par luy-mesme,' in Melchisedech Thévenot (ed.), *Relations de divers voyages curieux*, vol II. Paris: Cramoisy. A new edition is Augustin de Beaulieu 1996. *Mémoires d'un voyage aux Indes Orientales*, in Denys Lombard (ed.) Paris: Maisonneuve & Laroche, and a partial English translation is in Anthony Reid (ed.) 1995. *Witnesses to Sumatra: a Travellers' Anthology*. Kuala Lumpur: Oxford University Press, 64–81.

Benda, H. J., J. K. Irikura and K. Kishi (eds.) 1965. *Japanese Military Administration in Indonesia: Selected Documents*. New Haven: Yale University Centre for Southeast Asian Studies.

Berg, C. C. 1927. 'Kidung Sunda. Inleiding, tekst, vertaling en aantekeningen,' *BKI* **83**.

Bertrand, Jacques 2004. *Nationalism and Ethnic Conflict in Indonesia*. Cambridge University Press.

Blumenbach, Johann Friedrich 1775 [1865]. *De generis humani varietate nativa*. English translation in *The Anthropological Treatises of Johann Friedrich Blumenbach*, London: Longman.

Blumentritt, Ferdinand 1882. *Versuch einer Ethnographie der Philippinen*. No. 27 in Petermann's Mittheilungen. Gotha: Justus Perthes.

BP. Borneo Post, Kota Kinabalu, daily.

BPS 1990. *Penduduk Indonesia: Hasil Sensus Penduduk 1990*. Jakarta: Badan Pusat Statistik.

1992. *Penduduk Sumatra Utara. Hasil Sensus Penduduk 1990* (S2.02), Jakarta: Badan Pusat Statistik.

1994. *Indikator Kesejahteraan Rakyat 1993*. Sumatera Utara. Medan: Badan Pusat Statistik.

2001. *Penduduk Sumatera Utara: Hasil Sensus Penduduk Tahun 2000* (L2.2.2). Medan: Badan Pusat Statistik.

2006. *Pendudok Indonesia: Hasil Survei Penduduk Antar Sensus 2005* (S1. 3302). Medan: Badan Pusat Statistik.

Brown, C. C. 1952. 'The Malay Annals, translated from Raffles MS 18', *Journal of the Malaysian Branch, Royal Asiatic Society* **25**, 2 and 3.

Brown, David 2007. 'Regionalist Federalism: a Critique of Ethno-nationalist Federalism', in He Baogang *et al. Federalism in Asia*. Cheltenham, UK: Edward Elgar, 57–81.

Brunei Census 1971: 1972. Negeri Brunei, *Laporan Banchi Pendudok Brunei 1971*. Bandar Seri Begawan: Star Press.

Bruner, Edward 1961. 'Urbanization and Ethnic Identity', *American Anthropologist* **63**, 508–21.

1972. 'Batak Ethnic Associations in Three Indonesian Cities', in *Southwestern Journal of Anthropology* **28**, iii: 207–29.

1983. 'Emergent vs Invariate Models', in Rita Kipp and Richard Kipp (eds.) *Beyond Samosir: Recent Studies of the Batak Peoples of Sumatra*. Athens, Ohio: Ohio University Center for International Studies, 13–20.

Bunnag, Tej 1977. *The Provincial Administration of Siam, 1892–1915*. Kuala Lumpur: Oxford University Press.

Burma Census 1986. *1983 Population Census*. Rangoon: Immigration and Manpower Department.

Burney, Henry 1971. *The Burney Papers*, 2 vols. Farnborough: Gregg International.

Butcher, John and Howard Dick (eds.) 1993. *The Rise and Fall of Revenue Farming: Business Elites and the Emergence of the Modern State in Southeast Asia*. Basingstoke: Macmillan.

Callahan, William 2006. 'History, Identity, and Security: Producing and Consuming Nationalism in China?' *Critical Asian Studies* **38**: 2, 179–208.

Castles, Lance 1972. 'The Political Life of a Sumatran Residency: Tapanuli 1915–1940', Unpublished Ph.D. dissertation, Yale University.

Cense, A. A. 1979. *Makassaars-Nederlands Woordenboek*. The Hague: Nijhoff for Koninklijk Institut voor Taal-, Land-, en Volkenkunde.

Census of India 1933. *Census of India 1931, Vol. XI, Burma*. Rangoon: Government Printing and Stationery.

CGI (Crisis Group International) 2007. *Indonesia: how GAM Won in Aceh*. Crisis Group Asia Briefing No. 61, 22 March 2007.

Chakrabarty, Dipesh 2000. *Provincializing Europe: Postcolonial Thought and Historical Difference*. Princeton: Princeton University Press.

Chandler, David 1983. *A History of Cambodia*. Boulder: Westview.

Cheah Boon Kheng 1980. 'The Social Impact of the Japanese Occupation of Malaya (1942–1945)', in Alfred W. McCoy (ed.) *Southeast Asia under Japanese Occupation*. New Haven: Yale University Southeast Asia Studies, 75–103.

Chin, James 2004. 'Sabah and Sarawak: the More Things Change the More they Remain the Same', in *Southeast Asian Affairs*. Singapore: Institute for Southeast Asian Studies.

Chirot, Daniel and Anthony Reid (eds.) 1997. *Essential Outsiders: Chinese and Jews in the Modern Transformation of Southeast Asia and Central Europe*. Seattle: University of Washington Press.

Chua, Haji Abdul Malek 1995. *YB for Sale*. Kota Kinabalu: Zamantara.

Chau Ju-kua 1970 [orig. c. 1250]. *His Work on the Chinese and Arab Trade in the Twelfth and Thirteenth Centuries, entitled Chu-fan-chi*, trans. Friedrich Hirth and W. W. Rockhill. St Petersburg, 1911. Reprinted Taipei.

Clark Roff, Margaret 1974. *The Politics of Belonging. Political Change in Sabah and Sarawak*. Kuala Lumpur: Oxford University Press.

Clifford, Hugh 1926. *A Prince of Malaya*. New York: Harper & Brothers. Reprinted 1989 as *Saleh: a Prince of Malaya*. Singapore: Oxford University Press.

Coedes, G. 1968. *The Indianized States of Southeast Asia*, trans. Susan Cowing. Honolulu: East-West Center Press.

Cohen, Paul A. 2003. *China Unbound: Evolving Perspectives on the Chinese Past*. London: Routledge Curzon.

Collins, William 1979. 'Besemah Concepts. A Study of the Culture of a People of South Sumatra', Ph.D. dissertation, University of California.

Connor, Walker 1994. *Ethnonationalism: the Quest for Understanding*. Princeton: Princeton University Press.

Cooke, Nola and Li Tana (eds.) 2004. *Water Frontier: Commerce and the Chinese in the Lower Mekong Region, 1750–1880.* Lanham, MD: Rowman & Littlefield, and Singapore: Singapore University Press.

Coppel, Charles 1983. *Indonesian Chinese in Crisis.* Kuala Lumpur: Oxford University Press for Asian Studies Association of Australia.

Crane, Robert I. 1967. *Regions and Regionalism in South Asian Studies: an Exploratory Study.* Durham, NC: Duke University Program in Comparative Studies on Southern Asia.

Crawfurd, John 1820. *History of the Indian Archipelago*, 3 vols. Edinburgh: A. Constable.

Croo, M. H. du 1943. *General Swart: Pacificator van Atjeh.* Maastricht: Leiter-Nypels.

Cullinane, Michael 1998. 'Accounting for Souls', in Daniel Doeppers and Peter Xenos (eds.) *Population and History: the Demographic Origins of the Modern Philippines.* Madison: University of Wisconsin: Centre for Southeast Asian Studies.

Cunningham, Clark 1958. *The Postwar Migration of the Toba-Bataks to East Sumatra.* New Haven: Yale University Southeast Asia Studies.

Davidson, Jamie 2008. *From Rebellion to Riots: Collective Violence on Indonesian Borneo.* Madison: University of Wisconsin Press.

Day, Tony 2002. *Fluid Iron: State Formation in Southeast Asia.* Honolulu: University of Hawai'i Press.

DE. *Daily Express.* Kota Kinabalu, daily.

Dikötter, Frank 1992. *The Discourse of Race in Modern China.* Stanford: Stanford University Press.

Dion, Stéphane 1996. 'Why is Secession Difficult in Well-established Democracies?' *British Journal of Political Science* 26, 2, 269–83.

Drakard, Jane 1990. *A Malay Frontier: Unity and Duality in a Sumatran Kingdom.* Ithaca: Cornell University Southeast Asia Program.

1999. *A Kingdom of Words. Language and Power in Sumatra.* Shah Alam: Oxford University Press.

Duara, Prasenjit 1995. *Rescuing History from the Nation: Questioning Narratives of Modern China.* Chicago: University of Chicago Press.

Elson, R. E. 2008. *The Idea of Indonesia: A History.* Cambridge: Cambridge University Press.

Emerson, Rupert 1937. *Malaysia: a Study in Direct and Indirect Rule.* New York: Macmillan.

Encyclopedie van Nederlandsch-Indië, 2nd edn., 8 vols. The Hague: Nijhoff, 1917–1939.

EPU 2006a. *Mid-Term Review of the Ninth Malaysia Plan, 2006–2010.* Putrajaya: The Economic Planning Unit, Prime Minister's Department.

2006b. *Ninth Malaysia Plan, 2006–2010.* Putrajaya: The Economic Planning Unit, Prime Minister's Department.

Evans, I. H. N. 1953. *The Religion of the Tempasuk Dusuns of North Borneo.* Cambridge: Cambridge University Press.

Fujiwara Iwaichi 1966. *F-kikan.* Tokyo: Hara Shobo.

Geertz, Clifford, 1980. *Negara: the Theatre State in Nineteenth-century Bali.* Princeton University Press.

Gellner, Ernest 1983. *Nations and Nationalism*. Oxford: Blackwell.

Giddens, Anthony 1985. *The Nation-state and Violence*. Cambridge: Polity Press.

Glyn-Jones, Monica 1953. *The Dusun of the Penampang Plains*. 2 vols. London: Colonial Social Science Research Council.

Godley, Michael and Grayson Lloyd (eds.) 2001. *Perspectives on the Chinese Indonesians*. Adelaide: Crawfurd House Publishing.

Goscha, Christopher E. 1999. *Thailand and the Southeast Asian Networks of the Vietnamese Revolution, 1885–1954*. Richmond, Surrey: Curzon.

Graaf H. J. de and Th. G. Th. Pigeaud 1974. *De eerste moslims vorstendommen op Java*. The Hague: Nijhoff.

1984. *Chinese Muslims in Java in the 15th and 16th Centuries*, ed. M. C. Ricklefs. Clayton, Vic.: Monash Papers on Southeast Asia.

Greenfeld, Liah 1992. *Nationalism. Five Roads to Modernity*. Cambridge: Harvard University Press.

Guillot, Claude (ed.) 1998–2003. *Histoire de Barus*, 2 vols. Paris: Association Archipel.

Hamid, Haji Hashim Abd. 1992. 'Konsep Melayu Islam Beraja: Antar Ideologi dan Pembinaan Bangsa', in Dato Seri Laila Jasa Awang Haji Abu Bakar bin Haji Apong (ed.). *Sumbangsih*. Gadong: Akademi Pengajian Brunei.

Hamilton, Alexander 1930. *A New Account of the East Indies*, 2 vols, ed. William Foster. London: Argonaut Press.

Harper, Tim 1999. *The End of Empire and the Making of Malaya*. Cambridge: Cambridge University Press.

Harris, Peter 1997. 'Chinese Nationalism: the State of the Nation', *The China Journal*, 121–37.

Harrison, R. 1971. 'An Analysis of the Variation among the Ranau Dusun Communities of Sabah, Malaysia'. Ph.D. dissertation, Columbia University.

Hasan, Abdul Hadi bin Haji 1925–30. *Sejarah Alam Melayu*, 3 vols. Singapore: Education Department.

He Baogang, Brian Galligan and Takashi Inoguchi (eds.) 2007. *Federalism in Asia*. Cheltenham, UK: Edward Elgar.

Hefner, Robert 2000. *Civil Islam: Muslims and Democratization in Indonesia*. Princeton: Princeton University Press.

Heidhues, Mary Somers 1974. *Southeast Asia's Chinese Minorities*. Hawthorn, Vic: Longman Australia.

Henley, David 1996. *Nationalism and Regionalism in a Colonial Context: Minahasa in the Dutch East Indies*. Leiden: KITLV Press.

Hikajat Bandjar: A Study in Malay Historiography 1968. Ed. J. J. Ras. The Hague: Nijhoff.

Hikayat Hang Tuah 1971. Ed. Kassim Ahmad. Kuala Lumpur: Dewan Bahasa dan Pustaka.

Hikayat Patani 1970. Ed. A. Teeuw and D. K. Wyatt, 2 vols. The Hague: Nijhoff.

Hill, A. H. 1961. 'Hikayat Raja-Raja Pasai', romanised and translated by A. H. Hill, *Journal of the Malaysian Branch, Royal Asiatic Society* **33**, 2.

Hirosue Masashi 1996. *Sumatran port-cities and 'cannibalism' in the hinterlands.* Paper presented at the 14th Conference of the International Association of Historians of Asia, Bangkok, 22 May 1996.

Hirschman, Charles 1987. 'The Meaning and Measurement of Ethnicity in Malaysia', *Journal of Asian Studies* **46**, 3, 555–82.

HKBP (Huria Kristen Batak Protestan) 1984. *Almanak HKBP 1984.* Tarutung. 1995. *Almanak HKBP 1995.* Tarutung.

Ho, Engseng 2006. *The Graves of Tarim: Genealogy and Mobility across the Indian Ocean.* Berkeley: University of California Press.

Hoadley, Mason 1988. 'Javanese, Peranakans and Chinese Elites in Cirebon: Changing Ethnic Boundaries', *Journal of Asian Studies* **47**, iii, 503–17.

Hobsbawm, E. J. 1990. *Nations and Nationalism since 1780.* Cambridge: Cambridge University Press.

Hobson, J. A. 1902. *Imperialism: a Study.* New York: Pott.

Hugo, G. J., T. H. Hull, V. J. Hull and G. W. Joncs 1987. *The Demographic Dimension in Indonesian Development.* Singapore: Oxford University Press.

Humboldt, Alexander von, 1847–8. *Cosmos: Sketch of a Physical Description of the Universe*, translated under the superintendence of E. Sabine, 2 vols. London: Longman, Brown, Green & Longmans.

Humboldt, Freiherr Wilhelm von 1836–9. *Über die Kawi-sprache auf den insel Java: nebst einer einleitung über die verschiedenheit des menschlichen sprachbaues und ihren einfluss auf die geistige entwickelung des menschengeschlechts*, 3 vols. Berlin: Königlichen Akademie der Wissenschaften.

Huntington, Samuel P. 1993. 'Clash of Civilizations?', *Foreign Affairs*, **72**.

Hutagalung, W. M. 1991. *Pustaha Batak: Tarombo dohot Turiturian ni Bangso Batak*, ed. R. T. Sirait. No place: Tulus Jaya. [Orig. publ. as Waldemar Hoeta Galoeng, *Poestaha taringot toe tarombo ni halak Batak*, Laguboti: Zendingsdrukkerij, 1926.]

Ileto, Reynaldo 1979. *Pasyon and Revolution. Popular Movements in the Philippines, 1840–1910.* Manila: Ateneo de Manila University Press.

Ismail Hussein 1998. 'Kata Alu-aluan', in Zeus Salazar, *The Malayan Connection*, Quezon City, xi–xv.

Jenner, W. A. 1992. *The Tyranny of History: the Roots of China's Crisis.* London: Penguin Books.

Jomo, K. S. 1997. 'A specific idiom of Chinese Capitalism in Southeast Asia: Sino-Malaysian capital accumulation in the face of State Hostility', in Daniel Chirot and Anthony Reid (eds.) *Essential Outsiders: Chinese and Jews in the Modern Transformation of Southeast Asia and Central Europe.* Seattle: University of Washington Press, 237–57.

Jones, L. W. 1966. *The Population of Borneo: a Study of the Peoples of Sarawak, Sabah and Brunei.* London: Athlone Press.

Jones, Russell 1997. *Chinese Names: the Traditions Surrounding the Use of Chinese Surnames and Personal Names.* Kuala Lumpur: Pelandok.

Joustra, M. 1910. *Batak-Spiegel.* Leiden: van Doesburgh.

Kangle, R. P. 1969. *The Kautilya Arthasastra.* Bombay: Bombay University.

Ke, Fan 2001. 'Maritime Muslims and Hui Identity: a South Fujian Case', *Journal of Muslim Minority Affairs*, **21**: 2.

Keating, Michael 2001. *Plurinational Democracy: Stateless Nations in a Post-Sovereignty Era.* Oxford: Oxford University Press.

Kell, Timothy 1995. *The Roots of Acehnese Rebellion 1989–1992.* Ithaca: Cornell University Southeast Asia Program.

Khoo Kay Kim 1979. 'Local Historians and the Writing of Malaysian History in the Twentieth Century', in Anthony Reid and David Marr (eds.) *Perceptions of the Past in Southeast Asia.* Singapore: Heinemann, 299–311.

Kingsbury, Damien and Lesley McCulloch 2006. '*Military Business in Aceh,*' in Anthony Reid (ed.) *Verandah of Violence: the Background to the Aceh Problem.* Singapore: Singapore University Press, 199–224.

Kipp, Rita Smith 1990. *The Early Years of a Dutch Colonial Mission: the Karo Field.* Ann Arbor: University of Michigan Press.

1993. *Dissociated Identities. Ethnicity, Religion and Class in an Indonesian Society.* Ann Arbor: University of Michigan Press.

Kitingan, Jeffrey 1994. *Komoiboros Dusunkadazan/Dusunkadazan Dictionary.* Kota Kinabalu: Mongulud Boros Dusun Kadazan.

Klein, Martin (ed.) 1993. *Breaking the Chains: Slavery, Bondage and Emancipation in Modern Africa and Asia.* Madison: University of Wisconsin Press.

KLF (Kadazandusun Language Foundation) 2007. *Fakta-fakta Penting Mengenai Bahasa Kadazandusun di Sekolah.* Kota Kinabalu: Kadazandusun Language Foundation.

Klinken, Gerry van 2001. 'The Maluku Wars: Bringing society back in', *Indonesia* **71**, 1–26.

2007. *Communal Violence and Democratization in Indonesia: Small Town Wars.* London: Routledge.

Knaap, Gerrit 1996. *Shallow Waters, Rising Tide. Shipping and Trade in Java around 1775.* Leiden: KITLV Press.

Knaap, Gerrit and Luc Nagtegal, 1991. 'A Forgotten Trade: Salt in Southeast Asia, 1670–1813' in Roderich Ptak and Dietmar Rothermund (eds.). *Emporia, Commodities and Entrepreneurs in Asian Maritime Trade, c.1400–1750.* Stuttgart: Franz Steiner.

Kobata Atsushi and M. Matsuda (eds.) 1969. *Ryukyuan Relations with Korea and South Sea Countries.* Kyoto: Kobata & Matsuda.

Kohn, Hans 1944. *The Idea of Nationalism: a Study in Its Origin and Background.* New York: Macmillan.

Krasner, Stephen 2001. 'Organised Hypocrisy in Nineteenth-century East Asia', *International Relations of the Asia-Pacific* **1**, 173–97.

Kroeber, A. L. and C. Kluckhohn 1963. *Culture: a Critical Review of Concepts and Definitions.* New York: Vintage.

Kwok Kian Woon 1998. 'Singapore', in Lynn Pan (ed.) *The Encyclopedia of the Chinese Overseas.* Singapore: Archipelago Press, 200–17.

Laffan, Michael 2005. *Finding Java: Muslim Nomenclature of Insular Southeast Asia from Śrīvijaya to Snouck Hurgronje,* Singapore: Asia Research Institute Working Paper Series no. 52, www.ari.nus.edu.sg/publications.

Landon, Kenneth P. 1941. *The Chinese in Thailand.* London: Oxford University Press.

Langenberg, Michael van 1976. 'National Revolution in North Sumatra: Sumatra Timur and Tapanuli, 1942–1950'. Ph.D. dissertation, University of Sydney.

    1985. 'East Sumatra: Accommodating an Indonesian Nation within a Sumatran Residency', in Audrey Kahin (ed.) *Regional Dynamics of the Indonesian Revolution: Unity from Diversity*. Honolulu: University of Hawaii Press, 113–44.

Lasimbang, Rita 2004. 'To Promote the Kadazandusun Languages of Sabah', *Asian/Pacific Book Development* **34**, 2, 10–12.

Lavy, Paul 2004. 'Visnu and Harihara in the Art and Politics of Early Historic Southeast Asia'. Unpublished Ph.D. dissertation, University of California, Los Angeles.

Lee Kam Hing 1995. *The Sultanate of Aceh: Relations with the British, 1760–1824*. Kuala Lumpur: Oxford University Press.

    2006. 'Aceh at the Time of the 1824 Treaty', in Anthony Reid (ed.) *Verandah of Violence: the Background to the Aceh Problem*. Singapore: Singapore University Press, 72–95.

Lenin, V. I. 1948 [1916]. *Imperialism: The Highest Stage of Capitalism. A Popular Outline*. London: Lawrence and Wishart.

Liddle, William 1970. *Ethnicity, Party, and National Integration: an Indonesian Case Study*. New Haven: Yale University Press.

Lieberman, Victor 2003. *Strange Parallels: Southeast Asia in Global Context, c.800–1830. Vol. I: Integration on the Mainland*. Cambridge: Cambridge University Press.

Lim, G. 2004. 'The BN has Reshaped Sabah Politics to its Desires; now it must Deliver on its side of the Bargain', *Aliran Monthly* **3**.

Lindsay, Jennifer and Tan Ying Ying 2003. *Babel or Behemoth: Language Trends in Asia*. Singapore: Asia Research Institute, National University of Singapore.

Lodewycksz, Willem 1915 [1598]. 'Historie van Indien', in G. Rouffaer and J. W. Ijzerman (ed.) *De Eerste Schipvaart*, Vol. I. The Hague: Linschoten-Vereniging.

Loh Kok Wah, Francis 1992. 'Modernisation, Cultural Revival and Counter-Hegemony: the Kadazans of Sabah in the 1980s', in Joel Kahn and Francis Loh (eds.) *Fragmented Vision: Culture and Politics in Contemporary Malaysia*. Sydney: Allen & Unwin for Asian Studies Association of Australia, 225–53.

Luping, Herman 1989. 'The Making of a Huguan Siou: Facts and Fiction', in *Pesta Ka'amatan '89 Peringkat Negeri*. Penampang.

    1994. *Sabah's Dilemma: The Political History of Sabah (1960–1994)*. Kuala Lumpur: Magnus Books.

Maddison, Angus 2001. *The World Economy: a Millennial Perspective*. Paris: Organisation for Economic Co-operation and Development.

McCoy, Alfred W. (ed.) 1980. *Southeast Asia under Japanese Occupation*. New Haven: Yale University Southeast Asia Studies

Macdonald, Charles and Zheng Yangwen 2009. *Personal Names in Asia: History, Culture and Identity*. Singapore: National University of Singapore Press.

McGibbon, Rodd 2006. 'Local Leadership and the Aceh Conflict', in Anthony Reid (ed.) *Verandah of Violence: the Background to the Aceh Problem.* Singapore: Singapore University Press, pp. 315–359.

McGregor, Katherine 2007. *History in Uniform: Military Ideology and the Construction of Indonesia's Past.* Singapore: National University of Singapore Press.

McNeill, William H. 1985. *Poly-ethnicity and National Unity in World History: the Donald G. Creighton Lectures.* University of Toronto Press.

Mackie, J. A. C. 1996. 'Introduction', in Anthony Reid (ed.) *Sojourners and Settlers: Histories of Southeast Asia and the Chinese.* Sydney: Allen & Unwin, xii–xxx.

McVey, Ruth (ed.) 1992. *Southeast Asian Capitalists.* Ithaca: Cornell Southeast Asia Project.

Mahadhir, Mahanita and Lydie Tumin 2008. 'Language Attitudes of the Kadazandusun towards their Mother Tongue', Proceedings of the 9th Borneo Research Council Conference, Kota Kinabalu, July 2008.

Mahathir bin Mohamad 1970. *The Malay Dilemma.* Singapore: Donald Moore.

Ma Huan 1433. *Ying-Yai Sheng-lan: 'The Overall Survey of the Ocean's Shores',* trans. J. V. G. Mills 1970. Cambridge: Hakluyt Society.

Maier, H. M. J. 1988. *In the Center of Authority.* Ithaca: Cornell University Southeast Asia Program.

Malaysia 1995. *Laporan Am Banci Penduduk/General Report of the Population Census, 1991.* Kuala Lumpur, Department of Statistics.

Marr, David 1981. *Vietnamese Tradition on Trial, 1920–1945.* Berkeley, University of California Press.

Marsden, William 1811 [1966]. *The History of Sumatra.* Kuala Lumpur: Oxford University Press.

    1812 [1984]. *A Dictionary and Grammar of the Malayan Language.* 3 vols. Singapore: Oxford University Press.

Martin, François 1604. *Description du Premier Voyage faict aux Indes Orientalers par les François en l'an 1603.* Paris: Laurens Sonnius.

Matheson, Virginia 1979. 'Concepts of Malay Ethos in Indigenous Writing', *Journal of Southeast Asian Studies* **10**, ii: 351–71.

Miksic, John 1979. 'Archeology, Trade and Society in Northeast Sumatra'. Ph.D. dissertation, Cornell University.

    1996. *Indonesia Heritage: Ancient History.* Singapore: Editions Didier Millet.

Miksic, John and Cheryl-Ann Mei Gek Low (eds.) 2004. *Early Singapore, 1300s–1819: Evidence in Maps, Texts and Artefacts.* Singapore History Museum.

Miller, Michelle Ann 2006. 'What's Special about Special Autonomy in Aceh?' in Anthony Reid (ed.) *Verandah of Violence: the Background to the Aceh Problem.* Singapore: Singapore University Press, 292–314.

Milner, Anthony 1982. *Kerajaan: Malay Political Culture on the Eve of Colonial Rule.* Tucson: University of Arizona Press for the Asian Studies Association of Australia.

    1995. *The Invention of Politics in Colonial Malaya: Contesting Nationalism and the Expansion of the Public Sphere.* Cambridge: Cambridge University Press.

Milner, A. C., E. Edwards McKinnon and Tengku Luckman Sinar 1978. 'A Note on Aru and Kota Cina', *Indonesia* **26**, 1–42.

Mojares, Resil 2006. *Brains of the Nation*. Quezon City: Ateneo de Manila Press.

Morris, Eric 1983. 'Islam and Politics in Aceh: a Study of Center–Periphery Relations in Indonesia'. Unpublished Ph.D. dissertation, Cornell University, Ithaca.

Morris-Suzuki 1995. 'The Invention and Reinvention of "Japanese Culture"', *Journal of Asian Studies* **54**, iii, 759–81.

Muller, Hendrik (ed.) 1917. *De Oost-Indische Compagnie in Cambodja en Laos: Verzameling van Bescheiden van 1636 tot 1670*. The Hague: Linschoten-Vereeniging.

Myrdal, Gunnar 1968. *Asian Drama: an Enquiry into the Poverty of Nations*. New York: Twentieth Century Fund.

Nagata, Judith 1981. 'In Defence of Ethnic Boundaries: the Changing Myths and Charters of Malay Identity', in Charles Keyes (ed.) *Ethnic Change*. Seattle: University of Washington Press, 87–116.

Nagtegal, Luc 1996. *Riding the Dutch Tiger: the Dutch East Indies Company and the Northeast Coast of Java, 1680–1743*. Leiden: KITLV.

Naim, Mochtar 1984. *Merantau: Pola Migrasi Suku Minangkabau*. Yogyakarta: Gadjah Mada University Press.

Nandy, Ashis 1995. 'History's Forgotten Doubles', *History & Theory* **34**, 2: 44–66.

National Operations Council 1969. *The May 13 Tragedy: a Report*. Kuala Lumpur: National Operations Council.

Naval Intelligence Division 1943. *Indo-China*. Geographical Handbook Series. London: Naval Intelligence Division.

NBAR (North Borneo Annual Report), Jesselton, various years.

Nessen, William 2006. 'Sentiments Made Visible: the Rise and Reason of Aceh's National Liberation Movement', in Anthony Reid (ed.) *Verandah of Violence: the Background to the Aceh Problem*. Singapore: Singapore University Press, 177–98.

Newbold, T. J. 1839 [1971]. *Political and Statistical Account of the British Settlements in the Straits of Malacca*, 2 vols. Kuala Lumpur: Oxford University Press.

Ng Chin Keong 1991. 'The Case of Ch'en I-lao: Maritime Trade and Overseas Chinese in Ch'ing Policies, 1717—54', in Roderich Ptak and Dietmar Rothermunde (eds.) *Emporia, Commodities and Entrepreneurs in Asian Maritime Trade, c. 1400–1750*. Stuttgart: Franz Steiner, 373–400.

Noer, Deliar 1979. 'Yamin and Hamka: Two Routes to an Indonesian Identity', in Anthony Reid and David Marr (eds.) *Perceptions of the Past in Southeast Asia*. Singapore: Heinemann.

Olthof, W. L. (ed.) 1987. *Babad Tanah Djawi. Javaanse Rijkskroniek*. Dordrecht: Foris for KITLV.

Omar, Ariffin 1993. *Bangsa Melayu: Aspects of Democracy and Community among the Malays*. Kuala Lumpur: Oxford University Press.

Ong, Aihwa 1999. *Flexible Citizenship: the Cultural Logics of Transnationality*. Durham: Duke University Press.

Ongkili, James P. 1972. *Modernization in East Malaysia, 1960–1970.* Kuala Lumpur: Oxford University Press.

Our Cultural Heritage n.d. [1985?]. Kota Kinabalu: Koisaan Koubasanan Kadazan Sabah.

Palma, Rafael 1949. *Pride of the Malay Race*, trans. Roman Ozaeta. New York: Prentice-Hall.

Pan, Lynn (ed.) 1998. *The Encyclopedia of the Chinese Overseas.* Singapore: Archipelago Press.

Parfahn, Ahmed Ibn 1957/1967. *Malayan Grandeur (a Narrative of a History by a Hundred Seers) and our Intellectual Revolution.* Cotabato City: High School Press, 1957; Davao City: San Pedro Press, 1967.

Parlindungan, Mangaradja n.d. [1965?]. *Tuanku Rao: Terror Agama Islam Mazhab Hambali di Tanah Batak, 1816–1833.* Jakarta: Tandjung Pengharapan.

Paterno y de Vera Ignacio, Pedro 1887. *La Antigua Civilización Tagálog.* Madrid: Manuel Hernandez.

Pederson, Paul 1970. *Batak Blood and Protestant Soul.* Grand Rapids, MI: William B. Eerdmans.

Pelly, Usman 1994. *Urbanisasi dan Adaptasi: Peranan Misi Budaya Minangkabau dan Mandailing.* Jakarta: LP3ES.

Pelzer, Karl 1982. *Planters Against Peasants: the Agrarian Struggle in East Sumatra, 1947–1958.* 's-Gravenhage: Nijhoff.

Pemberton, John 1994. *On the Subject of 'Java'.* Ithaca: Cornell University Press.

Perret, Daniel 1995. *La Formation d'un Paysage Ethnique: Batak et Malais de Sumatra Nord-Est.* Paris: Presses de l'EFEO.

Perret, Daniel, Heddy Surachman, Lucas Koestoro and Sukawati Susetyo 2007. 'Le Programme Archéologique Franco–Indonésien sur Padang Lawas (Sumatra Nord). Réflexions préliminaires' *Archipel* **74**: 45–82.

Pigafetta, Antonio 1969. *First Voyage Round the World*, trans. J. A. Robertson. Manila: Filipiniana Book Guild.

Pigeaud, Th. G. Th. 1960. *Java in the Fourteenth Century: a Study in Cultural History*, 5 volumes. The Hague: Nijhoff.

Pinto, Mendes 1989. *The Travels of Mendes Pinto*, transl. Rebecca Catz. Chicago: University of Chicago Press.

Pires, Tomé 1515. *The Suma Oriental of Tomé Pires*, (trans. Armando Cortesão, 1944.) London: Hakluyt Society.

Polo, Marco 1958 [1292]. *The Travels of Marco Polo*, trans. R. E. Latham. Harmondsworth: Penguin.

Prinst, Darwan 1996. *Adat Karo.* Medan: Kongres Kebudayaan Karo.

Proudfoot, Ian 1993. *Early Malay Printed Books.* Kuala Lumpur: The Academy of Malay Studies and the Library, University of Malaya.

Purba, O. H. S. and Elvis Purba 1998. *Migran Batak Toba di luar Tapanuli Utara: Suatu Deskripsi.* Medan: Monora.

Purdey, Jemma 2006. *Anti-Chinese Violence in Indonesia, 1996–1999.* Singapore: Singapore University Press for Asian Studies Association of Australia.

Quirino, Carlos 1940. *The Great Malayan.* Makati City: Tahanan Books.

Raben, Remco 1996. 'Batavia and Colombo: the Ethnic and Spatial Order of Two Colonial Cities, 1600–1800'. Ph.D. Dissertation, Leiden University.

Rae, Simon 1994. *Breath Becomes the Wind: Old and New in Karo Religion.* Dunedin: University of Otago Press.

Raffles, Sophia 1835. *Memoir of the Life and Public Services of Sir Thomas Stamford Raffles Particularly in the Government of Java, 1811–1816, Bencoolen and its Dependencies, 1817–1824,* 2 vols. London: Duncan.

Raffles, Thomas Stamford 1818. 'On the Maláyu Nation, with a Translation of its Maritime Institutions', *Asiatic Researches* **12**.

1821. *Malay Annals: Translated from the Malay Language by the Late Dr John Leyden, with an introduction by Sir Thomas Stamford Raffles, FRS.* London: Longman.

Raniri, Nuru'd-dinar-1644 [1966]. *Bustanu's-Salatin, Bab II, Fasal 13,* ed. T. Iskandar. Kuala Lumpur: Dewan Bahasa dan Pustaka.

Regis, Patricia 1989. 'Demography', in Jeffrey Kitingan and Maximus Ongkili (eds.) *Sabah: 25 Years Later, 1963–1988.* Kota Kinabalu, Sabah: Institute of Development Studies.

Reid, Anthony 1969a. *The Contest for North Sumatra: Atjeh, the Netherlands and Britain, 1858–1898.* Kuala Lumpur, Oxford University Press/University of Malaya Press.

1969b. 'Indonesian Diplomacy. A Documentary Study of Atjehnese Foreign Policy in the Reign of Sultan Mahmud, 1870–1874', *Journal of the Malayan Branch, Royal Asiatic Society* **42**, 2, 74–114.

1969c. 'The Kuala Lumpur Riots and the Malaysian Political System', *Australian Outlook* **23**, iii (December 1969), 258–78.

1974. *The Indonesian National Revolution.* Melbourne: Longman.

1979a. *The Blood of the People: Revolution and the End of Traditional Rule in Northern Sumatra.* Kuala Lumpur: Oxford University Press.

1979b. 'The Nationalist Quest for an Indonesian Past,' in Anthony Reid and David Marr (eds.) *Perceptions of the Past in Southeast Asia.* Singapore: Heinemann.

1988–93. *Southeast Asia in the Age of Commerce, c.1450–1680,* 2 vols. New Haven, Yale University Press.

1993. 'The Unthreatening Alternative: Chinese Shipping in Southeast Asia 1567–1842', *Review of Indonesian and Malaysian Affairs* **27**: 13–32.

1996. 'Flows and Seepages in the Long-term Chinese Interaction with Southeast Asia', in Reid (ed.), *Sojourners and Settlers: Histories of Southeast Asia and the Chinese.* Sydney: Allen & Unwin, 15–49.

1997. 'Entrepreneurial Minorities, Nationalism and the State', in Daniel Chirot and Anthony Reid (eds.) *Essential Outsiders: Chinese and Jews in the Modern Transformation of Southeast Asia and Central Europe.* Seattle: University of Washington Press, 33–71.

2001. 'Understanding Melayu (Malay) as a Source of Diverse Modern Identities,' *Journal of Southeast Asian Studies* **32**, iii, 295–313.

2002. 'Island of the Dead: Why do Bataks erect Tugu?' in H. Chambert-Loir and A. Reid (eds.) *The Potent Dead: the Cult of Saints, Ancestors and Heroes in Modern Indonesia.* Sydney: Allen & Unwin for the Asian Studies Association of Australia, 88–102.

2004. 'War, Peace and the Burden of History in Aceh', *Asian Ethnicity* **15**, 3 (Oct), 301–14.

2005. *An Indonesian Frontier: Acehnese and other Histories of Sumatra.* Singapore: Singapore University Press.

Reid, Anthony (ed.) 2006a. *Verandah of Violence: the Background to the Aceh Problem.* Singapore: Singapore University Press.

Reid, Anthony 2006b. *Hybrid Identities in the Fifteenth Century Straits,* Working Paper Series no. 67, Asia Research Institute, Singapore, www.ari.nus.edu. sg/publications.

2006c. *Is There a Batak History?* Singapore: Working Paper Series no. 78, Asia Research Institute, www.ari.nus.edu.sg/publications.

2007. 'Indonesia's post-revolutionary aversion to federalism,' in He Baogang *et al.* (eds.) *Federalism in Asia.* Cheltenham, UK: Edward Elgar, 144–64.

Reid, Anthony and Zheng Yangwen (eds.) 2009. *Negotiating Asymmetry: China's Place in Asia.* Singapore: National University of Singapore Press.

Ricklefs, M. C. 1992. 'Unity and Disunity in Javanese Political and Religious Thought of the Eighteenth Century', in V. J. H. Houben *et al.* (eds.) *Looking in Odd Mirrors: The Java Sea,* Leiden: Leiden University Department of Southeast Asian Studies, 60–75.

1998. *The Seen and Unseen Worlds in Java, 1726–1749: History, Literature, and Islam in the Court of Pakubuwana II.* Honolulu: University of Hawai'i Press, for the Asian Studies Association of Australia.

Rinder, Irwin, 1958–9. 'Strangers in the Land: Social Relations in the Status Gap', *Social Problems* **6**, 253–60.

Rizal, José (ed.) 1961. *Sucesos de las isles Filipinas por el Dr Antonio de Morga.* Manila: Comision Naciónal del Centenario de Rizal.

Rizal–Blumentritt 1961. *The Rizal–Blumentritt Correspondence,* Vol. II. Manila: José Rizal Centennial Commission.

Robinson, Geoffrey 1998. 'Rawan is as Rawan Does: the Origins of Disorder in New Order Aceh', *Indonesia* **66**, 127–56.

Robison, Richard 1986. *Indonesia: the Rise of Capital.* Sydney: Allen & Unwin.

Robson, Stuart (ed.) 1995. *Deśawarana (Nāgarakrtāgama) by Mpu Prapañca.* Leiden: KITLV Press.

Rodenburg, Janet 1997. *In the Shadow of Migration: Rural Women and their Households in North Tapanuli, Indonesia.* Leiden: KITLV Press.

Rodgers Siregar, Susan 1981. *Adat, Islam and Christianity in a Batak Homeland.* Athens, Ohio: Ohio University Center for International Studies.

Rodgers, Susan 1991a. 'The Ethnic Culture Page in Medan Journalism' *Indonesia* **51** (April), 83–104.

1991b. 'Imagining Tradition, Imagining Modernity: a Southern Batak Novel from the 1920s', *BKI* **147**, 2–3, 273–97.

1997. *Sitti Djaoerah: a Novel of Colonial Indonesia.* Madison, WI: University of Wisconsin Center for Southeast Asian Studies.

2005. *Print, Poetics, and Politics: a Batak Literary Epic in the Indies and New Order Indonesia.* Leiden: KITLV Press.

Roff, Margaret 1969. 'The Rise and Demise of Kadazan Nationalism', *Journal of Southeast Asian History* **10**, ii: 326–43.

Roff, William 1967. *The Origins of Malay Nationalism.* Kuala Lumpur: University of Malaya Press.

Roolvink, R. 1975. *Bahasa Jawi: de Taal van Sumatra.* Leiden: Universitaire Pers.

Rooney, John 1981. *Khabar Gembira. A History of the Catholic Church in East Malaysia and Brunei (1880–1976).* London: Burns & Oates.

Rutter, Owen, 1929. *The Pagans of North Borneo.* London: Hutchinson.

Ryter, Loren 2002. 'Youths, Gangs and the State in Indonesia'. Ph.D. dissertation, University of Washington.

Salazar, Zeus A. 1998. *The Malayan Connection. Ang Pilipinas sa Dunia Melayu.* Quezon City, Palimbagan ng Lahi.

Salmon, Claudine 1996. 'Ancestral Halls, Funeral Associoations, and Attempts at Resinicization in Nineteenth Century Netherlands India', in Anthony Reid (ed.) *Sojourners and Settlers: Histories of Southeast Asia and the Chinese.* Sydney: Allen & Unwin, 183–214.

Salmon, Claudine and Myra Siddharta 2000. 'The Hainanese of Bali: A Little Known Community'. Paris: *Archipel 60.*

Sangermano, Vincentius 1966 [1818]. *A Description of the Burmese Empire*, trans. William Tandy. Rome and Rangoon. Reprinted London: Susil Gupta.

Sangti, Batara 1977. *Sejarah Batak.* Balige: Karl Sianipar.

Sani, Rustam A. 2008. *Failed Nation? Concerns of a Malaysian Nationalist.* Kuala Lumpur: Strategic Information and Research Development.

Schreiner, Klaus 1995. *Politischer Heldenkult in Indonesien.* Hamburg: Dietrich Reimer.

Schulte Nordholt, Henk 1993. 'Leadership and the Limits of Political Control: A Balinese "Response" to Clifford Geertz', *Social Anthropology* 1, 3.

Schulze, Kirsten E. 2006. 'Insurgency and Counter-Insurgency: Strategy and the Aceh Conflict, October 1976–May 2004', in Anthony Reid (ed.) *Verandah of Violence: the Background to the Aceh Problem.* Singapore: Singapore University Press 225–271.

Scott, Edmund 1606 [1943]. 'An Exact Discourse', in Sir William Foster (ed.) *The Voyage of Henry Middleton to the Moluccas.* London: Hakluyt Society, 81–176.

Scott, James C. 1998a. *Seeing Like a State.* New Haven: Yale University Press.
  1998b. 'State Simplifications', in David Kelly and Anthony Reid (eds.) *Asian Freedoms.* Cambridge: Cambridge University Press.

Scott, W. H. 1982. *Cracks in the Parchment Curtain.*

Sherman, George 1990. *Rice, Rupees and Ritual. Economy and Society Among the Samosir Batak of Sumatra.* Stanford: Stanford University Press.

Shim, P. S. 2007. *Inland People of Sabah, Before, During and After Nunuk Ragang.* Kota Kinabalu: Borneo Cultural Heritage Publisher.

Shiraishi, Takeshi 1997. 'Anti-Sinicism in Java's New Order', in Daniel Chirot and Anthony Reid (eds.) *Essential Outsiders: Chinese and Jews in the Modern Transformation of Southeast Asia and Central Europe.* Seattle: University of Washington Press, 187–207.

Singarimbun, Masri 1975. *Kinship, Descent and Alliance among the Karo Batak.* Berkeley: University of California Press.

Situmorang Sitor 1993. *Toba Na Sae: Sejarah Lembaga Sosial Politik Abad XIII–XX.* Jakarta: Komunitas Bambu.

Skinner, Cyril 1963. *Sja'ir Perang Mengkasar (The Rhymed Chronicle of the Macassar War) by Entji' Amin*. The Hague: Martinus Nijhoff.

Skinner, G. William 1957. *Chinese Society in Thailand: an Analytical History*. Ithaca: Cornell University Press.

1996. 'Creolized Chinese Societies in Southeast Asia', in Anthony Reid (ed.) *Sojourners and Settlers: Histories of Southeast Asia and the Chinese*. Sydney: Allen & Unwin, 51–93.

Smail, John R. W. 1968. 'The Military Politics of North Sumatra, December 1956–October 1957', *Indonesia* 6 (October), 128–87.

Smith, Anthony D. 1986. *The Ethnic Origins of Nations*. Oxford: Blackwell.

1991. *National Identity*. London: Penguin.

1995. *Nations and Nationalism in a Global Era*. Cambridge: Polity Press.

So, Billy 2000. *Prosperity, Region and Institutions in Maritime China: the South Fukien Pattern, 946–1368*. Cambridge, MA: Harvard University Press.

ST. Sabah Times. Kota Kinabalu, daily.

Stapel, F. W. 1922. *Het Bongaais Verdrag*. Published dissertation, University of Leiden.

Steedly, Mary 1996. 'The Importance of Proper Names: Language and "National" Identity in Colonial Karoland', *American Ethnologist*, **23**: 447–75.

Sulaiman, M. Isa 1997. *Sejarah Aceh: Sebuah Gugatan Terhadap Tradisi*. Jakarta: Pustaka Sinar Harapan.

2000. *Aceh Merdeka: Ideologi, Kepimimpinan dan Gerakan*. Jakarta: Pustaka al Kausar.

2006. 'From Autonomy to Periphery: a Critical Evaluation of the Acehnese Nationalist Movement', in Anthony Reid (ed.) *Verandah of Violence: the Background to the Aceh Problem*. Singapore: Singapore University Press, 121–48.

Suryadinata, Leo 1992. *Pribumi Indonesians, the Chinese Minority and China*, 3rd. edn. Singapore: Heinemann Asia.

Suryadinata, Leo, Evi Nurvidya Arifin and Aris Ananta 2003. *Indonesia's Population: Ethnicity and Religion in a Changing Political Landscape*. Singapore: Institute for Southeast Asian Studies.

Swettenham, Frank 1906. *British Malaya*. London: John Lane.

Tagliacozzo, Eric 2005. *Secret Trades, Porous Borders: Smuggling and States along a Southeast Asian Frontier 1865–1915*. New Haven: Yale University Press.

Tan Chee Khoon 1986. *Sabah: a Triumph for Democracy*. Kuala Lumpur, Pelandok.

Tan Pek Leng, 1992. 'A History of Chinese Settlement in Brunei', in *Essays on Modern Brunei History*. Department of History, Universiti Brunei Darussalam,

Thongchai Winichakul 1991. *Siam Mapped. A History of the Geo-body of a Nation*. Honolulu: University of Hawaii Press.

Tichelman, G. L. 1936. 'Batak-trek', *Koloniaal Tijdschrift*.

[Tiro,] Hasan Muhammad 1958. *Demokrasi Untuk Indonesia* [Democracy for Indonesia]. Np. Penerbit Seulawah.

1948. *Perang Atjeh, 1873–1927* Stencilled, Jogjakarta.

1981. *The Price of Freedom: the Unfinished Diary of Tengku Hasan di Tiro, President, National Liberation Front of Acheh Sumatra* [stencilled].

Tiro, Tengku Hasan M. di 1979. *The Drama of Achehnese History; 1873–1978. A Play in VIII Acts*. State of Acheh: Ministry of Education [stencilled].

Tobing, Adniel L. 1957. *Sedjarah Si Singamangaradja I-XII*, 4th edn. Medan: Firman Sihombing.

Tønnesson, Stein and Hans Antlöv (eds.) 1996. *Asian Forms of the Nation*. Richmond, Surrey: Curzon.

Topin, Benedict (n.d). 'The Origin of the Kadazan/Dusun: Popular Theories and Legendary Tales'. Typescript.

Toynbee, Arnold J. 1931. *A Journey to China or Things which are Seen*. London: Constable.

Tsu, Jing 2005. *Failure, Nationalism, and Literature: the Making of Modern Chinese Identity, 1895–1937*. Stanford: Stanford University Press.

Twang Peck Yang 1998. *The Chinese Business Elite in Indonesia and the Transition to Independence, 1940–1950*. Kuala Lumpur: Oxford University Press.

Umar, Pehin Orang Kaya Laila Wijaya Dato Haji Abdul Aziz 1992. 'Melayu Islam Beraja Sebagai Falsafah Negara Brunei Darussalam', in Sumbangsih (ed.) *Dato Seri Laila Jasa Awang Haji Abu Bakar bin Haji Apong*. Gadong: Akademi Pengajian Brunei.

Vella, Walter 1978. *Chaiyo: King Vajiravudh and the Development of Thai Nationalism*. Honolulu: University of Hawaii Press.

Vergouwen, J. C. 1964 [1933]. *The Social Organisation and Customary Law of the Toba-Batak of Northern Sumatra*. The Hague: Nijhoff for KITLV.

Vlieland, C. A. 1932. *British Malaya: a Report on the 1931 Census and on Certain Problems of Vital Statistics*. London: n.p.

Vliet, Jeremias van 2005. *Van Vliet's Siam*, ed. and trans. Chris Baker, Dhiravat na Pombejra, Alfons van der Kraan and David K. Wyatt. Chiang Mai: Silkworm Books.

Volkstelling 1930. 8 vols. Batavia: Departement van Economische Zaken, 1933–36.

Wade, Geoffrey 1994. 'The *Ming Shi-lu* (Veritable Records of the Ming Dynasty) as a Source for Southeast Asian History: Fourteenth to Seventeenth Centuries'. Ph.D. dissertation, 8 vols. University of Hong Kong.

Wade, Geoffrey and Sun Laichen (eds.) 2009. *Southeast Asia in the Fifteenth Century: the Ming Factor*. Singapore: Singapore University Press.

Wang Gungwu 1981. *Community and Nation: Essays on Southeast Asia and the Chinese*. Singapore: Heinemann for Asian Studies Association of Australia.

1996. 'Sojourning: the Chinese Experience in Southeast Asia', in Anthony Reid (ed.) *Sojourners and Settlers: Histories of Southeast Asia and the Chinese*. Sydney: Allen & Unwin, 1–14.

2000. *The Chinese Overseas: from Earthbound China to the Quest for Autonomy*. Cambridge, MA: Harvard University Press.

Wang Tai Peng 1994. *The Origins of the Chinese Kongsi*. Petaling Jaya, Malaysia: Pelanduk.

Warnaen, Suwarsih 1982. 'Identitas Sosial Suku Bangsa dan Nasional Sudah Stabil', *Sinar Harapan*, 16 October.

Wickberg, Edgar 1965. *The Chinese in Philippine Life 1850–1898*. New Haven: Yale University Press.

Wiener, Margaret 1995. *Visible and Invisible Realms: Power, Magic and Conquest in Bali*. University of Chicago Press.

Winstedt, R. O. 1923. *Malaya: the Straits Settlements and the Federated and Unfederated Malay States*. London: Constable.

Winstedt, R. O. (ed.) 1938. 'The Malay Annals or *Sejarah Melayu*', *Journal of the Malaysian Branch, Royal Asiatic Society* XVI, pt. III.

Winstedt, R. O. and Abdul Hadi bin Haji Hasan 1918. *Kitab Tawarikh Melayu*. Singapore.

Wolf, Eric 1982. *Europe and the People without History*. Berkeley: University of California Press.

Wolters, Oliver 1999 [1982]. *History, Culture and Region in Southeast Asian Perspectives*. Singapore: Institute for Southeast Asian Studies.

Womack, Brantly 2006. *China and Vietnam: the Politics of Asymmetry*. Cambridge: Cambridge University Press.

Woodside, Alexander 1976. *Community and Revolution in Modern Vietnam*. Atlanta: Houghton Mifflin.

Wright, Arnold and H. A. Cartwright 1908. *Twentieth Century Impressions of British Malaya: its History, People, Commerce, Industries, and Resources*. London: Lloyds.

Yen Ching-hwang 1995. *Studies in Overseas Chinese History*. Singapore: Times Academic Press.

Ypes, W. K. H. 1932. *Bijdrage tot de Kennis van de Stamverwantschap, de Inheemsche Rechtsgemeenschappen en het Grondenrecht der Toba- en Dairibataks*. The Hague: Nijhoff for Adatrechtstichting.

Yule, Henry and A. C. Burnell 1979. *Hobson-Jobson*. New Delhi: Munshiram Manoharial.

Zawawi, Ibrahim 2001. *Voices of the Crocker Range: Indigenous Communities in Sabah. Social Narratives of Transitioin in Tambunan and its Neighbours*. Kuching: Institute of East Asian Studies, Universiti Malaysia Sarawak.

Zenner, Walter 1991. *Minorities in the Middle: a Cross-cultural Analysis*. Albany: State University of New York Press.

Zentgraaff, H. C. 1938. *Atjeh*. Batavia: De Unie.

Zheng Yangwen 2009. 'The Peaceful Rise of China after a Century of Unequal Treaties', in Reid and Zheng (eds.) 159–91.

Index

Abdul Rahman, Prime Minister Tunku
74, 194
Abdullah, Munshi 102, 103
Abdullah Badawi 106
Aceh 115–28, 151–4
and Bataks 151–5, 158
conflict with Dutch 119, 121–4
language 130, 143
nationalism 22, 23, 132, 134–5
rebellion 125–6
against Sultan 119, 121
(1953) 131–3, 167
(1976–2005) 133–9
resistance motif 118–19, 121–6, 128,
133–5
sultans 8, 29, 30, 39, 116–17, 120
Aceh Independence Movement, see GAM
Aceh Referendum Information Centre
(SIRA) 138
adat (custom) 177–8
agriculture 190
cash cropping 58, 62, 119
rice 19, 43, 46, 90, 97, 168, 173, 195
unsuitability for 41
aircraft factories (Indonesia) 71
Alauddin Muhammad Syah, Sultan
(Aceh) 155
Alexander the Great 100, 116, 159
Ali Haji ibn Ahmad, Raja (Riau) 87, 88
Ali Hasjmy 132
Ali Mughayat Syah, Sultan (Aceh) 116
Alliance Party (Malaya) 74–5
America (US) 122, 141
traders 119, 120
ancestral cults 178–80, 181
Anderson, B. 3, 5, 214
print capitalism and 3, 13, 26
Anderson, John 153
Angkola (Batak) 160, 161–2, 175
Angkor Wat 42, 216
Anglo–Aceh Treaty (1819) 121
Anglo–Dutch London Treaty (1824) 31, 121

anti-Chinese violence 56–7, 66, 71,
72–7, 78
anti-imperial nationalism 8–10, 12, 13,
30, 136
defined 9
anti-Semitism 77, 78
Antonissen, A. 192, 195
Anwar Ibrahim 106, 202
APEC (Asia-Pacific Economic
Cooperation) 217
Arabic: influence 117, 120, 123
language 25, 35
names 35–6
overseas ethnie nationalism 211
scholars 117
script 27–8, 29
architecture, Batak 181–3
Arendt, H. 72, 77–8
Armstrong, J.A. 3, 15
Army, Indonesian National (TNI) 129,
139–40, 141, 166–7, 211
'Arsip Bakkara' manuscripts 155
Arthasastra 50
Aru (Sumatra) 148–9, 151, 152, 153
ASA (Association of Southeast
Asia) 216
Asahan (Sumatra) 146
ASEAN (Association of Southeast Asian
Nations) 140, 216–17
Association of British Malaya 95
Association of Southeast Asia (ASA) 216
Association of Southeast Asian Nations
(ASEAN) 140, 216–17
ASEAN+3 217
Regional Forum 217
Australia 14, 141, 197
and Colombo Plan 192

baba, see peranakan
Babad Tanah Jawa 52
Bakkara (Tapanuli) 154, 156
Bali 20, 21, 29, 45, 164

Bangkok 57, 64
bangsa (nation/race) 7, 102–6, 109, 110,
    143, 144
  Indonesia 107–11
  Melayu 102–7
Banjarmasin 88, 117
  Banjarese 29
  chronicle 52
Banten (Sultanate) 8, 55, 88, 115
Baperki party (Chinese-Indonesian) 69,
    136–7
Barisan Nasional coalition 204–5
Barros, J. de 54, 85, 86, 152
Barus (Sumatra) 121–2, 149, 152, 154,
    155
  chronicle 154
Batak 46, 47, 145–86
  church (HKBP) 157, 160, 170, 185
  diaspora identity 173–83
  early history 146–53
  ethnie nationalism 22, 25, 162–3,
    173–5
  genealogy 158–60, 176–7
  Islam and Christianity among 155–8,
    160–1, 174–5
  languages 157, 160, 185
  literature 160, 163, 175
  names 36, 159, 176
  outmigration 165, 166–7, 168–73
  script 149, 159
  see also Karo, Mandailing, Simalungun,
    Toba
Batak Bible 185
Batak Christian Association (Hatopan
    Kristen Batak, HKB) 162–3
Batam 133, 217
Batavia (Jakarta) 56, 57, 89–90,
    115, 119
Beaulieu, Augustin de 118
Bencoolen (Sumatra), *see* Bengkulu
  temples 42
Bengkulu (British Bencoolen) 94, 119
Betawi ethnie 108, 114
Beureu'eh, Daud 125, 131–6
Black Death 84
Blumenbach, Johann Friedrich 91, 97–8
Blumentritt, Ferdinand 98–9
boddhisatva (incarnations of the
    Buddha) 38
Bonifacio, Andres 44
boundaries
  as identity markers 30–2
  imperial 2, 121, 214–15
  national 215–18
Boxer movement 10

Brawijaya, King (Majapahit) 52
Breda, Treaty of 31
Britain 91–3, 93–7
British: imperialism 22, 30, 31–2, 33–4, 37,
    40–1, 118, 121, 212
  British Malaya journal 95
  in Malaya 40–1, 91–7, 100–2,
    103–5, 212
  nationalism 17, 30–1
  in Sumatra 118–121, 155
Brooke, James 112
Brooke government (Sarawak) 200
Brunei 51, 52, 55, 57, 58, 86, 87, 88,
    111–3, 200
Brunei nationality Enactment (1961) 112
Bruner, E. 170, 177, 178, 214
Buddha, incarnations of 38
Buddhism 8, 28, 149
Bugis ethnie (Sulawesi) 29, 87, 89,
    90, 115
Bukit Siguntang (Palembang) 81–2
bumiputra 106, 195–7, 199–200
Burma 19, 22, 38–40
  kings 8, 18, 25, 26, 28, 38
  language 27
  nationalism 26
Burney, H. 30
Burton, R. 155

cakravartin (world-rulers) 38
Cambodia 11, 12, 32, 40–3, 58,
    216, 217
  kings 25, 41, 42
cannibalism 149–51, 152, 153
Catalogo de Apellidos 36
Catholicism 21, 29, 180, 191, 198
  Sabah 201, 208
census 32–4, 47
  Brunei 112–3
  Burma 33, 47
  Indonesia 34, 111, 161–2
  Malaya 33–4, 100–2
  Sabah (Malaysia) 114, 187, 191, 199,
    205, 207
Cessation of Hostilities Agreement
    (CoHA) (Indonesia) 140, 141
Cham ethnie 20, 38, 41
  Champa 17, 88, 102, 116
Chandra Asri (Indonesia) 71
Chau Ju-kua 151
Chin ethnie 46–7
China: conflict with Japan 10–11, 66
  Imperial 15–18, 21, 38, 49–53
  nationalism 10–11, 17, 23
  term 49–51

Chinese: business 65–6, 67, 70–2, 74
   Europeans and 53–7
   hybridities 59–63
   language 35, 38, 70, 77
   names 34–5, 36
   nationalism overseas 61–6
   princess (*puteri Cina*) 51–2
   in Sabah 188, 196
   settlers in Southeast Asia 39, 43, 51–9
   sources 20, 27, 81–2, 151
Chinese Communist Party 11, 69
Chinese New Year (*Imlek*) 77, 194
'Chinese war' (Java) 80
Christianity: Aceh and 116, 138
   among Bataks 156–8, 162–3, 175, 180
   Chinese and 62
   conflict with Islam 117, 138, 158, 183
   and identity 12, 28–9, 116, 157–8
   in Sabah 197–8, 201
   see also Catholicism
Chulalongkorn, King (Siam) 39, 121
church membership, Jakarta 170
CIA (Central Intelligence Agency) 134
Claveria, Governor-General
      (Philippines) 36
Clifford, Sir Hugh 93, 97
CoHA (Cessation of Hostilities
      Agreement) (Indonesia) 140, 141
Cold War 13, 216
Colombo Plan 192
'colonial nationalism' 5
communism 69, 131, 176, 217
   anti-communism 70, 216
Cong Po 52
Crawfurd, J. 57, 91, 95
creole identities 59–63
Crimean War 120
Crisis Management Initiative (Helsinki) 142
culturalism theory 53

da Conti, Nicolo 151
Daendels, Herman Willem 31
Dai Viet 116
Daily Express (Kota Kinabalu) 193, 202–3
Dairi (Pakpak) Batak 183
Dampu Awang 52
Damrong, Prince 39
dance, Batak 177–8, 180–1, 186
DAP (Democratic Action Party)
      (Malaysia) 106
Darul Islam (DI) 134, 135, 136
Darwin, Charles 98
Datuk Sundang 195
Dayak 29, 46, 164, 165
   Persatuan Daya (PD) 164
De Molac 155

Deli (Sumatra) 145
democracy 77–80, 183–6
   democratisation 1–2, 3, 136–44
Democratic Action Party (DAP)
      (Malaysia) 106
diaspora
   Batak 173–83
   Malay 57–9, 87–91
Diponegoro Division, Central Java 70–1
Djalal (author) 139
Dompok, Bernard 204, 205–7, 208
dress, traditional 179–80, 208
Dusun ethnie 187, 190, 201–3, 208
   language 201–2
   see also Kadazandusun
Dusun Lotud Association 201
Dusunkadazan Dictionary 203
Dutch: imperialism 21–2, 30, 31, 43–5,
      107, 122–5
   East India Company *see* VOC
   language 25, 28, 44
   missionaries 27, 29, 157–8
   schools 66
   sources 88–9, 117, 129
Dutch Missionary Society (Nederlandsch
      Zendingsvereniging, NZG) 158
dynasties 7
   Barus Hilir 154
   Han 16
   Ming 58, 83–5
   Qin 50; *see* Manchu
   Riau 41
   Singamangaraja 147, 154–5, 156
   Tang 16, 81

East India Company: English 119;
      Dutch, *see* VOC
education 8
   Aceh 124–5, 133, 136, 143
   Bataks and 171–3
   Chinese 64, 70, 191
   Indonesia 130, 168, 172–3, 211, 215
   Islamic 128
   Malaya/Malaysia 62–3, 95–7
   Sabah 191–2, 201, 202–3, 207
elections: Indonesia 136, 137, 138, 164,
      183, 186
   Malaysia 75, 104, 106
   Sabah 199–201, 204–5
Elizabeth I, Queen 118
Elson, R.E. 65, 211, 214
Ence Amin 88
Encik Amat 89
English (*see* British): language 26, 44, 144,
      188, 191–2, 198

ertutur 176
'essential outsiders' 49, 68
ethnic labelling 89
ethnie 5
  defined 6–7
  formation 164, 187–8, 191–5, 200–3,
    206, 208
ethnie nationalism 5–7, 17, 25, 26, 102–7
  Aceh 23, 132, 134, 136
  Kadazan 194–5
  Malay 4, 23, 104, 106–111
  overseas Chinese and 63
  Philippines and 25
Europe, nationalism and 12–15

Far Eastern Economic Review (*FEER*) 76
Federal Malaysia 212–14
federalism 132, 133, 208, 212–13
Federated Malay States (FMS) 93, 94
Federation of Malaya 104–5
Fiji 75
Filipinos, in Sabah 188
  see also Philippines
'First Emperor' (*Qin Shih Huangdi*) 16
Flowery (Middle) Kingdom 49, 50
France 31–2, 130
  imperialism 32, 37, 39–42, 118
  in Indo-China 42–3
Fujiwara, Iwaichi 67, 125

GAM (Gerakan Aceh Merdeka) 132,
    135–6, 138–40, 143
  peace talks with RI 139, 141–3
Gani, A.K. 165
Gayo ethnie 124, 146
GBKP *see* Gereja Batak Karo Protestan
Geertz, C. 18, 20–1
Gellner, E. 3, 157
genealogy, Batak identity and 158–63,
    176–7
Gereja Batak Karo Protestan (GBKP,
    Karo Batak Protestant Church)
    158, 171
Gereja Kristen Protestan Indonesia (GKPI,
    Indonesian Protestant Christian
    Church) 170, 185
Gereja Protestan Indonesia Barat (GPIB,
    Protestant Church of West
    Indonesia) 169
Gerakan Acheh Merdeka *see* GAM
Ghaddafi, Muammar 135
Gintings, Lt. Col. Djamin 167
Giyugun (volunteer force) 166
GKPI *see* Gereja Kristen Protestan
    Indonesia

global factors, nationalism and 12–15
globalisation 13
Golkar party 111
Goscha, C.E. 40, 216
GPIB *see* Gereja Protestan Indonesia Barat
Great Britain, Malaya and 91–3, 93–7
Greenfeld, L. 4, 6
Guided Democracy period (Indonesia)
    68, 129, 147
Gujarati: traders 82
  scholars 117
'gunpowder empires' 8, 115
guojiazhuyi (state nationalism) 7–8, 17

Ha Tien 57, 58
Habib Abdur-rahman az-Zahir 123
Habibie, President B.J. 71, 77, 137
Hamilton, A. 91
Hamzah, Jafar Siddiq 139
Han dynasty 16
Hanoi 116
Harris Salleh 198–9, 200
harvest feast (*kerja tahun*) 178
harvest festivals 194–5, 200, 209
Hasan, A.H. bin H. 96
Hasan, Bob 70–1
Hasan Ali 132
Hatopan Kristen Batak (HKB, Batak
    Christian Association) 162–3
Havel, Vaclav 12
He Baogang 213
Henry Dunant Centre 139
Herder, Johann Gottfried 92, 157
hero, national 80, 129, 147, 178
Hikajat Bandjar 52
Hikayat Aceh 152
Hikayat Hang Tuah 86, 95
Hikayat of Imam Jun 143
Hikayat Patani 52–3
Hikayat Raja-Raja Pasai 51
Hikayat Tanah Melayu 96
Hikayat Tanah-Tanah Melayu 96
Himpunan Ulama Daya Aceh (HUDA,
    Association of Ulama of [traditional]
    Aceh Religious Schools) 138
Hindu-Buddhist influences, Batakland
    149, 153
historiography 95–6, 128–30, 146–7
history as identity 7, 129, 135–6
Hitler, Adolph 76
Hoeta Galoeng *see* Hutagalung
HKB *see* Hatopan Kristen Batak
HKBP (Toba Batak church) 163, 165,
    169–70, 172, 185
HKI *see* Huria Kristen Indonesia

Hobson, J.A. 10
Hoi An 55
holy war 117, 127, *see jihad*
HUDA (Himpunan Ulama Daya
    Aceh, 138
Huguan Siou (Kadazan leader) 200–1, 205
'Humanitarian Pause' (Indonesia) 139
Humboldt, Alexander von 98
Humboldt, William von 98
Huminodun (mythical maiden) 194
Hun Sen 217
Huria Kristen Indonesia (HKI, Indonesian
    (formerly Batak) Christian Church)
    163, 170
    membership 170
Hutagalung, W.M. 159, 185
hybrid identities, Malay 83–7, 174

Iban ethnie (Sarawak) 202, 208
Ibn Battuta 116
Ibrahim, Sultan (Barus Hilir) 154
Ibrahim Mansur Shah, Sultan (Aceh)
    120, 122
Ibrahim Yaacob 104
identity
    Batak diaspora 173–83
    genealogy and 158–63
    layered 162–3, 183–6, 212, 215
    markers 26–37
ilustrados 25, 61, 98–9
Indonesia 43–5, 212–5
    Aceh within 126–44
    bangsa 107–11, 163
    censuses 34, 111, 161–2
    and Chinese 67–72, 75–7, 79–80
    identity 32, 44–5, 107–11
    language 184–5
Indonesia Merdeka (journal) 45, 109
Indonesian Protestant Christian Church
    (Gereja Kristen Protestan Indonesia,
    GKPI) 170, 185
Indonesian Youth Congress 109
Insulinde party 45
International Court of Justice
    (The Hague) 216
Irwandi Yusuf 143
Iskandar Muda, Sultan (Aceh) 119, 152
Islam 11, 108, 114, 115
    as Batak 'other' 151–3
    and Chinese 50–1, 55
    and identity 8, 28–30, 108, 130
    Islamization (Malaysia) 197–9, 205
    OSH-flavoured 22
Ismail Hussein 100, 102
Italy 75–6, 122

Jakarta, as capital 167
    as magnet for migrants 169–70
Jakarta, church membership 170
Jakarta Post 77
Jambi 82, 101
Japan 14, 17, 217
    conflict with China 9, 10–11
    5th column operations 67, 125
    nationalism 8
    rule in Southeast Asia 1, 9, 26, 66–7,
        126, 147, 164, 165, 216
Jauhar al-Alam, Sultan (Aceh) 130
Java, pre-colonial 43, 52, 54, 83, 85, 86–7,
    99, 117
    as base of Dutch empire-state 43–4
Javanese: identity 29, 36, 108, 211
    language 25, 28, 29, 86
    in Melaka 86
    in Sumatra 175, 186
    writing 20, 29, 50–1, 52, 149
Jawa ethnonym 85
Jawi 85–6
Jews, compared with Chinese 75
jihad (holy war, *perang sabil*): in Aceh 117,
    123, 127, 132, 152
John Paul II, Pope 180
Johor 93, 95, 102, 112
*Journal of the Straits Branch of the Royal
    Asiatic Society* 94
Joustra, M. 154
JSB (Young Sumatran Union) 163
jus sanguinis (China) 64

Kaamatan festival 196, 200, 202, 208
Kadazan 187–203
    ethnie nationalism 191–5
    revival 197–200
'Kadazan Corner' 192
Kadazan Cultural Association (KCA)
    196, 199–200, 201–3
Kadazan Dictionary and Grammar 192
Kadazan Dusun Cultural Association
    (KDCA) 203
Kadazan Dusun Malay English Dictionary 204
Kadazandusun (KD): economy 208
    identity 187–8, 201–3
    language 187, 191–4, 196, 197–8,
        201–2, 204, 207, 208
    Language Foundation (KLF) 207
Kang Yuwei 64
'Kapitan Melayu' 89
Karen 40, 46, 47, 48, 49
Karo (Batak) 111, 146, 149, 150, 159–161,
    165, 167, 169, 175–7
    Christianity 158, 165, 166, 171

Cultural Congress 173
diaspora 171, 173–5, 177–9
education 171–2
identity 157–8, 183, 186
origins 149, 152–3, 154, 159
Protestant Church (GBKP) 158, 171
Kartosuwirjo, Sekarmadji Maridjan 131
Keningau (Sabah) 201, 209
Khmer 7–8, 38
  see also Cambodia
Kitingan, Jeffrey 203
Kitingan, Joseph Pairin 199–200, 202–3,
  205–7, 208
KMM (Young Malays' Union) 67
KMT see Kuomintang
Koding, Mark 202–3
Korea 9, 10, 14, 16–17, 217
  kings 8
  language 8, 35
Kuomintang (KMT) 10, 64, 66, 95

labour, international movement of 14
Lamri (Sumatra) 116
Lancaster, James 118
landaarden 34, 108, 161
Langkat (Sumatra) 122, 146
Laos 8, 11, 40–3
Laurel, Jr., Jose P. 100
layered identity 162–3, 183–6, 212, 215
Lee Kuan Yew 62, 105, 196
Lenin, V.I. 10
Leydekker (Malay) Bible 27, 62
Leyden, J., 91–2
Liang Qichao 63, 64
Libya 135
Liem Sioe Liong 67, 70, 71
Light, Francis 119
Lim Boon Keng 66
Linnaeus, Carl 98
Lodewycksz, W. 55, 56
Louis Napoleon 120
Louis-Philippe, King 120
Low, Hugh 112
Luzon ethnonym 86, 87, 111–2
Luther, Martin 157

Ma Huan 84
Mac Cuu 58
Macapagal, Diosdado 100
Madagascar 98, 102
Maddison, A. 76, 213–14
Magindanao 22
Mahathir bin Mohamad, Prime Minister
  78, 105–6, 204, 213, 217
Mahavihara ordination 8

Mahmud, Sultan (Melaka) 51
Mahmud Shah, Sultan (Aceh) 122, 123
Mahmud Syah, Sultan (Aceh) 119
Makassar 8, 31, 88, 115
  language 29
malaria 146, 173
Malay (Melayu) 81–104
  in Brunei 111–14
  as diaspora 87–91
  ethnie nationalism 12, 67, 102–7,
    111, 114
  hybridities 83–7
  language 25–7, 44, 60–1, 80–1, 85, 91,
    107, 109, 157, 191, 209
  literature 87, 109, 116–7, 130
  origins 81–3
  as race 91–2, 97–102
  in Sabah 188, 199, 205–7
  as suku (ethnie) 110–1, 186
  traders 54
'Malay Annals' (Raffles) 92
'Malay Association' 99
Malay Bible 27, 62
Malay Cultural Fair 111
Malay Dilemma (Mahathir) 105
Malaya 40–3, 93–7
Malayan Chinese Association 69, 196
Malayan Civil Service 97
Malayan Communist Party (MCP) 66, 95
Malayan Emergency 213
Malayan Miscellanies 94
Malayan Union 69, 104
Malaysia 215
  elections 74, 75, 106
  as federal model 212–4
  formation (1963) 2, 75, 105, 194–5
  race relations 72–5; see also Malaya, Sabah
Malik Mahmud 134, 139
Manchu period 58
Manchu (Qing) rule in China 9, 39, 58
  resistance to 58
Mandailing (Batak) 155, 156, 160, 161,
    162, 165, 169
Manila 56–7, 86, 112
Mansur, Sultan (Melaka) 51, 52
Manullang, Mangihut Hezekiel 162–3
Maoism 11
Maphilindo 100
Marsden, W. 85, 90–1, 95
Marxism 10, 11, 41, 68, 108, 127, 165
Masjumi 165
massacres, military excesses 132, 133, 136,
    138, 139
Mataram (Java) 8
May Fourth movement (China) 10

May riots 72–7
MCP *see* Malayan Communist Party
Mecca 117
Medan 110, 111, 128, 131, 149
  Batak migrants in 160–1, 167, 168–9,
    173, 175–6, 182–3
  as North Sumatran capital 167, 175, 186
Medan Fair (theme park) 175, 183
Megawati Sukarnoputri, President
    137, 141
Mejidie (Ottoman honour) 120
Melaka: British 93
  chronicle ('Malay Annals') 82, 92
  Dutch 56, 59–60, 91
  Portuguese 52, 82–3, 86, 116
  sultanate 51–2, 82, 84, 86
Melaka royal chronicle 82, 92
  'Malay Annals' 92
Melayu Islam Beraja (MIB, Malay, Islam,
    Monarchy) (Brunei) 113
Merga Si Lima (journal) 158
Middle (Flowery) Kingdom 49, 50
Mill Hill Mission 191, 198
Minahassa 153, 157, 164, 211
Minangkabau ethnie 18, 25, 29,
    88, 92, 95, 101, 156, 163,
    174, 182
Ming Dynasty 50, 51, 55, 58, 83–5, 87
Ming government 53, 54
Mingguan Malaysia (newspaper) 106
Minh Mang, King (Vietnam) 18, 42
Mobil Oil 133
Modigliani, E. 155
Mohammad Amir 109
Mohammad Daud, Sultan 123
Mojuntin, Peter 193, 196, 198–9, 209
Mon ethnie 47
monarchy
  fragile 40–3
  as resistance 116–17
Mongkut, King 121
Mongol rule in China 83
monkhood (*sangha*) 8, 28
Moreno, Cesar 122
Muhammad Shah, Sultan (Aceh) 130
Muhammadiah 124, 125, 172
Murut ethnie (Sabah) 188–91, 200
museums 182–3, 212
music, Batak 180–1
muslimin (guerrillas) 124
Mussolini, Benito 76
Mustapha, Datuk (Tun) 196–7,
    198, 213
Myrdal, G. 26
'mysterious killings' (Indonesia) 213

NAD (Nanggroe Aceh Darussalam)
    Law (2001) 140
Names, as identity-markers 34–7
'national humiliation days' (China) 11
nationalism,
  Asia and 1–8
  case study overviews 22–3
  enduring states 15–18
  overlapping time-scales 12
  post-nationalism 12–15
  Southeast Asia and 25–48
    colonial states/ethnies 37–48
    identity-markers 26–37
  see also anti-imperial nationalism;
    ethnie nationalism; state
    nationalism; outrage at state
    humiliation (OSH)
Negara Sumatera Timur (NST) 165–6
New Economic Policy (NEP) (Malaysia)
    74, 106
New Order regime (Indonesia) 70, 137,
    168, 174, 179
  prosperity, Bataks and 168–73
New Year festivities
  Chinese 55, 77
  Toba Batak 178
Newbold, T.J. 58
Nias 183
Nommensen, Ludwig 156
non-governmental organisations (NGOs)
    14, 138, 139, 141
Norodom, King (Cambodia) 42
Northeast Asia 15–18
Notosusanto, Nugroho 129
NST (Negara Sumatera Timur)
    165–6
Nurdin, Major-General Tengku
    Rizal 111
NZG (Nederlandsch Zendingsvereniging,
    Dutch Missionary Society) 158

Oevaang Oeray 164
oil and gas 133, 134, 140
Olympic torch fiasco 11
Ong Sum Ping 52
Ongkili, J.P. 195, 197, 199
Onn bin Jaafar 95
Opium War 11
OSH *see* outrage at state humiliation
Ottoman, *see* Turkey
Our Cultural Heritage 190
outrage at state humiliation (OSH) 6, 9,
    10–23, 63, 119
  Aceh and 121–2, 130, 136
  -flavoured Islam 22, 119

Padang Lawas (Sumatra) 149, 159, 161
Padri Islamic reformers 155–6
Palembang 52, 82, 84, 86, 117
Pan Malaysian Islam Party (PAS) 106
Pane (Sumatra) 149
Papar (Sabah) 198, 200, 201–2
Papua 183–4
Pardede, T.D. 181
Parfahn, Ahmed Ibn 100
Parkindo (Indonesian Christian Party) 165
Parlindungan, M. 147, 155, 156
PAP (People's Action Party) (Singapore) 106
party politics: Indonesian 164–5, 175
    Sabah 195–7, 198–205
PAS (Pan Malaysian Islam Party) 106
Pasai (Sumatra) 116, 117 n.1
Pasemah ethnie (Sumatra) 18, 46
Pasok Momogun 195
Patani 55, 88, 89
    chronicle of 52–3
Paterno, P. 44
PBS (Sabah Unity Party) 200–1,
    204–5, 207
PD (Persatuan Daya) 164
peace-making 139–40, 141–3
Penampang (Sabah) 191, 193, 200,
    201–2, 205
Penang 91, 93
    and Aceh 121
    establishment (1786) 119
People's Action Party (PAP) (Singapore) 106
People's Daily 11
pepper 58, 116, 118–20, 123, 130
peranakan (or baba) Chinese 59–63, 65, 67,
    68, 108
perang sabil, see jihad
'Perhimpunan Indonesia' students'
    association 109
Persatuan Daya (PD) 164
Persatuan Ulama Seluruh Aceh (PUSA)
    125–6, 127–8, 129, 131
petrochemical industry (Indonesia) 71
Philippines 21, 25, 43–5, 140, 216
    names 36
    nationalism 25, 26, 29, 44, 61, 81, 99–100
Pidië (Aceh) 116, 125, 128
Pigafetta, A. 83
Pinto, Mendes 151–2
Pires, Tomé 51–2, 82, 148, 151
PKI (Indonesian Communist Party) 165
PNI (Indonesian Nationalist Party) 165
Polo, Marco 50, 116, 151
Pontianak (Borneo) 66, 87
population 169–71, 173
    Sabah 188, 191

Portugal 30, 31, 32
    imperialism 29, 116
    sources 117, 148, 151, 152
PPD (United Dayak Party) 136
Prabowo, General 72
Prajogo Pangestu 71
Pridi government (Thailand) 216
print 26–8: Batak identity and 157–9, 185
    capitalism 3, 13, 26–7
    Kadazan identity and 191–4, 202–3
    newspapers 108
    urban culture and 59–63
protective model of colonialism 40–3,
    93–4, 96–7
Protestantism 158, 170, 171, 185, 201
    GBKP 158, 171
    HKBP 163, 165, 169–70, 172, 185
PRRI rebellion 134, 136, 166, 167
Ptolemy 50, 81, 149
PUSA see Persatuan Ulama Seluruh Aceh
Putri Ijo 153

Qin Dynasty 50
Qin Shih Huangdi ('First Emperor' or
    world-ruler) 16
Qing see Manchu
Quanzhou 51, 83–4

race: and nation, ethnie 4–5, 7, 92,
    99–101
    as census category 32–4, 100–2, 188
    factor in violence 71–7, 78, 183, 213
Raden Patah 52
Radio Sabah 192, 201
Raffles, T. Stamford 18, 31, 85, 91–2,
    96, 121
Rama I, King (Thailand) 42
Rama VI, King (Thailand) 36, 56
Ranau (Sabah) 190, 193, 194, 202
Raniri, Nuru'd-din ar-50, 116, 130
Razak, Prime Minister Tun Abdul 74,
    119, 198
religion 28–30
    see also Catholicism; Christianity; Islam;
    Protestantism
Residencies, Dutch administrative
    division 166
resistance
    Aceh (1873–1945) 54–5
    monarchy as 116–17
revolution: path to national identity 2–3,
    44–5, 110, 212–8
    and centralism 2, 212–4
Revolutionary League (China) 64
Rhenisch mission 156–7, 157–8

Rhodes, Alexandre de 27
Riau archipelago 58, 62, 87, 90, 217
Riau dynasty (Malay) 41
riots 78, 105
  see also anti-Chinese violence
Rizal, José 25, 44, 99
Romulo, Carlos P. 100
Roxas, Manuel 100

Sabah 187–209
  economy 208
  elections 204–5, 199–200
  pastoral council 198
  population 114, 188, 206
Sabah Alliance 195–6
Sabah Chinese Association (SCA) 196
Sabah Cultural Association 199
Sabah National Party (SANAP) 196
Sabah Times (ST) 192, 194, 201–2
Sabah Unity Party see PBS
Sabang port (Aceh) 132, 133
Said Abu Bakar 125, 126
St Michael's secondary school 191
Salazar, Z.A. 99–100
SANAP (Sabah National Party) 196
sangha (monkhood) 8, 28
Sarawak 69, 187, 198, 208
Sarekat Islam (Islamic Association) 30, 65,
  108, 124, 163
SCA (Sabah Chinese Association) 196
Scott, Sir Walter 92
SEATO (Southeast Asian Treaty
  Organisation) 216
Selim II, Sultan (Ottoman) 117
Seulimeum (Aceh) 126
Shan ethnie 18, 40
Shi Huangdi 50
Shi-zong, Emperor 18
'shorn Chinese' 55
Si Pokki 156
Si Raja Batak 162
Siam 19, 22, 32, 38–40, 42, 52, 84, 88–9,
  93, 120–1, 210
  see also Thai; Thailand
Siau Giok Tjhan 69
SIJORI (Singapore-Johore-Riau) 217
Simalungun (Batak) 154, 157–8, 161, 165,
  168, 183
Simbolon, Colonel Maludin 167, 185
Singamangaraja IX 155
Singamangaraja X 156
Singamangaraja XII 146–7, 148, 178
Singamangaraja dynasty 147, 154–5, 156
Singapore 14, 33, 56, 59, 60, 62–3, 75, 93,
  102, 216–7

as base for Chinese 59, 68
Chinese movements in 64, 66
in Malaysia 2, 75, 105, 197
pre-colonial 84
Singkil (Sumatra) 121–2, 151, 155
SIRA (Aceh Referendum Information
  Centre) 138
Situmorang Sitor 147
Sjafruddin Prawinegara 129, 134
Smith, A.D. 3, 4, 5, 6, 15
Soara Batak (journal) 163
social Darwinism 109
social revolution (Sumatra, 1945–6)
  128, 165
Society of Kadazans 192, 194
Southeast Asian League 216
Southeast Asian Treaty Organisation
  (SEATO) 216
sovereignty 30–2, 87–8
'sovereign equality' principle 1
Soviet Union 3, 215
Spain 99
  imperialism 21, 26, 29–31, 37, 43–5
  language 26
Spencer, Herbert 63
Sri Lanka 8, 89, 102
Srivijaya 81, 83, 84, 115, 151
ST (Sabah Times) 192, 194, 201–2
state
  -averse societies 18–22, 22–3, 115, 145
  power, lack of 203–9
  stateless peoples 19–20, 45–8, 145–6, 164
state nationalism 7–8, 17, 107–11, 141, 187
status gap 67–8
Steedly, M. 157, 159
Stephens, Donald (Tun Fuad) 204, 208
  Kadazan and 193–5, 196, 197,
    198–9, 200
Straits Settlements 60, 62, 65, 93, 94,
  96, 103–4
Subroto, General Gatot 71
Suharto, President 67, 69, 70, 147, 168, 214
  Aceh and 129, 133, 136–7, 138
  Chinese and 69, 72, 76–7, 79
  wife of 183
Suharto era 45
  architecture 181–3
  ethnie competition and 175–6
  outsider insiders and 70–2
  radio and 180–1
Sukarno, President 45, 68, 69, 110, 214
  Aceh and 129, 132, 133, 141
  Bataks and 147, 164–5, 167
  Japan and 67, 127
Sukarno period 176, 180

Sulaiman, Isa 128–9, 133–4
Sumatra: environment 19
    identity 85, 90, 109, 163, 166
Sumatra Treaty (1871) 122
Summer Institute of Linguistics 201
Sun Yat Sen 64
Swart, Governor (Aceh) 125
Sweden 139
Swettenham, Sir Frank 94
Syafiie, Teungku Abdullah 139
Syair Perang Mengkasar (Ence Amin) 88
Syiah Kuala (Abdurra'uf as-Singkili) 130

Tagalog: language 25, 26, 27
    nationalism 44
Tai family of languages 18, 19
Taksin, King (Thailand) 42
Taman Mini Indonesia (theme park) 71, 183
Tambunan (Sabah) 198, 200, 201
    harvest festival (1982) 202
Tamil (South Indian) influences 94, 100, 119
Tan Chee Khoon 200
Tan Kah Kee 66
Tan Singko (Singseh) 80
Tanah Melayu 93–7
Tang dynasty 16, 81
tax farming 57, 64
Teuku Umar 129
Thai: language 7, 19
    monarchy 8, 36, 38–9, 42
    names 36–7
    nationalism 8, 36–7, 39, 64
Thailand 2, 81, 140, 216
    race relations in 79
    see also Siam
'Theatre State' (Geertz) 20
Tian-shun, Emperor 53
Tiro, Hasan 128–9, 130, 131–6, 139, 142
Tiro, Teungku Syech Saman di 123, 124,
    127, 128, 129
TNI *see* Army
Toba (Batak) 146, 147
    church 165, 175, *see also* HKBP
    ethnie nationalism 162, 186
    language 156–8, 174–5
Toba, Lake 151, 156, 157, 168, 186
Tokugawa Ieyesu 17
Toraja ethnie (Sulawesi) 164, 190
Toynbee, A. 65–6
trade empires 43–5
treaties
    Anglo-Aceh (1819) 121
    London (Anglo-Dutch) (1824) 31, 121
    Sumatra (1871) 122
Treaty of Breda 31

Treaty of London (1824) 31, 121
Treaty Ports 62
tributary relations 38, 39, 51–2, 84
Truong Minh Giang 18
tsunami 141–2
Tuanku Rao 156
Tuaran (Sabah) 201–2
Turkey 30, 31, 117, 118, 120, 152
Tuuk, H. N. von der 155

UFMS ('Unfederated Malay States') 94
ulèëbalang (Aceh aristocracy) 119, 122,
    123, 124, 126–8, 129, 130, 131
UMNO *see* United Malays National
    Organisation
'Unfederated Malay States' (UFMS) 94
United Dayak Party (PPD) 136
United Malays National Organisation
    (UMNO) 69, 104, 106, 192, 196,
    199, 204–5
United National Kadazan Organisation
    (UNKO) 194, 196
    see also United Pasok-momogun
        Kadazan Organization (UPKO)
United Nations 1, 13, 138
United Pasok-momogun Kadazan
    Organization (UPKO) 195–7,
    198, 204
United Sabah Dusun Association
    (USDA) 201–3
United Sabah National Organisation
    (USNO) 195–7, 198
University, Aceh 132, 133
UNKO *see* United National Kadazan
    Organisation
Untung coup 69
UPKO *see* United Pasok-momogun
    Kadazan Organization
urban print culture 59–63
USDA *see* United Sabah Dusun
    Association
USNO *see* United Sabah National
    Organisation
Uti, Raja 154
Utusan Melayu (newspaper) 104

Vajiravudh *see* Rama VI, King (Thailand)
Vatican II 180
Vietnam 38–40, 216, 217
    language 27, 35
    names 35–6
    nationalism 9, 17, 22, 38, 40, 42
    pre-colonial 7–8, 12, 16–18, 19, 21, 38,
        42, 116
Workers' Party 40

Vinzons, Wenceslao 99–100
violence
    Indonesia and 138, 183, 213
    Medan 175
    spice trade and 120
    see also massacres
Vision 2020 (Malaysia) 106
Vlieland, C.A. 33–4, 101–2
Vliet, Jeremias van 88–9
VOC (United East India Company)
    (Dutch) 29, 31, 115, 116, 119

Wahid, President A. 77, 137, 139–40
Warta Malaya (Malayan News) 95
West Kalimantan Council 164
Westphalia system 1
William, Prince 118
Winstedt, R.O. 52, 92, 94, 96
Wolf, E. 146
Womack, B. 38
women 171, 179

World Bank 13
World Trade Organisation 13
world-rulers
    cakravartin (Burma) 38
    Qin Shih Huangdi (China) 16

Xiamen (Amoy) 171, 179
Xiao-zong, Emperor 53

Yamin, Muhammad 109
Yasovarman, King (Khmer) 50
Young Sumatran Union (JSB) 163
Youth Congress (Indonesia) 25, 163
Ypes, W.K.H. 159
Yuan Shikai government 10
Yudhoyono, President S.B. 137, 141
Yung-lo Emperor 83

Zentgraaff, H.C. 123, 129
Zheng family (shipowners) 58
Zheng He 50, 51, 52, 84

www.ingramcontent.com/pod-product-compliance
Ingram Content Group UK Ltd.
Pitfield, Milton Keynes, MK11 3LW, UK
UKHW042155280225
455719UK00001B/352